SHIRDI SAI:
THE SUPREME

SHIRDI SAI: THE SUPREME

> "I am Allah, I am Mahalakshmi, Maha Ganapati, Sri Krishna, Sri Rama, Dattatreya, Lakshmi Narayana, Maruti, and Vittobha. All forms are Mine."
>
> –Sri Shirdi Sai Baba

Compiled and Edited By
DR. S.P. RUHELA
Founder & Secretary
Sai Divine Research Centre,
126, Sector 37, Faridabad-121003 (INDIA)

DIAMOND BOOKS

ISBN : 81-7182-040-9

© S.P. Ruhela (1997)
Published in collaboration with
"Sai Divine Research Centre"
126, Sector-37, Faridabad-121003

Published by :	Diamond Pocket Books (P) Ltd.
	X-30, Okhla Industrial Area, Phase-II
	New Delhi-110020
Phone :	011-51611861-865
Fax :	011-51611866
E-mail :	sales@diamondpublication.com
Website :	www.diamondpocketbooks.com
Edition :	2004
Price :	Rs. 95/-
Printed by :	Adarsh, Shahdara, Delhi-110032

Shirdi Sai: The Supreme
E.D. by S.P. Ruhela   Rs. 95/-

Dedication

*Sri Sai Baba, who is the
embodiment of
all that is the highest,
all that is the holiest,
all that is the noblest,
and
to all His devotees and
Spiritual Seekers.*

* * *

Offering to Lord Sai Baba

*O Lord of Lords, how can we offer Thee the things
When every thing in the world is Thine,
Can we pray Thee to accept our souls
While every soul is Thine?*

*The only thing we pray O Sai,
In the airs of They sweet name let us sway,
Make us remember They looks gay
Every moment and every minute of the day.*

*O Sai, the Saviour, let the, nectar of Thy words intoxicate us,
In the waters of Thy Love let our minds swim,
Wend our way round Thy heaven,
Make us, O Lord, rest at Thy feet haven.*

—L. V. Kistaiah,
(From: *Shri Sai Leela*)

"I am in this world as well as in the higher worlds and in all. I am pervading the whole animate and inanimate worlds as the inner most Being."

"I am all pervading. Nothing can be concealed from Me. The innermost thought of your heart are known to me. I am the Creator, Preserver, Dissolver. All you Karmas can be destroyed and all you sins wiped out by the mere touch of My hand."

—*Sri Shirdi Sai Baba*

* * *

PRAYER TO THE SADGURU

"Oh Sai! Oh Sai Baba! God-realisation cannot be explained through the written words. To love You is to know You. To know You is to love You. God-realisation is to know You and to love You. It is silly to attempt the expression of this love through physical senses.

Let me bow to You, Oh Sai! May I live always in the paradise of the dust of Your Feet repeating:

"May my mind and movements lead me to the dust of Sai's Lotus Feet! Let my tongue repeat Sai's Name. Let my body prostrate at His Feet. Whatever deeds are done by me as an instrument of Sai may become pure enough to bear the fruit of unsullied Love for Sai!"

Om Sai Shri Sai Jai Jai Jai Sai
Shirdi Sai Baba Temple Society
(Charitable trust Regd at Faridabad vide deed No 319 dt 7-4-98)
Offerings qualify exemption u/s 80-G of the Income Tax Act, 1961

शिरडी साई बाबा टैम्पल सोसायटी
(धर्मार्थ न्यास पंजीकृत फरीदाबाद सं० 319 दि० 7-4-98)
भेंट आयकर धारा 80G के अंतर्गत छूट के योग्य है

Sai Dham, Tigaon Road, Faridabad (Haryana), India • Phone : 8-296388

Sai Sewak
Motilal Gupta
Founder Chairman

31, Kailash Hills, New Delhi-110065, India
Phones Off : 6843693 & 6845404 Res : 6984517 & 6880483
Fax : 011-6984640, e-mail : Sapoonam@giasdl01.vsnl.net.in

October 8, 1997

MESSAGE

Sadguru Shri Sai Baba of shirdi is a unique phenomenon on the horizon of spirituality. His eyes full of compassion and concern for the suffering humanity, with the torn kafni on his body, He presents a picture of the age old sage who has decended on this earth to show the path of Love and Brotherhood to the people in distress. He has very emphatically shown how 'Faith and Patience' can bring complete peace and happiness to His followers.

To enlighten devotees, Prof. S P Ruhela, an ardent devotee, is bringing out a book titled as "Shirdi Sai:The Supreme".

I hope this book will throw lot of light on the Divinity of Lord Shri Sai Baba of Shirdi and would impart immense knowledge to the spiritual seekers.

May Shri Sai's Grace be on him and the readers of this book.

Bow to Sri Sai: Peace be to all.

(Sai Sewak Motilal Gupta)
Founder Chairman,
Shirdi Sai Baba Society, Faridabad &
Chairman of International Convention of
Shirdi Sai Devotees(October 19-21, 1997)
Sai Dham Tigaon Road
Faridabad-121002

HOW SAI BABA WORKS

How Sai works is unique. He allows the creation to go on untrampled and brings in subtle changes in the relationship and minds of the beings. He helps people in distress and woe, by cutting across the jargon of karma and gives them ample scope to rectify and develop. Sai looks after minutes needs to the highest requirement of emancipation. The constant faith in Him and the prayer to Him (Sai), wards off many dangers and isolation. The trust in Him slowly develops to spirited love for Him and for everything one is made to depend on Him only. Finally, *He enriches His devotees to love everyone and the creation to serve with steadfast faith. The advanced devotee perceives only Sai Baba in everything.* Sai Maharaj trains His lovers to face several ordeals of life with case and without the desire of seeking anything at all. The greatest transformation He brings in His devotees in desirelessness and slowly, but steadily march to the Summom Bonum of life of the realisation, that He is God.

When Sai Baba plays a miraculous part all over, the grip and influence of Him is so expanding every nook and corner and all is bless to see the world, the creation fast moving to an ideal plane of Self-realisation and utmost satisfaction.

This is a Golden Era, Let all take to His Bhakti and directions and it is so sure, all doubts of the creation will cease and everyone shall ultimately see the creation as a play, which should be effectively and happily acted by all, while their merging in the Totality of Sai is a definite certainty.

The part played by Sai Bhagwan is the miracle, which is far wider and greater than all the miracles of the creation.

—O.V.G. Subrahmaniam, F.F.I.I.
18/286 Ambari Agraharam,
Machilpatnam, Kisna Dist., A.P.
(*Shri Sai Leela*, April 1990)

PREFACE

Sri Shirdi Sai Baba occupies the most prominent place among all the great Godmen and saints of the 19th and 20th centuries. His Name and fame as a very caring, compassionate and loving saviour of the distressed people and earnest seekers of his divine intervention and spiritual knowledge, have already spread in the four corners of the world. Each day more and more people — needy ones, spiritual seekers, intellectuals as well others, of all religions and lands, are coming under the fold of his divinity and becoming his devotees. Sri Shirdi Sai Baba is a unique and most fascinating divine personality who is venerated as a Prophet. He is much different from other Saints and Godman. His uniqueness lies in his extreme simplicity of the style of his living, his catholicity and nobility of his teachings, his promptness in responding to the earnest call from any devotee's heart, his genuine integrative secular approach, and his universalistic and altruistic pattern variables in his role functioning as the great Prophet of the Age.

I consider it to be my rare fortune that in this birth I have been privileged to be under the umbrella of the grace of such a great divine Master. Since 1974 I have been his devotee. I have visited his holy place Shirdi in Maharashtra State many times and have read almost all important books and articles in English and Hindi written on him so far. As a social science researcher as well as as an ardent devotee, I have felt that although there are so many books written on him, yet most of them are not comprehensive and complete; they usually present a very sketchy or superficial description of his Avataric career and focus mainly on his miracles, while neglecting the most crucial aspects of his divine charismatic personality and his spiritual significance and relevance to the human society in the modern times and the fast-approaching 21st Century.

With the spread of education and emergence of the age of logic, science and concern for functionality in every sphere of life, educated people of today do not have much interest and faith in divine or spiritual personalities and spiritual matters, their miracles and teachings which they usually consider to be rather very traditional, superstitious or out of tune with the modern times. But on the other hand, the sociological fact is that there is a widespread *anomie* (normlessness), misery, immorality and resultant insecurity and unhappiness in the world. Only the intervention of Prophets, Saints and their teachings of the right kind of moral and spiritual values, which focus on universality and nobility of man's existence, can save the crisis-ridden contemporary world. Everyone in the spiritual and religious circles throughout the world is now talking of the coming 'Dawn of a New Era of Peace and Enlightenment' for the humanity soon.

It is in this sociological and religious contexts that I have realized the need to bring out this book of selected readings on Sri Shirdi Sai Baba under the title *"SHIRDI SAI: THE SUPREME"* to present a very comprehensive, up-to-date, and authentic information on this great divine personality.

The articles included in this book are, the cream of the perceptible writings on Sri Shirdi Sai Baba by Sai devotees scholars and spiritual seekers during the last sixty years or so. They include the contributions of such great spiritual luminaries like revered Sri Basheer Baba, Sri B.V. Narasimhaswamiji, Yogi Minocher K. Spencer, Acharya E. Bhardawaja and Sri Sai Padananda who, having shown us the Sai path, have departed from this world many years back, as well as of those eminent Sai devotees and spiritual seekers living today who are seriously addressing themselves to the study of the spiritual significance and relevance of Baba's Avatarhood for the modern world, as well as for the future world.

The twenty-seven articles included in this book present a comprehensive profile of Sri Shirdi Sai Baba. I earnestly believe that this book will go a long way in creating interest among people throughout the world to know about Baba more and more, and also it will quench the spiritual thirst of Sai devotees, spiritual seekers and intellectuals and all others. It will enlighten both the masses and the elites who are keen to understand Sri Shirdi Sai Baba, His divine mystery and His relevance to our modern and future society.

I am most grateful to Bhagavan Sri Shirdi Sai Baba for giving me the inner prompting, motivation, capacity, opportunity, facilities and resources for compiling this book now after 23 years of my first knowing him and two decades of my keen interest in study and research on him.

Baba had mysteriously conveyed to me, through Sri Lakshman Swamiji, Spiritualist of Bangalore whom I met in a train in June

1992, his divine wish that I should bring out a set of books on Him. Accordingly, I have brought out a number of books viz. *'Sri Shirdi Sai Baba: The Universal Master'* (1994), its Hindi translation under the title *'Sant Shiromani Sri Shirdi Sai Baba'* (1997), *'What Researchers Say on Sri Shirdi Sai Baba'* (1995), *'My Life With Sri Shirdi Sai Baba'*, 'Thrilling Memories of 102 Year Old Sai Devotee Shivamma Thayee' (1992), *'Divine Grace of Sri Shirdi Sai Baba'* - Experiences of Sai Devotees in the Post-Samadhi Period (1918-1997), *'Shirdi Sai Baba Speaks to Yogi Spencer in Vision'* (1998), *'Divine Revelations of A Sai Devotee' 'Hamara Pyare Sri Shirdi Sai Baba'* (In Hindi: 1997) and now this one *'Shirdi Sai: The Supreme'* (1997) The last four books are being published on the happy occasion of the International Convention of Shirdi Sai Devotees (Oct. 19-21, 1997) at Faridabad, which is a matter of great happiness to me.

This book is most lovingly, reverentially and gratefully dedicated to the lotus feet of Sri Shirdi Sai Baba.

I am grateful to all the contributors to this book. Grateful thanks are due to the Editor, *'Shri Sai Leela'* Shirdi, from which a number of illuminating articles have been taken by me for inclusion in this book.

I am very much grateful to Sai Sevak Sri Moti Lalji Gupta, President of Shirdi Sai Temple Society, Sai Dham, Faridabad and the Chairman of the International Convention of Shirdi Sai Devotees, for sending his message for this book. He is a very inspiring Sai Sevak who has for several years been doing great service in missionary spirit to propagate the Name of Baba and promote Sai Consciousness among people. It is a privilege to have his words of blessings in the form of the Foreword of this book.

October 8, 1997

SATYA PAL RUHELA
Compiler & Editor
Sai Divine Research Centre,
126, Sector 37,
Faridabad-121003

ACKNOWLEDGEMENTS

The following articles have been reprinted from *Shri Sai Leela*, monthly published by Sri Sai Baba Sansthan, (Shirdi)

1. Sai Bindu, 'Sai is Universal Truth', *Shri Sai Leela*, Nov. 1988.
2. K.B. Kher, 'Daily Routine of Sri Sai Baba', *Shri Sai Leela*, March, 1990.
3. D.M. Mishra, 'Avatar Sai Baba '*Shri Sai Leela*', Sept.-Oct. 1996.
4. V.B. Kher, 'The Siddhis of Sri Sai Baba', *Shri Sai Leela*,.
5. O.K. Vaide Rao, 'Sai Baba and the Univesality of Religion' *Shri Sai Leela*, Jan. 1989.
6. R.K. Kapoor, 'Teaching of Sri Shirdi Sai Baba and Dattareya', *Shri Sai Leela*, March, 1988.
7. K.Ventakataramiah, 'Sai Baba's Sayings and Teachings', *Shri Sai Leela*, Jan. 1990.
8. V.H. Desai, 'The Relevance of Sai Spiritualism Today', *Shri Sai Leela*, Jan.-Feb., 1995.
9. R. Rukmani, 'The Need For Baba's Technique to the Present World', *Shri Sai Leela*,
10. S.M. Bannerjee, 'We Devotees', *Shri Sai Leela*, May, 1988.

I am highly grateful to my esteemed Parsee Sai devotee friend Sri Jal Mani Chinoy, B/3, Khullar Apartments, Byramji Town, Nagpur, for giving me the old issues of *Shri Sai Leela*, magazine and for providing me much enlightenment, inspiration and help.

I am grateful to my esteemed friends and well-wishers among Sai devotees like Sri Chakor Ajgaonkar (Thane), Sri T.R. Ram Nathen (Sarangabad), Sri T.R. Naidu (Hyderabad), Sri Meenakshi Sundaram 'Sai Dasan' (Madras), Sri Radhakrishnan 'Sai Jeevi', (Hubli), Sri. B.Umamaheswara Rao (Guntur), Sri M.G. Bavanarayan (Madras), Sri Putanna (Bangalore), Sri H.D. Lakshmana Swami (Bangalore), Sri Subhas C. Chowfla (Solan),

Sri A. Somasundaram (Markapur), Smt. R. Seethammal 'Baba Paatti' (Madras), Sri M.R. Raghunaathan (Madras), Sri Janak Raj Laroria (NOIDA), and Sri R. Seshadri (Bangalore) Sri B.M. Sharma (Faridabad).

Grateful thanks are due to all the contributors whose valuable contributions have been included in this book of readings on Sri Shirdi Sai Baba.

I am also grateful to Mr. Brian Steel (Australia), Mr. Lucas Ralli (UK), Mr. Hans Hopfgartner (Austria), Mr. Rohit Kumar Dewan (Brunei) for their help to me in this Sai Service done under the auspices of 'SAI DIVINE RESEARCH CENTRE', Faridabad.

I am thankful to my friend eminent sociologist Prof. T.K.N. Unnithan, Former Vice-Chancellor, Rajasthan University, Jaipur, for his encouragement and advice to me to do research on Sri Shirdi Sai Baba in the 'SAI DIVINE RESEARCH CENTRE'.

Last but not the least, I wish to place on record my most sincere thanks to Mr. Javed Khan, Mr. Shiv Singh Bisht and Mr. Saghir Alam of *datapro systems*, for excellent and prompt laser typesetting of this book, and also to Sri Jai Prakash Singh, my student of M A (Education) in Jamia Millia Islamia, for his help to me in this work.

Satya Pal Ruhela
SAI DIVINE RESEARCH CENTRE
October 19, 1997   125, Sector 37,
Faridabad - 121003 (INDIA)

CONTRIBUTORS

1. (Late) SRI B.V. NARASIMHASWAMIJI : The greatest Apostle of Sri Shirdi Sai Baba Founder President of All India Sai Samaj, Madras, Author of a number of most important books on Sai Baba.

2. (Late) BASHEER BABA : Eminent Muslim Godman and Sai Pracharak.

3. (Late) SRI SAIPADANANDA RADHAKRISHNA SWAMIJI: Eminent Apostle of Sri Shirdi Sai Baba.

4. (Late) YOGI MINOCHER K. SPENCER : Great Yogi, Medium and Spiritualist whom Fakir Sai Baba, the God Almighty, Spiritual trained and enabled to see God face to face; Compiler of the book "*HOW I FOUND GOD*" (1957).

5. (Late) ACHARYA E. BHARADAWAJA : Eminent Spiritualist and author of "*SAI BABA: THE MASTER*".

6. (Late) MRS. MANAGER : Eminent Parsi Sai Devotee who had visited Sri Shirdi Sai Baba a number of times in the 1910's.

7. (Late) V.V. GIRI : Eminent Trade Union Leader who later became President of India.

8. SRI JAL MANI CHINOY : Eminent 72 years old Parsee Sai Devotee from Nagpur: B/3, Khullar Apartments, Byramji Town, Nagpur.

9. SRI S.M. BANNERJEE : President, Sri Sai Samaj Calcutta (Regd) and Editor, SRI SAI AVATARS; 28/6, Bipin Pal Road, Calcutta - 700026.

10. SRI V.B. KHER : Eminent Sai devotee, researcher on Sai Baba, and author of "*SAI BABA OF SHIRDI THE UNIQUE SAINT*".

11. PROF. C.R. NARAYANAN : Eminent scholar, Sai devotee and author of "THE GOD AND THE APOSTLE" (1992). Retired Professor of Botony. American College, Madurai; Resident (12) Sri P. Reddy Citizens Home, Abdhra Mahila Sabha, Madras - 600028.

12. DR. R. RUKMANI : Eminent Sai devotee and author of several learned articles on Sri Sai Baba : No.7, Sixth Street, Ram Nagar, Nanaagandullur, Madras - 600061.

13. SRI RADHAKRISHAN 'SAI JEEVI' : Eminent Sai Devotee and Pracharak, President, Akhanda Sai Nama Saptaha Samithi, Bangalore, 560046. 10/B. MTS Colony, Railway Qrs. Hubli - 580024.

14. DR. VIJAY KUMAR, Eminent Sai Devotee, has contributed a number of illuminating articles Sai Baba's mission in Sai journals.

15. K. VENTAKATRAMAIAH, Eminent Sai devotee from Guntur: Retired Deputy Director of Cooperative Societies,; 'Sudarshan Krishna Nagar, II Lane, Guntur--522006 (A.P.).

16. R.K. KAPOOR, Sai Devotee.

17. O.K. VAIDE RAO, Eminent Sai devotee from Hyderabad, 50 Mehdipatanam, Hyderabad.
18. V.H. DESAI, Sai Devotee.
19. SAI BINDU, Sai devotee from Goa; C-26, 50(2), Colaco House, Near Power House, Aguer, Margao,--403601 (Goa).

20. DR. S.P. RUHELA, Professor of Education (Sociology), Sai devotee and author of several research based books on the Sai phenomna; Founder & Secretary, 'Sai Divine Research Centre', 126 Sector 37, Faridabad-121003.

THE DIVINE LIFE OF SRI SHIRDI SAI

Dr. S.P. Ruhela

"Realise first who am I. Do not be concerned with My eternity and birthlessness. I am all pervasive, all engulfing spirit of the world and its entire manifestations is none else than Me. My Divine nature will be revealed to the entire humanity with lightening speed. I am a nutshell, I am the Goal, Abode, Refuge, Friend, Origin, Dissolution, Foundation, Treasure-house and imperishable seed of things. I am existence and non-existence, aught and naught, is and is-not, I am the ineffable cosmic mystery."

—Sri Shirdi Sai Baba

I

Sri Sai Baba, popularly known as Sri Shirdi Sai Baba, was born on 27th September, 1838 in the forest near Pathri village in Aurangabad District of Maharashtra State of India. His parents were high caste Brahmins belonging to Bhardwaja Gotra. His father's name was Ganga Bhavadia and his mother was Devagiriamma. His parents lived near a *bavdi* (water tank), called *'Kumhar bavdi'* on the ontskirts of Pathri village, where there still stands the old Hanuman temple worshipped by them. It is likely that because of his living close to the *bavdi*, his father was known as Ganga Bavadia (or Bhavadia). A keen researcher on Baba, B.V. Kher, (1976, 1991) has mentioned, on the basis of his field research in 1970s that Baba most probably belonged to the Bhusari Family of the Brahmins of Pathri village, and his parental house (No. 4-438-61) was situated in Vaishnav Gali. That house has some years back been bought by local people forming "*Shri Sai Samarak Mandir Samiti*" and they have erected a shed and temple for where local Sai devotees to perform *aarti* (worship) of Sri Shirdi Sai Baba.

Pathri is now an important place. There are two trains on Central Railway from Bombay to Selu or the next station Manwat or the next Parabhani. They halt at both Selu (Sailu) and Manwat. Pathri is about 15 kms from Selu and about 10 kms from Manwat. Tapovan Express does not halt at either of these but only at Parabhani from which Pathri is 40-45 kms. One can catch these trains also at Manwat if one is at Shirdi. There are direct State Transport buses from Bombay to Pathri which is a taluka town.

Sri Shirdi Sai Baba's father was a boat man. It was a poor family. Baba's parents were religious people who worshipped Hanuman, Shiva, Shakti and other gods of the Hindus. They did not have any child. Once when Ganga Bhavadia had gone to the riverside to save his boat in the rainy and stormy night and Devagiriamma was alone in the house, at about 9 p.m., first Lord Shiva disguised as an old man came to her house and asked for shelter and food, and then Goddess Shakti (Lord Shiva's Consort), also came there in the form of a village woman of low caste to massage the legs of the old man. Being happy at the hospitality, good character and pity of Devagiriamm, the old man and the woman then gave their darshan as the divine couple Devagiriamma and blessed her that she would have three children --one son, then a daughter and then one son, adding further that the third child would be the incarnation of Shiva himself.

This divine blessing materialised in course of a few years. First a son was born and then a daughter. When the third child was going to be born, suddenly Ganga Bhavadia developed *vairagya* (detachment with the worldly life) and decided to leave the house and family and become a renunciate. Devagiriamm, being a devout wife, decided to follow her husband's path; she sent both her children to her mother's home, and accompanied her husband. On 27 September, 1838 they left Pathri village very early in the morning. While they were passing through a forest, a few miles away from their village, birth pangs set in. Devagiriamma implored her husband to wait for a while till the child was born, but he would not heed and went ahead. So Devaririamma gave birth to her third child all alone in the forest. Placing the child on the ground and covering him with *peepal* leaves near the forest path around mid day, she hastened after her husband. This child later on became known as the famous Sri Sai Baba of Shirdi.

After some time, an elderly Muslim Faqir, named Patil, and his wife, called Faqiri, who were returning from his in-law's house in a *tonga* (horse carriage), reached near that spot where the new born baby was lying. Faqiri alighted the tonga to answer the short call of nature, and then she heard the cries of the new born baby. Exited at this, she called her husband to the spot. As they were a childless couple, they thought that Allah had sent that child for them. They took the child to their village Manwat. They named the child as 'Babu'. They brought up the child as their own son. Unfortunately, the Faqir died after four years, i.e. in 1842. The foster mother of Babu soon got tired of him as he was becoming uncontrollable. He was doing very strange and offensive acts like visiting Hindu temples and reciting the Quran there, visiting the mosque and installing a stone Lingam there and worshipping it, singing songs in praise of Allah in Hindu temples and saying that "Rama is Allah, Shiva is Allah" etc. etc. This irritated the people of Manwat. Disgusted with the daily complaints of neighbours against her son, Faqiri ultimately decided to carry Babu to Sailu village and leave him there in the ashram of a Hindu Saint Gopal Rao 'Venkusha' who looked after a number of abandoned, orphaned and poor boys. He had been the ruler of that place and so his ashram was in a big building and there was no dearth of food and clothing for the inmates.

In one of his past lives, Venkusha had actually been Guru Ramanand, the teacher of the eminent saint poet Kabir. It is said that Venkusha had a dream one night in 1842 in which Lord Shiva appeared before him and told him that He himself would be coming to his ashram at 1 a.m. the next day. So when Faqiri, carrying the four year old child Babu on her back, reached Guru Venkusha's Ashram and asked the gateman to let her meet Vankusha at 11 a.m., Venkusha immediately came out and accepted the child. Faqiri also lived for eight years in the *Ashram* till her death there. Babu stayed in Venkusha's Ashram for 12 years from 1842 to 1854. He was loved very much by Venkusha due to his staunch respect and devotion for the Guru. Lateron Sri Shirdi Sai Baba recalled this about his Guru to one of his devotees at Shirdi :

> "I had Guru. He was great saint and most merciful. I served him long, very very long; still he would not blow any *mantra* in my ears. I had a keen desire, never to leave him, but to stay with him and serve him and at all cost receive some instruction from him...I resorted to my Guru for 12 years. He brought me up. There was no dearth of food and clothing. He was full of love, nay, he was love incarnate. How can I describe him? When I looked at him, he seemed as if he was in deep meditation and then we both were filled with bliss. Night and day, I gazed at him with no thought of hunger and thirst. Without him I felt restless. I had no other object to meditate, nor any other thing than my Guru to attend... He always protected me by his glance, just as the tortoise feeds her younger ones whether they are near or away on the other side of the river bank, by her loving looks."

Because of Venkusha's great love for Babu, other boys of the ashram grew very much jealous of him. In 1854 one day when Babu had been sent by his Guru to the forest to bring *bilva* leaves for worship, a group of the Ashram boys beat him there and one of them hit his forehead with a brick and Babu bled profusely. The boys ran to the ashram; Babu came to the Guru with that brick. Venkusha tore his loin cloth and bandaged Babu's forehead wound. He was deeply grieved. He shed tears. He told Babu: "Now the time has come for me to part with you. Tomorrow at 4 p.m. I shall leave this body. I shall vest my full spiritual personality in you. For that purpose, bring milk from a black cow." Young Babu went to Hulla, the Lambadi (herdman). He had only one black cow, but she was not giving milk. Babu, nevertheless, came with the cow to the Guru. The Guru touched the cow from horns to tail and asked the Lambadi, "Now pull at the teats." The Lambadi's pull drew out plenty of milk, and the whole of that milk was given by Venkusha to Babu to drink then and there. The Guru's blessings and full spiritual powers immediately were thus passed on to the 16 year old Babu.

At the same time, the boy whose brick had hurt Babu, fell dead. His friends ran to Guru Venkusha to request him to revive the dead boy. Venkusha asked them to request Babu for this, as all his powers had already been transferred by Venkusha to him.

Babu touched the dead body, and immediately he came back to life. This was the first great miracle that Sri Shirdi Sai Baba did in his life.

Thereafter, Babu was asked to leave the Ashram and go towards Godavari river. The Guru gave Babu his old sheet of cloth and the brick which had hit him. Carrying these two things as gifts from his Guru Venkusha, the young Baba travelled on foot for several days and ultimately reached Shirdi village, which is a few miles away from Godavari river.

He quietly reached Shirdi and stayed under a neem tree outside the village. It was the same *neem* tree which we now find at Gurusthan at Shirdi - the place of Shirdi Sai Baba's Guru in one of his previous births. An old woman of Shirdi, the mother of Nana Chopdar, then saw the young Baba and she left behind his portrait of him:

> "This young lad, fair, smart and very handsome, was first seen under the neem tree, seated in an *asana* (yogic posture). The people of the village were wonderstruck to see such a young lad practising hard penances, not minding heat and cold. By day he associated with none, by night he was afraid of none....Outwardly he looked very young but by his action he was really a great soul. He was the embodiment of dispassion and was an enigma to all...."

After about two months, one day he suddenly left Shirdi and for four years shrouded in mystery he wandered without disclosing his identity. During these four years, he visited a number of places, lived in some mosques, and influenced a number of people.

> "I grew up in Meurgad (a place sanctified by the presence of Lord Dattatreya). When people pestered me I left for Girnar; there too people pestered me much and I left for Mount Abu (a hill station in Rajasthan). There too the same thing happened. Then I came to Akkalkot and from there to Daulatabad. Then I went to Pandarpur; from there I came to Shirdi."

But prior to this as per his own revelation, he walked on foot for eight days on the path from Pathri (his parental village) via Selu (Sailu), Mannoe (Manwat where he had spent the first four years of his life in the Muslim Faqir's house), and Jalnapur; "trodding over the grass and sleeping at night in the grass," he reached Paithan, Aurangabad, where he stayed in an old mosque and guided and begged for an old Muslim Faqir for some years.

Baba once disclosed to his devotee Upasani Maharaj's elder brother Balkrishna Govind Upasani that he had seen the battle in which the Rani Laxmi Bai of Jhansi took part as he was then in her army. Rani Laxmi Bai was one of the foremost freedom fighters in the first Battle of Independence of the Indians with the then British rulers in 1857 and she was killed in the battle in late June in that year. It is likely that soon after her death in 1857, Baba might have left the army service, and then he might have gone to Meurgad, Girnar, Mt. Abu, Akkalkot, Daulatabad and Pandarpur as mentioned above.

It appears that from Paithan the young Baba went towards the twin villages Sindhon--Bindhon. In the forest near these twin villages, one noon he was sitting, and just then a Muslim landlord of Dhoopkhera village Chand Bhai Patil passed by that side. Seeing him sad, the young Baba addressed him by his name, called him near, did the miracles of calling Chand Bhai's lost mare there and of materialising live amber and water by thrusting his tongs in the ground. These miracles of the young Baba greatly thrilled Chand Bhai Patil. He invited Baba to his house. Baba did not go with him, but He reached his village a few days later. At Dhoopkheda, the curious villagers' crowd became unruly and started pinching and pestering the young Baba. So Baba became furious and started pelting stones at the crowd. Two stones hit a mad adolescent girl (who used to roam about naked) and a lame boy. They were immediately cured of their ailments by the miraculous hitting of Baba's stones. These miracles immediately impressed the villagers. Baba stayed at Chand Bhai's house for some days. He accompanied Chand Bhai's nephew's marriage party on bullock carts to Shirdi where the bridegroom was going to be married to Chand Bhai's sister's daughter. The carts of the marriage party halted near the Khandoba temple outside Shirdi village. Baba was the first one to alight from the cart. He moved a few steps towards the Khandoba temple.

The priest of the Khandaba temple Mhalsapati, who was somewhat friendly with Baba when He had first came to Shirdi in 1854, welcomed him with these words. *"Ya Sai"* (Come Sai). This new name 'Sai' (which means Saint, Divine Father) given by Mhalsapati was accepted by Baba, and from that memorable day in 1858 he became known as Sai Baba.

Although Sai Baba moved to a nearby village for a few weeks, yet He soon returned to Shirdi and permanently settled down here. He made an old discarded mosque his home. Throughout his life, till his MahaSamadi on 15 October, 1918, he lived in this mosque which He had named as 'Dwarkamai'. In the beginning He was considered to be a cynical, half-mad Faqir, and children used to pelt stones at him, but gradually He became the favourite of all the villagers of Shirdi and the neighbouring villages.

In his early years, he used to cure people by his herbal medicines, but when one patient, who was a leper died due to the violation of food and other precaution (he indulged in sex relations with his wife during treatment which was prohibited by Sai Baba), Sai Baba stopped giving medicines. Gradually, Dwarka Mai Masjid became the heart of Shirdi, and Baba did all his *leelas*, miracles, teachings and spiritual transformation of his devotees there for six decades.

He used to live on alms collected only from five specific families. He shared his food freely with his devotees as well as other creatures like dogs, cats, birds etc. His external appearance of a simple, modest, illiterate, moody, very indulgent, yet at times very fiery and sometimes abusive in speech and aggressive fakir was in fact his mask of *maya* (illusion) put on by him just to hide his real identity as God Incarnate.

However, the villagers of Shirdi and nearby places soon discovered by their experiences of his thrilling miracles and compassionate instant mysterious help that He was no ordinary saint, but was in fact a divine personality of a very high order. Rarely did He declare publicly that He was God. Mostly he uttered the name of Allah, and advised people to remember, depend on and venerate whatever God or Goddess they had been worshipping in their families. He demonstrated that he was the incarnation of Shiva, Dattatreya, (the Incarnation of the Trinity of Brahma, Vishnu and Mahesh) and that all other Gods and Goddesses were within Him.

He incessantly worked for Hindu-Muslim unity in Shirdi. Despite the then prevailing fundamentalism and opposition on the part of some Muslims as well as Hindus, he was ultimately successful in making them appreciative and tolerant of each other's faith. He taught them spirituality and morality in very simple words. During 1985 he died for three days, but again came back into life. During his sixty years stay at Shirdi he performed many thrilling miracles. His fame spread fast from 1910; people from far and near started coming in crowds and presenting *dakshinas* (cash gifts) as demanded by him from whomsoever He wanted. During the last 10-15 years of his life, he daily received hundreds of rupees as *dakshina*, but by evening he would distribute all of it among his devotees, beggars and poor people. Before his MahaSamadhi in 1918 he had assured that all his miracles and grace would be available to all those who would remember him and visit his Samadhi Masjid complex temple at Shirdi. And rightly so, innumerable people have actually been benefitting by praying Sri Shirdi Sai Baba and visiting Shirdi, and many have witnessed the miracle of seeing Him in person even now in different forms or in his usual attire and in their dreams.

The name of Sri Shirdi Sai Baba has been spreading very fast throughout the world. Now there are hundreds of Shirdi Sai Temples not only in India, but even in London, Los Angels, Loredo (U.S.A.), Canberra, (Australia), Durban (South Africa), Logos (Nigeria) Mauritius, Nepal, and many other cities of the foreign countries. Not only the Indians are his devotees, even many Germans, Americans, Australians, Africans, British, Italians etc., are also deeply impressed by him and becoming his devotees. The name of Sri Shirdi Sai Baba and the Sai movement are spreading like wild fire in the world. The simple village Fakir of Shirdi who lived 80 years back in the litle known interior village of India, has now become the object of deep veneration and adoration of countless seekers of peace, bliss, and spirituality.

Mehar Baba, the disciple of Upasani Maharaj who was the only disciple of Sri Shirdi Sai Baba, had seen Sri Shirdi Sai Baba in 1915. Mehar Baba himself is considered to be an important incarnation of God. According to him :

> "You will never be able to understand thoroughly how great Sai Baba was. He was the personification of Perfection. If you know him as I knew him, you will call him the Master of Creation."

Sri Sathya Sai Baba has revealed about Sri Shirdi Sai Baba as under:

> "Shirdi Sai was a *Brahma-jhani*. He was the embodiment of Universal Consciousness-*Gnaaswaroopa*.

He was also the Sadguru teaching his devotees the reality and guiding them along the path of Truth.

He was a *Poornavatar* (Full or Integral Incarnation of God) and possessed the attributes of Divine *Shakti* (Power) but he held them in check and did not reveal them fully. He was like a learned musician who exhibits his musical skill occasionally; He was like a gifted poet who gave voice to his verse only rarely. He was like a skilled sculptor who revealed his artistry some times.

Siddhis (miracles) and *Leelas* (sport) were merely outpourings of His love for his devotees. They were not meant to attract but only to safeguard and protect. He did not use them like visiting cards. He used his *Shakti* only to save the devotees from distress and trouble, from sorrow and pain...His advent was for revealing divinity."

Sri Sai Baba's miracles were of many kinds--miraculous cures, removal of poverty and barrenness in women, warding of diseases, lighting lamps with water, saving lives, forecasting future calamities, giving blessings for prosperity, his own thrilling yogic exercise like khandyoga and removing his intestines and drying them in the sun and granting all kinds of boons. He would often tell people about the number of past births in which some of his close devotees had been associated with him.

His devotees and followers belonged to all religions, castes, social classes, and occupational groups. Even some foreigners came to have his darshan and they held Him in high esteem. There were then about fifty contemporary saints in Maharashtra and other adjoining states. They interacted with Sri Shirdi Sai Baba by paying visits to Him and many of them did so mysteriously remaining at their places. Baba remained a celibate all his life. Although he was loving and calm, yet at times he become furious and even abused, and some times he beat people. He was fond of smoking his *chilum* (pipe). He often danced and sang some bhajans. All kinds of village entertainers, dancing girls, musicians, acrobats, circus men, jugglers etc., often exhibited their skills at his Dwarkamai mosque. Although he was very kind and sympathetic towards every one in Shirdi, yet he had a towering personality and none except one or two very close devotees dared to take liberties with him. He was also humorous.

Daily he was telling parables and stories to instruct his devotees as also to reveal the working of spiritual laws like *Rinanubandha* (Bondage of give and take), *Sambhava* (principle of equality), *Karma* and *Punarjanma* (Action and Rebirth), unity of the souls of all creatures etc. He disliked casteism, practice of untouchability dowry, religious conversion, religious fundamentalism, conversion, and the traditional bar on women in matters of worship and social life. Baba said:

He was a mild and tolerant incarnation of Kabir, who instead of attacking the so-called superstitious beliefs and practices of the Hindus and the Muslims, allowed and encouraged each one of them to continue following his or her traditional beliefs and religious modes of worship. Thus he promoted intrinsic and genuine communal tolerance and emotional and national integration by allowing both the Hindus and Muslims to worship him according to their respective modes of worship in his Dwarkamai mosque. The Udi (Holy Ash) of his *dhuni* (fireplace) in Dwarkamai was his regular gift to all his visitors and devotees. It was and is still considered to be a unique miraculously beneficial substance much sought after by all devotees.

His image as an *Avatar* (Incarnation) - a Faqir clad in rags, begging alms for his sustenance and wishing well of all creatures, his austerity and superb poise and spiritual attainments have for decades been instantly turning millions of people into his devotees, and each day the number of his devotees is increasing in astronomical proportions. When He breathed his last, the only property he had consisted of 16 rupees in his pocket, some of his clothes and shoes, chilums, and *sadka* (a wooden stick), a handmill to grind grain and a tin pot, although during the later years of his life he had been daily getting hundreds of rupees as *dakshina,* so much so that the British Government Income Tax department once considered to tax his daily income which was during 1916-18 more than that of the British Governor General of India. In all wisdom they did not tax him for he was giving away all his daily income in charity, but they did tax some of the regular beneficiaries of his charity.

II

Five Stages of the Development of Sai Baba Movement:

Let us undertake a hurried review of the development of the spiritual movement associated with Sri Shirdi Sai Baba:

I Stage :
(a) From 1838 to 1886:
"Baba's main work was that of a Samarth Sadguru who had to diffuse religion and help the good and remove the evil that oppresses the good. Even before 1886 he was possessed of vast powers used for this purpose. In 1886, he had a small body of worshipers who might all have been benefited both temporarily and spiritually by reasons of *Poorva rinanubandha* or present contact." (Narasinhaswamiji, *Life of Sai Baba*, Vol. I, p. 183).

(b) From 1886 to 1918 :
Baba passed away in 1886 but returned after three days. "He had to get back into the same body to work out the same remaining portion of the present life". During this time Baba's name and fame spread in Maharastra.

(c) 1908-1918 :
During this time Baba's fame spread in South India; most of His prominent devotees came to Him from southern states and also from Gujrat and even northern states; most of his widely known miracles took place; Hindu-Muslim unity was fused through secular worship by both communities in Dwarkamai: lots of crowds came there, offerings of cash, food and other articles were given and distributed among devotees and the poor ones. Due to the publicity by Das Ganu and Upasni Baba, Baba's name and fame spread far and wide.

II. Stage (1920s-30s): Shirdi became known all over India, and Sai literature was created by Das Ganu, Dabholkar, H.S. Dixt etc. and *Sai Leela* sprang up. There were much less-crowd during this period. The number of persons approaching Sai Baba at Shirdi was pitiable small on ordinary occasions.

III Stage Sai: (1940s) The Sai Baba movement flared up in the thirties and forties and it attained all India character and drew thousands instead of hundreds to Baba's feet. Baba presence outgrew Shirdi and his presence was felt in the various temples that were built for him and in the bhajan halls, even in the homes.

IV : 1940s-1960s : Spread of Sai Baba's name throughout the country and also in many parts of the world. Due to the writings of Narasimhaswamiji, Shirdi became known all over.

V : 1980s & 1990s : Many propagated the name, fame and

message of Shirdi Sai Baba, e.g. Sri Sathya Sai Baba, Sri Narayan Baba, Smt. Sivamma Thayee, Sri Radhkrishnaji, Sri Sai Das Baba, etc. Many Sai Temples, organizations, journals were established all over India and in some countries of the world.

Now Baba's popularity as the foremost Avatar of the Kali Age is at its highest pitch all over the world.

III

Sri Sai Baba Universal Religion.

An eminent devotee Dr. K.V. GopaleKrishan has rightly said this of Baba's universal religion, the promotion of which was his mission:

"Shri Sai Baba of Shirdi was the greatest exponent of Universal religion. He embraced people of all religions with equal grace and never differentiated His *bhaktas* by religion, nation, state or caste as God is omnipresent and envelopes the entire movable and the immovable universe. One may observe at Shirdi people of all religions, castes and creeds joint in universal brotherhood as Sai devotees with no barriers at all. In fact, among Sai devotees there is never a question of who is of what religion or nation or state or caste. Caste is man-made barrier and the biggest hurdle in national and universal brotherhood. Shri Sai Baba's *bhaktas* have nothing to do with caste or any differences. Hindus, Muslims, Sikhs, Parsees, Jains, Christians and people belonging to various other religions came to Baba (come to him even now), prayed Him and were received equally and blessed by Him. Sai faith is multinational, multilingual and embraces people all over the globe with equality. At Shirdi even now and always every one can wash the Mahasamadhi, climb the steps of His Mahasamadhi, touch and worship the Mahasamadhi and visit and worship at Dwarakamai, Gurusthan and all other holy places without the least restriction or restraint. Sai Baba lived in a dilapidated mosque (which was later repaired by His devotees) which he called "Dwarkamai" where He had the sacred *Dhuni*, the ever burning fire according to Hindus custom and he was worshipped by aratis, blowing of conchs and *pada puja* etc. He had festivals of Hindus and Muslims performed with due eclat. When a devotee remarked about some one else that he was a Christian, Baba said, "He is my brother". He appeared at various places while being in Shirdi in His mortal coil. He is doing so more vigorously now after having shed His mortal coil.

    The strature of Shri Shirdi Sai Baba is beyond comprehension of the normal human mind. His spirituality, divinity and powers are immeasurable and even the greatest of devotees could not touch the fringe of His greatness. Sai Dabholkar (Hemadpant) who wrote Baba's biography 'Sri Sai Satcharita' said that it is impossible to describe the greatness of Baba. Sai Spirituality can only be experienced but not explained. As such it is not possible to narrate the spiritual experiences He gives. But the temporal benefits he confers. through miracles which we very much need in this *vyavaharik* state are innumerable. The great Avatar who can destroy Karma and is disposed to do so showers his grace upon his humble devotees who surrender to him, to ward off their calamities and takes care of them in mundane and spiritual spheres and takes them to the ultimate goal of deliverance."

                                                       (*Shri Sai Leela*, Dec. 1988)

2

CHRONOLOGY OF EVENTS IN THE LIFE OF SRI SHIRDI SAI BABA

Dr. S.P. Ruhela

"I am the Creator and Dissolver. All of you are subject to My will. Conduct yourselves with propriety and be guideless having due regard to what is proper and improper in the discharge of you duties."

— Sri Shirdi Sai Baba

27.9.1838:	Birth in forest near Pathri village at 12 Hrs. 5 Min. 25 Sec. Noon according to ancient Tamil Naadi records at Madras.
1838-42:	Was brought up by a Muslim Fakir Patil and his wife Fakiri at Manwat.
1842:	The Fakir's wife left the child Babu in the charge of Guru Venkusha at Sailu.
1842-1854:	Brought up and instructed by Guru Venkusha in his Ashram at Sailu;
1854:	Departure from the Ashram in 1854, with Guru's blessings; the Guru also died the same day.
1854:	First visit to Shirdi, stayed there for about two months.

Chronology of Events in the Life of Shirdi Sai

1854-58: Period of *Agyatvas*: (unknown wanderings)
- visited various places doing various jobs;
- lived with Bade Baba at Aurangabad;
- lived with Faqir Akbar Ali at Ahmad Nagar;
- moved with other faqirs and Hindu saints;
- visited Shivagaon Pathodi and asked Gadge Maharaj for bread.
- served in the army of Rani Laxmi Bai of Jhansi in 1851;

1858: Chand Bhai Patil met him in jungle near the twin villages, Sindhon-Bindhon; showed his lost mare, materialised live amber and water for his pipe.

Visited Chandbhai Patil's village Dhupkheda three days after meeting him in the forest.

1858: Reached Shirdi (second time) with Chandbhai's nephew's marriage party; Mhalapthy addressed him as "*Ya Sai*"; He assumed the name 'Sai' from that time.

1858: Went to Rahata village, stayed in *Chawdi* (village place for visitors) there for some days; wanted to stay in Rahata permanently, but soon decided to come back to Shirdi.

1859: Visit of Saint Gangagir who said of him to the villagers of Shirdi, "He is a precious gem."

1861: Occupied an old forsaken masjid and named it Dwarkamai Masjid. Many villagers and children teased him, pelted stones at him considering him to be a mad Faqir.

1873: Saint Bidkar Maharaj visited Baba.

1881: Mahadev Rao Deshpande, Shirdi village Primary School teacher, accepted Baba as his Guru. Baba nick-named him as 'Shama'.

1886: Severe attack of Asthma on Baba; Baba's *Prana* (life) left His physical body for three days entrusting it to the watch of Mhalasapathy.

1889: Arrival of Abdul as servant-devotee of Baba from Fakir Aminuddin of Nanded.

1890:	Baba went to live with a pseudo-Guru Javar Ali at Rahata; villagers of Shirdi persuaded Him and Javar Ali to return to Shirdi; Javar Ali was defeated in a spiritual contest by Saint Jankidas of Shirdi and so he fled away from Shirdi.
1891:	Nana Saheb Nimonkar first met Sai Baba at Rahata village.
1892:	(Diwali Day): Baba did the famous miracle of lighting his Dwarkamai Masjid lamps with water when oil was refused to him by the village grocers. This miracle spread his fame far and wide.
1904:	Baba's great miracle 'Jamner incident': Baba sent *Arti* and *Udi* (holy ash) with Ramgir Bua for Mina Tai daughter of Nana Saheb Chandokar at Jamner: materialised a horse carriage and servants to take Ramgir Bua from Jalgaon station to Nana Sahib's residence in night to be delivered to Mina Tai at the time of her painful delivery.
1906:	Baba appeared miraculously (in his other body) at Pallachi near Coimbatore with Sanyasi Thangavel Gounder; gave darshan to hundreds of villagers there for two days; blessed Rajamma Gounder, (lateron named on Shivrama Thayee) a 15 year old married girl, niece of Sanyasi Thangavel Gounder, and spoke to her in Tamil.
1908:	Baba gave *darshan* as a Sadhu to Chandrabai Borkar at Kopargaon.
1909:	Faqir Baba (Baba's first disciple at Aurangabad) came to stay with Baba in Masjid and lived there till Baba's *Mahasamadhi*.
1909:	Baba appeared in the form of Lord Rama in Dwarkamai Masjid to a doctor devotee of Lord Rama.
1909:	H.S. Dixit met Baba at Shirdi and became His ardent devotee.
1909:	From 19 December 1909, the rituals of worshipping Baba and taking out his procession from masjid to Chawri was started by his devotees which still continue.

Chronology of Events in the Life of Shirdi Sai

1910:	Dabholkar met Baba; Baba gave him the name of 'Hemadpant' and lateron permitted him to write his biography. *'Shri Sai Sat Charita'*.
1910:	Foundation of Dixitwada was laid on 10th February 1910; completed in April 1911.
1910:	Baba's *Shej Art* (Night worship) on every alternate day was started.
1910:	Baba's famous miracle of grinding wheat in Masjid and getting its flour thrown on the boundary of Shirdi village to prevent plague entering the village.
1910:	Baba stopped cooking *Prashad* (Handi Food) in Masjid due to very large number of devotees coming there by then.
1911:	Visit of Upasani Maharaj to Baba on 27 June.
1911:	Baba assumed the form of three-headed Child Lord Dattatreya in Masjid; witnessed by divine Balwant Kohojkar and others at Dattatreya Jayant day at 5 PM.
Dec.1911:	Visit of a noted Muslim Saint Durvesh Sahib to Baba; was cordially treated by Baba.
25Jan.1912:	Death of Megha, Baba's ardent devote; Baba wept and shed tears while putting flowers on his corpse.
1912:	Visit of Chinna Krishna Saheb, who become His great devotee.
1912:	Visit of Sagun Meru Naik.
1912:	Renovation of Dwarkamai Masjid; noted services done by three carpenter brothers Kundaji, Gawji and Tuka Ram.
1914:	Visit of famous singer Khan Sahib Kasim Khan (father of now famous singer Hirabai Badodekar), his party and wife Tahera and daughter Gulab Kavali (Hirabai Badodekar) to Baba; they sang a number of Bhajans of Kabir and *Abhangs* of Tuka Ram in a music session before Baba and hundreds of villagers in the night till 2 AM; were blessed by Baba with silver coins and sweets.

1915-17:	Training of Upasani Maharaj under Baba's guidance at Shirdi in Khandoba Temple.
1915:	Visit of young Parsi spiritual seeker Mehrun (Meher Baba); Baba directed him to become Upasani Maharaj's disciple.
1916:	Arrival of a 3½ year old abducted and abandoned child Narayan with pilgrims to Baba; Baba welcomed and looked after him till his *Mahasamadhi*; became famous as Sai Narayan Baba who had been given the power to materialise Baba's hot *Udi* and cure people.
1916:	Baba asked his devotee G.C. Narke to beg food for Baba attired in his European suit to teach him the lesson of egolessness.
1917:	Famous politician and spiritual seeker Lokmanya Tilak met Baba on 19 May, 1917; Baba told him, "*Ja, jap, Swaraj asta*". (Go, mediate, Independence follows).
1918:	Baba sent food offerings and Rs.250 to Fakir Samsuddin Mia and a garland of *Sevanthi* flowers to Faqir Banne Mia and His message of His *Mahasamadhi* in the near future giving its exact date, in June or July 1918, through Kasim son of Bade Raba and Imambhai Chote Khan.
8 Oct. 1918:	Baba gave *mukti* (Liberation) to an ailing tiger brought by a band of Fakirs to Dwarkamai Masjid, and then got it buried near the masjid.
28 Sept. 1918:	Baba developed high temperature; still he went out to beg alms.
15 Oct. 1918: (2.30 PM)	Baba achieved *Maha Nirvana*.
16 Oct. 1918:	Baba appeared in his usual form and white dress at his devotee Mataji Krishnapriya's cottage in Simla (Himachal Pradesh) in the evening; she offered him tea, *chapatis* (breads) and brinjal curry (Baba's favourite vegetable); Baba took the food, blessed her and finally disappeared from there.

3

WHAT 'SAI' MEANS

Sri Basheer Baba

"I am residing in the hearts of every one and I am the Ruler. I am the life thread of the world and I am mother of the world (Jagan Matha). Worshipping Me will make you disinterested in mundane affairs, and attain God-Realisation."

— Sri Shirdi Sai Baba

"Sai" means Bhagavan and Bhagavan has no such difference. Sai Samaj takes into its fold Christians, Muslims, Hindus, Sikhs, Parsis and devotees of various faiths and creeds who have developed 'faith' in Sri Sai Baba. Sai is *sarwaswarupi*. He is eternal and present everywhere. The mortal remains of Sri Sai Baba are enshrined in Shirdi. Sai Baba administered the holy ashes from the fire lit in Dwarakamayi and healed all kinds of prolonged and chronic ailments and relieved them of their physical and mental worries and transformed their gratitude into devotion. He gives courage to the disappointed and peace to the distressed.

Just as soap cleanses the body of the dirt, the Sai soap (*nama* of Sai) cleanses the *Atma* of *kama*, *krodha*, hatres and bad intentions and purifies the heart. Sri Sai Baba has demonstrated daily His various powers. He appeared as Krishna to Krishna *bhaktas* and as Sri Rama to Rama *Bhaktas*. He is "Sri Krishna-Ram-Siva-Marutyadi-rupa Sai". He is a '*Poorna-Avatara*'. Why should anyone go after new saints and seers when we already have such omnipotent ones like Sri Sai Baba? Why should anyone go in for new soaps that are advertised. one's belief in Baba washes away all sins.

4

AVATAR SAI BABA

D.N. Mishra

> *I am the Divine Power, Prime Power, Noble Form, Combination of twenty-four subtle elements, Supreme power which destroys the evil effects of evil actions. I am the Life-Power of movable and immovable objects of the world. I am the living power which protects My bhaktas.*
>
> — Sri Shirdi Sai Baba

We do not see the stars in the daylight but that does not mean that there are no stars in the sky. Standing by the bank of a pool, thickly overspread by scum and weeds we say that there is no water in it. If we desire to see the water we are to remove the scum in a surface of the pond. Likewise because we fail to conceive and grasp the existence of God or Avatar in the grip of our ignorance due to non-removal of the film of 'Maya' from our eyes that does not mean the absence of the existence of God or Avatar in the universe. So, as long as man remains subject to the dualistic delusions of nature, he can not know the Avatar who is God and is one only. When one removes the veil of Maya, he becomes able to uncover the secret of creation that ultimately leads him to know the Avatar or God.

The purpose of the Avatar is the descent of God for the ascent of the man. Avatar or incarnation is a highly concentrated and condensed centre of divine effulgence in human form. Avatar is actually the condensed beam of rays of the Lord. The divinity of the Avatar is all encompassing as it is the substance of all symbols. Its vision is universal and it embraces all the dimensions of time. There is always a double element in the Avatar, human in front, divine behind and we with our external eyes only see him as a human being, as many people looked and assessed Sri Shirdi Sai Baba during his life time. But Baba the Avatar was actually an integrated manifestation of the divine and was always at work and at rest.

The appearance of Baba as an Avatar was an extremely monumental event in the history of mankind and his appeal was universal. He represented the highest expression of man's potential consciousness without limit, love without boundary. He was all power, all love, capable of accomplishing anything imaginable and dictated history, whose activities benefit all mankind, and was the source of all knowledge, knowing past, present and future, and was at all places at all times, that was revealed from his Avataric activities.

Baba was really one who was conscious of the presence of the power of divine born in him or descended into him and governing from within his will, life and actions, identified inwardly with the divine power and presence and came to usher in a new age for humanity, to enable it to take another step in it's evolution towards it's ultimate goal.

The great saint Meher Baba found in Sai Baba the highest manifestation of the supreme reality and considered him as the master of universe. In Baba he found his spiritual pursuit and in the year 1915, when he sought Baba's grace and asked for a message Baba said "Love God to such an extent that you become God". Baba also confirmed through his utterances much earlier (though very scarcely) and the succeeding assessment and expression of Sri Meher Baba is reflected in the "Sri Sai Satcharita)".

Baba had decleared, "I am the inner-ruler of all and seated in their hearts. I envelope all the creatures, the movable and the immovable world. I am the controller, the wire-puller of the show of the universe... All the insects, ants, the visible movable and immovable word are in my body and form". (*Sai Satcharita, P.14*)

"Baba said that he was omnipresent occupying land, heaven". (*Sri Sai Satcharita 103*)

> "Barring your name and form, there exist in you as well as in all beings, a source of being or consciousness of existence. That is My-self, knowing this you see Me inside yourself, as well as in all beings". (*Sri Sai Satcharita 229*)

"My abode is in your heart and I am within you"
(*Sri Sai Satcharita* 85)

"I am roaming in their forms. He who see me in all creatures is my beloved. *(Sri Sai Satcharita* 56)

"Make me the sole object of your thoughts and actions, and you will, no doubt attain Paramartha Spiritual Goal of Life". *(Sri Sai Satcharit* 98)

Albert Einstein said the presence of a superior reasoning power revealed in the incomprehensible universe forms my idea of God ?

It is true that with the omnipotent divine consciousness i.e., God speaks through supermen, who are also the saviours and are called Avatars i.e., incarnations of God Himself, descending to humanity as occasion arises during the darkest days. Baba was a rare phenomenon, whose service to humanity, if judged calmly, would be found great enough to require a special corner in our Pantheon. His was a message of love, mutual forbearance and understanding. He was the most humane amongst all supermen and was most approachable and had boundless sympathy for all creatures.

In a subtle but very effective way he chiselled into men's hearts the truth that the only mission of life is to sense, God, living in the proximity of God grow on to like God, and ultimately to become one with God.

Baba was the central or common factor that bound the followers of various religions in the country and preached that there is only one God whom people pray in different names; He never identified himself with any particular race, religion, sect, creed or caste as he condemned all sectarian approach to religion that becomes the best instance, best means of founding the universal faith and as a result the Christians, Muslims, Hindus, Parsees and Jains unequivocally surrendered at his feet with intense faith. He preached no cult and was not the founder of any sect. He only showed the ways of life to the mankind through his living activities and messages.

As the Avatar of the age through his divine functioning he put an equilibrium amidst the doctrinal tussles of various religion, sects, admitting all as true, being different paths to the same God, just as many rivers proceeding through various zig-zag courses merge in to the same ocean.

Swami Paramahans Yoganand once to a questine of a man, as to how could God, the unmanifested absolute, appear in visible form to a devotee, gave a fitting reply, "If you doubt, you won't see and if you see, you won't doubt".

Baba, the incarnation of purity, has showed the mankind how there is illusion in reality and reality in illusion and through his invisible spiritual force has left behind such powerful perennial wave for global integration of mankind, the colossal impact of which shall surely sway the whole of humanity without being conscious of the process and ultimately shall assimilate all men in the divine ocean of true consciousness to establish universal faith and spiritual fraternity in the World.

(Shri Sai Leela, Sept-Oct. 1996)

5

DAILY ROUTINE OF THE CHARISMATIC SAI AVATAR

V.B. Kher

"Mine is the Divine powerful seat. I am the Indweller. I am the Supreme power. I will be seen in many beautiful appearances. I am the sweet smiling effulgence that emerges from the lotus like faces."

– Sri Shirdi Sai Baba

Most of the humanity live in chronological time and experience psychological time. Sometimes when human beings are engaged in work of their choice and liking, they experience that time flies. Any activity which is imposed on them may become a burden in which case time may hang heavy upon them. Those who have a sense of asthetics occasionally forget for some moments that there is anything like time. More often, for creative individuals like artists and poets time comes to a stop when they are in creative mood. This phenomenon has been studied in depth by the philosopher J. Krishnamurti whose observations on this topic are refreshing. He says,"It is interesting to realize that our lives are mostly spent in time - time, not in the sense of chronological sequence of minutes, hours, days and years, but in the sense of psychological memory. We live by time, we are the result of time. The present is merely the passage of the past to the future. Our minds, our activities, our being, are founded on time, without time we cannot think, because thought is the result of time, thought is the product of many yesterdays and there is no thought without memory. Memory is time, for there are two kinds of time, the chronological and the psychological. There is time as yesterday by the watch and as yesterday by memory. You cannot reject chronological time; it would be absurd — you would miss your train. But is there really any time at all apart from chronological time? Is there time apart from the mind? Surely time, psychological time, is the product of the mind.

Without the foundation of thought there is no time — time merely being memory as yesterday in conjunction with today, which moulds tomorrow — As I said, happiness is not of yesterday, happiness is not the product of time, happiness is always in the present, a timeless state — merely disciplining the mind in time, conditioning thought within the framework of time, which is memory, surely does not reveal that which is timeless".[1]

The opening sentence of the Dhammapada embodies the great psychological truth viz. `All that we are is the result of what we have thought : it is founded on our past thoughts and made up of our present thoughts, It is only a yogi whose involuntary activity of thought has ceased, whose mind is still and tranquil like a placed lake can transcend time. For him, time has come to a stop - not chronological time but psychological time. As for a Superyogi like Sai Baba, he is not only omniscient but omnipresent and omnipotent as well. The mental state of Sai Baba has been best described by Mrs. Tarabai Sadashiv Tarkhad as under. "One noticeable difference between Sri Sai Baba and other saints struck me. I have moved with other notable saints also. I have seen them in high Samadhi or trance condition entirely forgetting their body and effacing the narrow notion of the self confined to the body; and I have seen them later getting conscious of their surroundings, knowing what is in our hearts and replying to us. But with Sri Sai Baba there was this peculiar feature. He had not to go into trance to achieve anything, or to reach any higher position or knowledge. He was every moment exercising a double consciousness, one actively utilizing the Ego called Sri Sai Baba and dealing with other Egos in temporal or spiritual affairs, and the other — entirely Superceding all Egos and resting in the position of the Universal Soul or Ego; he was exercising and manifesting all the powers and features incidental to both the states of consciousness. Other saints would forget their body and surroundings and then return to it. But Sri Sai Baba always was in and outside the material world. Others seemed to take pains and by effort to trace the contents of others' minds and read their past history. But with Sri Sai Baba this was not a matter of effort. He was in the all knowing state always.[2]

For such a superyogi, time in the chronological and psychological sense has no meaning whatsoever. Naturally the title of this article too from the point of view of Sai Baba has no meaning. But to the humanity at large, to whom the world is relatively real, the title suggests the daily routine of Sai Baba as seen by an ordinary person as an observer.

Let us see how the day began for him. He would be seen sitting near the *dhuni* (sacred fire) in the masjid before 5 a.m. He would answer the call of nature, come back and sit quietly by the dhuni. His religious practice was hardly noticeable. He never had any books or writing material with him. And his instruction was only oral. It is said that he would wave his arms and fingers about, making gestures and saying "*Yade Haq*", People were not permitted to go near even within fifty feet of him. The *sevekaris* (attendants) would carry on their usual service of clearing, replenishing fuel for *dhuni* etc.[3] The first sevekari to arrive would be Bhagoji Shinde who would press the body of Sai Baba, fill His chillum with tobacco, light it and hand it over for smoking to Sai Baba. Sai Baba would have a puff and give it to Bhagoji for a puff. Then Sai Baba would have five or six puffs. A few close devotees would now come to do guruseva. Their seva over, Sai Baba would get up, wash and clean his hands, feet and face delicately with plenty of water.[4] Sai Baba was not known to take his bath daily. He would bathe once in eight or ten days as the spirit moved him but he was always scrupulously clean.

At about 8 a.m. Sai Baba would go to four or five houses in the village for alms. The houses he would visit for alms were those of Bayajabai Kote Patil, Patil buva Gondahri, Appaji Kote, Nandram Savairam and Narayan Teli. Standing outside he would cry out. "*Puri anage Chatkur Bhakri.*" He would collect all the dry bhiksha in his Jholi and the liquid things in his tumbler. After returning from the begging round he would partake of some food from the bhiksha and keep the rest in a corner from which any one was free to help himself. Even birds and animals were not prevented from eating from it.

The first sitting would then he held which would last upto 9.30 a.m. Many devotees would come to pay their respects to him. At this sitting he would buy bananas, guava and mangoes and distribute them among the devotees.

At 9.30 a.m. he would proceed to the Lendi stream accompanied by Abdul and spend an hour there. Sai Baba would sit behind the enclosed Nanda Deep from where the lamp was not visible to him. He did not gaze at the lamp. He would have two pots full of water from which He would make offerings to various directions. Whether He uttered any mantra while doing so is not known.

After returning from the Lendi He would remain in the masjid until 2 p.m. During this time He would hold a second sitting for an hour. The devotee would worship. Him individually and a congregational worship and arati would follow at noon time. It would then be time for the afternoon meal or lunch. Sai Baba would preside over the meal with two rows on either side of him and the seat to the left of Sai Baba would be reserved for Babe Baba.[6]

Between 1 p.m. and 2 p.m. when He would be alone, with a screen in front of him he would take out a pouch containing ten or fifteen old coins of various denominations such as 1 paise, 2 paise, 1 anna, 2 annas, 4 annas, 8 annas and a rupee. He would rub his finger tips constantly yet gently against their surface. Whether he would utter any mantras while doing so is not known. As he rubbed his fingers against the coins, he would say, "This is Nana's, this Bapu's, this Kaka's this Somya's etc. "If any one approached, he would gather the coins, put them back in the pouch and hide them. The surfaces of the coins had become smooth with rubbing. The bhaktas believed that Sai Baba did all this for their welfare.

At 2 p.m. Sai Baba would go again to the Lendi and return after forty-five minutes. Between 2.45 p.m. and 5 p.m. He would remain in the masjid. The third sitting would be held between 5 p.m. and 6.30 p.m. At 6.30 p.m. he would go out for his evening round for a few minutes. He would take a few steps in different directions and come back.

Thus during the day, He held there sittings in all; the first between 8.30 a.m. to 9.30 a.m. the second between 10.30 a.m. and 11.30 a.m. and the third between 5 p.m. and 6.30 p.m. At the three sittings he would instruct the devotees. His language was highly cryptic — full of symbology, parable, allegory and metaphor.[8] He would clear the doubts of and enlighten the devotees in such as manner that only the devotee concerned would understand. He preached no sermons, gave no discourses on Vedanta, Upanishad.

Bhagwad Gita etc. His instruction was mainly ethical. He imparted faith in God to those who lacked it, confirmed the faith of those who had it. He gave simple instructions about *namajapa*, spiritual practices etc. However if a yogi came to Him, He would meet him on his level and appropriately communicate with him. He counselled devotees to go on with their devotions and He would lead them slowly on the path of self-realization in accordance with their capacity and effort. He would use His supernatural powers to give direct experiences to the devotees who remembered him and fervently prayed to him.

When day passed into night would Sai Baba sleep at night? — is a question which an inquisitive reader may ask. The answer to this query is that "sleep" as such has no meaning in relation to a superyogi like Sai Baba. Upto the turn of the nineteenth century and the beginning of the twentieth century, it is said that Sai Baba would sleep on a plank of approximately 6'x1' about 7 or 8 feet above the ground level and 1 or 1 1/2 cubits below the roof. It was suspended from the ceiling by shreds of torn cloth and four lamps used to be placed on it. Nobody ever saw him getting on or down the plank and how He did it remained a mystery. Two devotees Mrs. Chandrabai Borkar and Das Ganu have recorded in their statements, they had seen him lying on the plank.[9] The plank was given to him by Nanasaheb Dengle. When crowds began to gather to watch him, Sai Baba gave up sleeping on the plank suspended from the rafter. Speaking with reference to sleeping on this plank Sai Baba once observed that it was joke to sleep on the suspended plank. He who is ever alert in body and mind and who can lie awake, alone can succeed in this feat. Only the divinely meritorions can achieve it.[10]

Notes

1. *Krishnamurti Reader*, compiled by Mary Lutyens, Penguins, 1970, p.86
2. *Devotee's Experiences of Sri Sai Baba*, Part I, p.92 at pp-96-97
3. *Ibid*, Part I, p.92 at p. 102 & p. 104, at p. 115 statements of Mrs. Tarabai Sadashiv Tarkhad and R.B. Puranadare respectively.
4. *Shri Sai-Sat-Charita* (Marathi), foreword by Hari Sitaram Dikshit.

5.	*Devotee's Experiences of Sri Sai Baba,* Part II, p.79 at pp. 80-81.
6.	*Shri Sai-Sat-Charita,* Chap XXIII
7.	*Devotee's Experiences of Sri Sai Baba.* Part II, p.43 at pp. 64-65 and p.127. At p.130 statements of Das Ganu and Somnath Deshpande.
8.	*Ibid,* Part I, p. 18 at p.25 — statement of Prof. G.G. Narke.
9.	*Ibid,* Part III, p.80 and Part II, p.43 at pp.48 and 64.
10.	*Shri Sai-Sat-Charita,* Chap. XXXXV, Verses 131, 135,136

(*Shri Sai Leela,* March 1990)

6

THE SIDDHIS OF SRI SAI BABA

V.B. Kher

"The nectar of My Grace will fill the vessel of you heart. I am the truth personified and God. All that you regard as yours in this world—spouse, progency, wealth and so forth—is actually Mine. You are only a temporary trustee."

— Sri Shirdi Sai Baba

In Chapter 15 of the Section XI of Shrimad Bhavwat and in Part III of Yoga-Sutras of Patanjali and in many other religious or yogic treatises there is description of siddhis which is more or less alike with some minor differences. Patanjali warns the yogi in his aphorisms that he should not be allured by *siddhis* lest he should fall into the vortex of birth and death again. The seeds of bondage are required to be destroyed to attain liberation. Hence it is only when intellect becomes as pure as the self that liberation follows.

For our purpose let us consider the *Siddhis* described in Shrimad Bhagavat as we have the authoritative commentary of one of the foremost saints of Maharashtra, Eknath, to guide us. In his preface to Chapter 15, Eknath warns that siddhis are an impediment on the path to liberation.

It is stated at the outset that siddhis stand with folded hands at the door of him, who has established mastery over his senses, conquered his *prana*, who is singularly devoted to the Lord and whose *chitta* is ever one with the Self.

The Siddhis of Sri Sai Baba

Classification of Siddhis

There are twenty-three siddhis in all, which have been graded into three classes: great, medium and small. The great siddhis are eight in number and are very difficult to acquire. Only he who is established in the Self, who has lost all consciousness of his body and of the sense of 'I' and 'mine', one can get them. The medium siddhis are ten and a seeker who is endowed with divine qualities and is pure in heart gets them. The small siddhis number five and he whose heart is purified through devotion or yoga can acquire them. Now let us examine the siddhis under each class.

Eight Great Siddhis:

Of these, the first three siddhis pertain to the body.

(1) *Anima*: The reduction of one's form to an atom, assuming the subtle and invisible state.

(2) *Mahima or Garima*: To make the body weighty or heavy.

(3) *Laghima*: To make the body light excessively and beyond what is natural.

(4) *Prapti*: To acquire objects of sense pertaining to the respective organs.

(5) *Prakashya*: To see and know invisible things in the other worlds.

(6) *Ishita*: To stimulate bodies and creatures; to have control over natural forces.

(7) *Vashita*: To have supremacy over the senses.

(8) *Yatkamastadavasyati*: Literally, the power to obtain joys in the three worlds effortlessly by mere willing. However, this power leads to the state of the highest bliss through ending of all desires.

It is only a rare Mahatma who has these eight siddhis.

Medium Siddhis:

1. *Anoormimattvam*: The six modifications of being (*oormis*), namely, hunger, thirst, grief or sorrow (*shoka*) and infatuation/stupefaction/delusion/confusion of mind (*moha*), old age and death do not disagree with and affect injuriously the body.

2. *Doorshravan*: To hear, sitting at one place, speech from however distant a place.
3. *Doordarshan*: To see, sitting at one place, events/things in all the three worlds.
4. *Manojava*: The body travels at the speed of mind to any place you desire.
5. *Kamaroopa*: To assume at once any form you desire.
6. *Parakayapravesh*: To enter into another body dead or alive, temporarily leaving one's own body.

    In this connection the story of Adi Shankaracharya is well-known. He had obtained an adjournment of six months in his debate with Saraswati, the wife of Mandanmishra, to answer her questions on sex. During this period Shankaracharya had entered the corpse of the King Amaruk who had died while he had gone for hunting, lived the life of the King, after reviving the corpse, for six months, acquired all the necessary knowledge of sex, and thus defeated Saraswati. Thereafter Saraswati had told Shankaracharya to initiate her husband Mandanmishra into sannyas and to make him his disciple. Shankaracharya agreed. Accordingly, Mandanmishra was given sannyas, renamed Sureshwaracharya and made the first head of the Shringery Sharadapeeth founded by Shankaracharya.[1]

7. *Swachhandamrutyu*: To die at one's own will, death having no control over him.
8. *Sahakridanudarshanam*: To see the sport of gods in heaven and capacity and prowess to participate in it.
9. *Yathasamkalpasamsiddhi*: To attain whatever desired.
10. *Ajnapratihatagatih*: Whereby whose command and movement have no obstruction and stoppage.

Little Siddhis:

1. *Trikalajnatvam*: The knowledge of past, future and present.
2. *Advandvam*: To be beyond the control of the duality of pleasure, pain, cold, heat, soft, very hard.

3. *Parachittadyabhijnata*: To tell about another's dream or to know his mind.
4. *Pratishtambah*: To stop the effect of fire, wind, water, weapon, poison and the sun.
5. *Aparajayah*: Not being defeated by any body; being victorious everywhere.

Sai Baba had, it would appear, all the above-mentioned siddhis and some others not mentioned here e.g. *Khandayoga*. Sometimes his action would be a combination of two or more siddhis. Now we will examine from testimony on record the siddhis he is known to have used. Let us now see the testimony on great siddhis.

Anima and **Laghima** - These siddhis pertain to the body. Upto the end of the nineteenth century Sai Baba was known to sleep on a wooden plank 6' x 11/4' suspended from the rafter by shreds of torn cloth and four lamps used to be placed on it. The plank would be about 7 to 8 feet above the ground and 4 to 5 feet below the ceiling. Two devotees Mrs. Chandrabai Borkar and Das Ganu have recorded in their statements that they had seen him lying on the plank *(Devotees' Experiences of Sai Baba* Part III, p. 80 and Part II, p. 43 at pp. 48 and 64). It is also known that in 1908 Sai Baba had assumed the form of a fly to taste the *naivedya* of puranpoli offered by Nanasaheb Chandorkar *(Devotees' Experiences of Sai Baba*. Part III, pp. 75, p.79). For Rao Bahadur M.W. Pradhan, Sai Baba had assumed the form of a crow and lifted the *naivedya* of puranpoli *(Devotees' Experiences of Sri Sai baba* Part II, p. 1 and p.5). That is why in verses 19-20 of Chapter X of "*Shri Sai Sat Charit*". Annasaheb Dabholkar says that he who could assume the form of a fly, insect or ant instantaneously at will and remain seated in the air or midspace, for him what is it to lie on a plank like the above ?

It is also on record that Sai Baba had entered the room of Megha and thrown *akshata* (consecrated rice) on his bed *(Shri Sai Sat Charit*, XXVIII, pp. 192 and 199) and later told him that he (Sai Baba) was everywhere, had no shape and size, and did not require a door to enter the room. He had also told Mrs. R. A. Tarkhad that he had been to their Bandra residence which he had entered at will and had to return hungry as no *naivedya* was offered to him *(Shri Sai Sat Charit*, IX, 108).

Mahima or Garima: This siddhi also relates to the body.

The body can be made as heavy as desired, even as heavy as a mountain. Bayaji Kote Patil on whose body Sai Baba leaned and gave up the ghost in 1918 records in his statement: "I used to boast and feel proud that I had Bhima's strength. So I tried to lift Baba up in my arms after the massage to carry him and place him before the fire. Many a day I have done so. That day I could not lift him. Baba laughed at me and he put down my pride." (*Devotees' Experiences of Sri Sai Baba*, Part II, p. 101, p. 103)

Prapti: Sri Baba had no desires whatever. He was *nishakama* par excellence as far as he himself was concerned. Chakra Narayan, the Christian Police Fauzdar observes in his statement. "I was Police Fauzdar at Kopargaon when Baba passed away (October, 1918). I was not a believer in Baba. We were watching Baba through our men. Even though I watched him skeptically, the result was to create in me a high regard for him. First and foremost was the fact that he was not moved by women or wealth. Many women would come to him and place their heads on his feet and sit before him. But he was unmoved. He would not care to cast one glance of admiration, or of lust at them. He was clearly an unmistakably unattached. About money also, we watched him people voluntarily gave him money. If any did not give him money, Baba would not curse or hate or be displeased with him. The same held good about his begging for bread. He did not care for what he got. Whatever he got, he scattered with a liberal hand. When he died, we took possession of his cash, that was only Rs. 16". (*Devotees' Experiences of Sri Sai Baba*, Part I, p. 125). In verse 60 of Chapter XIII of '*Shri Sai Sat Charita*', it is said that the state of Sai Baba was such that he did not have even a bit of worldly desire but he bestowed on his devotees whatever they desired.

Undoubtedly, *vairagya* of Sai Baba was of the highest order, (*Devotees' Experiences of Sri Sai Baba*, Part I, p. 18, p. 33) but for his devotees he desired to help them in temporal matters so that slowly he could lead them on to the path of spiritual progress. Prof. G.G. Narke has observed in his statement: "Baba gave experience to each devotee--experience of Baba's vast powers of his looking into the heart, into the distant regions of space and time, past or future and then and there, infused faith. One had not merely to swallow everything on trust. The solid benefit, temporal or spiritual reaped by the devotee, and his feeling that he is under the eye and power of Baba always wherever he may go and whatever he may do, give him incredible basis for his further spiritual and temporal guidance." (*Devotees' Experiences of Sri Sai Baba*, Part I, p.18, p. 35)

Prakashya: Of this siddhi of Sai Baba Prof. G.G. Narke says in his statement. "To one deeply observing Him, the startling fact came out into greater and greater prominence that Baba was living and operating in other worlds also, besides this world and in an invisible body. Baba was frequently talking of His travels with an invisible body across great distances of space (and time). In the mornings, sitting near His *dhuni* (fire) with several devotees. He would say to what distant place He went overnight and what He had done. Those who had slept by His side the whole night at the masjid or *chavadi* knew that His physical body was at Shirdi all the night. But His statements were literally true and were occasionally verified and found to be true. He had travelled to distant places in an invisible i.e. spirit form and rendered help there. Again He would frequently talk of post mortem experiences. This power to travel in invisible body to distant parts of the world, to traverse other realms than the earth life and note or conrol what takes places there, and to see the past and future alike revealed one great fact about his nature. Some of His own observations also brought that out clearly (*Devotees' Experiences of Sri Sai Baba*, Part I, pp 24, 25, 26, 27).

One of the examples cited by Narke is as follows: "A Shirdi Marwadi's boy fell ill and died. People returned from funeral to the Masjid with gloomy faces. Sai Baba then said of that boy, 'He must be nearing the river now, just crossing it'. I felt that the reference could only be to Vaitarini (Part I, 26-27).

In verse 68 of Chapter XV of *Shri Sai Sat Charita*, Dabholkar quotes Sai Baba's words: "Though my physical frame is here and you are far away, beyond seven seas, I come to know instantaneously whatever you do there".

Ishita : Prof. G.G. Narke states in this connection: "He (Sai Baba) also made occasional references to what his function was in this terrestrial sphere and in other worlds. He several times referred to His control of the destinies of the departed souls - indicating thereby His function in the Cosmic Order. Sai Baba never spoke an untruth, never meaningless jargon". (*Devotees' Experiences of Sri Sai Baba*, Part I, pp. 27-28).

When a mother came to Sai Baba and repeatedly implored him to revive her dead child, Kakasaheb Dikshit was standing nearby.

Moved by her grief, he also joined her in requesting Sai Baba to bring the dead child to life again. Then Sai Baba said to him, "Do not fall into delusioln. What has happened is for the good. His soul has entered a new body and in his new body will do good work which he could not have done in this body. If I drag his soul into this (old) body it will no doubt revive. I can do this for you. But have you thought of the consequences ? Are you prepared to shoulder the responsibility?" Dikshit immediately understood the wisdom of Saibaba's observations and no more pressed him to revive the dead body of the child.

Vashita : Sai Baba undoubtedly was the Master of His senses and was ever in the state of highest bliss. Prof. Narke observes. "His awareness exceeded the bounds of our space and time-extended over all the worlds and embraced the distant past and future as well as the present. He knew, therefore, what existence in any of the worlds and at anytime had to offer for the soul's enjoyment; and with such knowledcge he renounced all attachement. He was perfectly detached, amidst numerous attractions. His life was, therefore, real *Vairagya* and real *Nishkama Karma*. (*Devotees' Experiences of Sri Sai Baba*, Part I, p.33). Narke also says further that Sai Baba's *brahmacharya* was perfect and his glittering eyes spoke it out (p.38). Chakra Narayan, the Police Fouzdar at Kopargaon whose observations we have quoted earlier also bears out what Narke says.

Yatkamastadavasyati : Even as the waters subside in the ocean which though ever being filled by them, never overflows, in Sai Baba all longings had subsided and he was ever one in his infinite peace. His was a serene wisdom, for like the tortoise he had withdrawn all his senses from the attractions of the pleasures of sense. Therefore not only was He ever in a state of the highest bliss but He could ever give a taste of it to devotees like G.S. Khaparde, Krishnashastri Jageshwar, Bhishma and others. It is also recorded that in December, 1909, Sai Baba gave darshan in the form of Rama to a doctor who was a staunch Rama devotee and who did not want to accompany his Mamledar-friend to Shirdi as he thought he would have to bow at the feet of Sai Baba whom he regarded as a Muslim. At that time he stayed in Shirdi for three days and on the midnight of the third day, in his sleep he experienced bliss which lasted for 15 to 20 days even after his return home. (Preface by Hari Sitaram Dikshit to *Sainath Bhajanmala* by Raghunath & Savitri Tendulkar, *Shri Sai Sat Charita*, XII, 151-173).

We will now turn to medium siddhis.

Annormimattvam : Hunger, thirst, grief, delusion, old age and death, the six modifications of being, did not injuriously affect the body of Sai Baba. He led a life of austerity and tapas and established complete supremacy over His senses. In the process He came to have siddhis. It is said that He never took any medicine for any of his bodily ailments even when He drew upon himself the karmic sufferings of his devotees e.g. buboes of G.S. Khaparde's son and Mrs. Sadashiv Atmaram Tarkhad's eye-trouble. Mrs. S.A. Tarkhad says in her statement. 'My eyes have been giving me trouble constantly. On one occasion while I was at Shirdi, they were greatly paining me and water was freely flowing from them. In such a condition I went and sat up before Baba. He looked at me. My eyes ceased to pain and water. But His eyes were dropping tears. The accurate diagnosis of the disease at a glance was wondrous enough. Still more wondrous was His curing deep seated organic disease abruptly and suddenly without any visible application of remedy or treatment. Scientists or medical men may disbelieve this. But having actually experienced it in my own case and in that of others who came before Sri Sai Baba, I cannot disbelieve such cases and what is most peculiar - the drawing of diseases on to himself by pure will-power." (*Devotees' Experiences of Sri Sai Baba*, Part I, pp. 95-96).

Doorshravan* and *Doordarshan : There are innumerable instances of these siddhis both in '*Shri Sai Sat Charita*' and '*Shri Sai Leela*' magazine. To mention only two, when Dabholkar engaged in a controversy with Balasaheb Bhate in Sathewada in Shirdi which is at some distance from the masjid, Sai Baba sitting in the masjid immediately saw and heard everything and asked Dabholkar about it when the latter called on him. (*Shri Sai Sat Charita*, Chap. II) Another instance is that of Shankarrao and his friend Lakhmichand who borrowed money and went to Shirdi and during their travel by train did Bhajan and made enquiries with other passengers about Sai Baba. Sai Baba narrated all these details when the two of them called on Sai Baba the first time (*Shri Sai Sat Charita*, Chap XXVIII). To cap it all Shankar Rao has stated in an article in *Shri Sai Leela* (Vol. III, issue 12, p. 423) that Sai Baba told him his family history from his grandfather's time which was found to be correct on verification by Shankar Rao on returning home. But these siddhis pale into insignificance as compared to "*Prakashya*" one of the great siddhis described earlier.

Manojava and ***Kamaroopa*** : To travel at the speed of mind to any place, and to assume at once any form. The two telling instances of these powers are (1) Sai Baba assuming the form of a Bengali Sannyasi and attending with two lads the luncheon on the conclusion of a religious vow at B.V. Deo's residence at Dahanu (*Shri Sai Satcharita*, Chap XXXX) and conveying Ramgirbua to Jamner from Jalgaon Railway Station by materialising a tonga and a horse and himself assuming the form of tongawala for the purpose (*Shri Sai Sat Charita*, Chap XXXIII).

Parakayapravesh : There is no instance to my information and belief of the use of this siddhi by Sai Baba. Some devotees assume that the form of cat which Sai Baba assumed to cure the fondness for curds of a devotee named Hansraj is an example of this siddhi (*Devotees' Experiences of Sri Sai Baba*, Part II, PP. 117-119). But this does not seem to be correct. It is another instance of *Kamaroopa* siddhi mentioned earlier.

Swachhandmrutyu : Undoubtedly Sai Baba lay down his life of his own sweet will on October 15, 1918 the day of Vijayadashami as the mission of his life had been fulfilled (*Shri Sai Sat Charita*, XXXXII, 145). He who had told a devotee of his connections with him in past births as far back as 72 generations had full knowledge of the past, present and future. It would not, therefore, be a surprise if he had planned for his final departure carefully. Four months before his end, he had sent messages to two fellow fakirs in Aurangabad of his impending departure and got ceremonies performed according to Muslim practices. (*Devotees' Experiences of Sri Sai Baba*, Part III, pp.159-160). Similarly fourteen days before his end he had got a devotee to do *parayanas* of Rama Vijay before himself in the masjid. Two other incidents described in detail in *Shri Sai Sat Charit* aindicate how he had planned the finale carefully. (Shri Sai-Sat-Charit, XXXIX, 120-171 and XXXXII, 44-68).

Sahakridanudarshanam : This is a medium siddhi and to a yogi like Sai Baba of renunciation and detachment this siddhi is insignificant. In any case it is only an aspect of the great siddhis like *Prakashya* and *Yatkama Stadavasyati*.

Yathasamkalpa and ***Ajnapratihatagatih*** : These are the last two of the medium siddhis. The former is the power to attain whatever desired and the latter ensures that there is no stoppage of the command. But these are obviously subordinate to the great siddhis of *Ishita* and *Yatkamastadavasyati*. Further their jurisdiction would appear to be confined only to this world.

Perhaps lighting of lamps with water, taking karmic suffering of the devotees upon himself, curing of snake bites, stopping the further progress of diseases and such other siddhis would appear to be covered by these powers.

After having had a look at the medium siddhis let us now consider the small siddhis.

Trikalajnana : The knowledge of past, future and present.

Prof. G.G. Narke states in his statement: When He (Sai Baba) talked, He spoke as one seated in my heart, knowing all its thoughts, all its wishes, etc. This is God within. I had no hesitation in deciding that he was God. I tested him at times. Each test produced the same conviction that he was all--knowing, all--seeing and able to mould all things to his will. A few instances out of hundreds may be cited here which showed that nothing was beyond him or concealed from him, in the past, present and future." (*Devotees' Experiences of Sri Sai Baba*, Part I, p. 21). Only two instances which Prof. Narke cities in his statement may be quoted here : (1) In 1913 Sai Baba told Gopalrao Buti, Prof. Narke's father-in-law that he would construct a Dagdiwada (Stone edifice) at Shirdi and Narke would be in charge of it. It was only in 1915-16 that Buti began to build it. Body of Sai Baba was interred in the Dagdiwada in 1918 and that part is known as Samadhi Mandir (2). The entire future career of Prof. Narke was known to Sai Baba and he had told him way back in 1913 that he would settle in Poona and asked him to apply in 1917 for the post of Professor of Geology in Poona Engineering College which Narke considered out of his reach. We have also seen above that Shri Baba had told Shankarrao his family history from his grandfather's time which was absolutely accurate. No wonder the author of Shri Sai-Sat-Charit says:

"He had knowledge of the past, future and present. Whoever went to him for his darshan, Sai Baba would narrate his past, future and present, unasked, to the last detail. (*Shri Sai Sat Charita*, X, 71) In *Shri Sai Sat Charita* there are also three tales of past births of Mrs. R.A. Tarkhad (Chap XXVII), two she-goats (Chap. XXXXVI) and the serpent and the frog (Chap XXXXVII).

Advandvam : Sai Baba walked barefooted, sat on a bare sack cloth, wore only a kafni made of thick mandarpat and used no other covering throughout the year whether summer or winter.

(*Shri Sai Sat Charita*, V, 88,91). His was a spartan life. He was beyond the duality of pleasure-pain, cold-heat, soft-very hard etc. He had risen beyond the three gunas (forces), and beyond earthly pairs of opposites, beyond gains and possessions and was established in the consciousness of the Atman, always, as described in verse 45 of Chapter II of the Bhagwad Gita.

Parachittadyabhijnata : To tell about another's dream or to know his mind there are innumerable instances of this siddhi possessed by Sai Baba in full cited in *Shri Sai Sat Charita*, e.g. Dr. Hate's dream of offering naivedya of walpapadi vegetable to Sai Baba (Chap. XXIX, 145-159), also the desire of Dharamsey Thakkar to have seedless grapes from Sai Baba while others got grapes with seed (Chap. XXXV) the desire of Lakhmichand to eat sanja (Samolina pudding) (Chap. XXVIII).

Pratishtambah : Stopping the effect of fire, wind, water, weapon, poison and the sun. Examples of the use of this siddhi are found in Chap XI of *Shri Sai Sat Charita*. He had with his powers stopped the tornado accompanied by heavy showers, thundering of clouds and lightning. Even earlier he put his hand in a boiling dish being cooked over fire or in the burning fire it did not affect him. Also see (Chap. XXXVIII verses XI).

About stopping the effect of weapons, Swami Sai Sharan Anand, narrates an instance of this siddhi at p. 112 of the Biography of Sai Baba written by him in Gujarati. It is stated by him that in 1915 an intolerant Pathan drawn to Sai Baba due to his charisma turned hostile and planned to make short work of Sai Baba by dealing a mortal blow on his head from behind with a staff. Sai Baba merely glanced at him, caught hold of his wrist and the Pathan became lifeless and collapsed to the ground. It was only with support of two persons that he could get up. He left Shirdi for good thereafter.

Aparajaya : Not being defeated by any body, being victorious everywhere.

A man of *vairagya* (renunciation & austerity) and *nishkarma* (desireless and detached) like Sai Baba who had all the siddhis waiting at his door would accomplish whatever he desired for his devotees for he wanted nothing for himself. The question of defeating anybody has no meaning in a life like his.

Both in Patanjali Yogasutra as well as in Eknathi Bhagwat

the use of siddhis has been deprecated as they are a great impediment in liberation. What happens after liberation, whether the siddhis which have accrued naturally should be used by a *siddha* or *mukta* or a *paramhamsa* has not been stated in these books. Sai Baba also discouraged the use of siddhis and used the appellation `rand' (woman of easy virtue) in referring to them. R.A. Tarkhad was the secretary and manager of Makanji Omit Khatau Cotton Textile Spg. & Wvg. Mills of Bombay. He first had Sai Baba's darshan in September, 1910. He had been brought up for 45 years of his life in Prarthana Samajist tradition and could not understand Sai Baba's leelas. So he read the books of Marathi saints and works of Ramatirtha and Vivekanand; He particularly liked Raja yoga of Vivekanand. Being a science graduate he had made a study of physiology and comparative anatomy in depth. He then came to the conclusion that all the things of Rajayoga depended on gaining control over vasomotor nerve. So he started practising pranayama not for gaining siddhis but for realization of God. Soon he began to feel energetic, and his health improved. It was 12th September, 1912. At 7 p.m. he returned home. He had a bath of cold water and sat down for pranayama with his eyes concentrated on the tip of the nose. And he had a strange experience. He saw a rose coloured light which would not vanish. He got up, washed his face with cold water and sat down once more. Again the rose coloured light appeared before his sight which turned to dark red. It would not disappear. So he concentrated his attention on the light and he saw a house of fire. As soon as the thought about the house came to his mind, it became clear to him that particular part of his mill had caught fire. Immediately he got up from his seat, tears came to his eyes and he prayed to the Lord within, "Oh Lord, I started this *pranayama* for your realization, not for this siddhi. Hence I have stopped *pranayama* from today." So saying, he came out of his room, just then a peon from his mill came and told him that a fire had broken out in his factory. Tarkhad immediately went to the mill and by then the fire had come under control. He returned home at 1 a.m. There was a sequel to this. Two to three months after the above incident when Tarkhad went to Shirdi, as soon as he placed his head on Sai Baba's feet Sai Baba said, "Well, was the *rand* (woman of easy virtue-meaning siddhi) trying to attach itself to you ? But how shall I allow it ! We have nothing to do with these *rands*." This shows that Sai Baba also had no use for cultivation and/ or pursuit of *siddhis*. (*Shri Sai Leela,* Vol. VI, issues 4-5, p.1) For how a yogi ever one with Brahman like Sai Baba may use the siddhis- refer to Chap. *Riddhi-Siddhis* in Swami Sai Sharanand's book.

We have mentioned at the beginning that besides the siddhis etc. mentioned in Srimad Bhagavat Sai Baba possessed a unique siddhi known as *Khandayoga* - i.e. severing parts of the body and joining them to-gether. It is said that his different limbs would be seen lying scattered in the masjid but Sai Baba would later be seen whole seated on his usual place (*Shri Sai Sat Charita*, VII, 60-68). In this connection, the conversation between the above referred R.A. Tarkhad and Baba Madhavdas a renowned yogi is very instructive. First a few words about Baba Madhavdas. He hailed from Bengal and was a yogi of ChaitanyaPanth. His tapas was severe and unbelievable. He had spent twelve years in Kanakeshwar (forest on mountain in Raigad district near Bombay) on a diet of only chillis and one seer of ghee. He was therefore known as Mirchibaba in these parts. Later he went to Gujarat and in 1921 took samadhi in a village called Malsar on the banks of Narmada. Gaikwads, the ruling family of the erstwhile Baroda State and the owner of Makanji Khatau Textile Mills were, among others, his devotees. Tarkhad once witnessed a miracle wrought by Baba Madhavdas at Baroda. Tarkhad found while seated near Madhavdas that he had changed his sex to the female sex when a woman devotee approached him and had reverted to his original state when she left. He saw the whole thing with his own eyes and could not suppress his curiosity to ask Madhavdas about his change of sex at will. "How did this happen?' asked Tarkhad. Pointing to the two sides of his things, Madhavdas said, "There is a nerve here. When it is pulled/stretched your sex changes." Tarkhad queried him about *Khandyoga*. Madhavdas replied that Khandyoga exists but he had not experienced it in his present body but hoped to do so in his next body. From this Tarkhad obtained confirmation of the report of the practice of Khandyoga by Sai Baba. (*Shri Sai Leela*, Vol. II. issue 2, p. 301).

The above is a very sketchy and incomplete description of Sai Baba's powers.

7
TWO GREAT MIRACLES OF SRI SAI BABA

Prof. C.R. Narayanan

"The unworldly life and miracles of Sai Baba are universally acclaimed. The secular humanitarian approach of Baba, his amazing deeds have created a dazzling and awe-inspiring aura round his life and sainthood."

–Chakor Ajgaonkar,
Shri Sai Leela, May, 1989

Of the numerous miracles of Sai Baba of Shirdi well known as '*Sai Leelas*', to lofty height astounding was His donning the mantle of death in the year 1886 for a period of three full days (or seventy two hours) and recovering to life exactly as He had predicted before the phenomenon. Of course the Avatarship of Baba was established by Him when he lighted the oil lamps of the Masjid with consecrated water, when once the oil managers of Shirdi refused to give oil gratis to Him and when the lamps burnt as brightly with water as with oil, the eyes of the world were opened fully to His incarnation as god.

More thrilling, however, are His other miracles in the eyes of His numerous devotees. One of these is mentioned already in the beginning of the article viz. His entering into a period of absolute death for a period of three full days and His subsequent recovery to life as according to His prediction. Only a brief account of this miracle entitled as "The Seventy--two Hour Samadhi" is furnished in Hemadpant's *Sai Satcharita*. A slightly larger account is presented in "Baba's Charters and Sayings", Putting the two together the phenomenon may be described as follows :

One day in 1886 (the month and date are not given), following an attack of asthma, Baba of Shirdi told His *bhakta* Mahalsapathy (the goldsmith born but brahmin by merit) that he would be going to Allah for a period of three days during which Mahalasapathy should to guard his body and if he did not return after the stipulated seventy--two hours, His injunction to His devotee was to bury His body in an adjacent field.

The thrill of Baba's *'Chamatkar'* is about to commence. Completing His words and injunction Baba leaned on the body of Mahalasapathy and in the eyes of the outside world passed away as completely dead or turned into a corpse. His breathing had stopped, His pulse ticked no more and His eye bids were closed. What more evidence of death including the absence of heart beat would confirm Baba's Samadhi ?

A wail of sorrow swallowed the inhabitants of Shirdi and with mortals understanding prepared for the burial of the dead. The body of Baba had to be recovered from the lap of Mahalsapathy. This indeed posed the most difficult problem. True to the word of Baba a word which was unto the goldsmith inviolabloe as a command of God, Mahalsapathy stubbornly refused to part with His God's body and with almost superhuman stamina guarded it on this lap for a full period of hours seventy two. The ordained seventy two hours passed and wonder of wonders Baba's heart ticked again, the pulse beat again, the breathing was restored again and the eyes of the God opened to the world outside "watching with bated breath and whispering humbleness". It was a pandemonium of the purest joy that broke loose in the village of Shirdi. Baba of Shirdi was alive again to the chorus of joyful acclamation of the villagers.

Thus began and ended the miracle number one of Baba of Shirdi. Is there any example in the annals of any religion the miracle of an Avataar passing away as dead completely and recovering as alive in full ? Only Baba of Shirdi did this wonder and so undoubtedly an Incarnate of the Absolute unparalled or unique in event undoubtedly He is.

In this context the observations or deductions of Mataji Krishna Priya, authoress of a new edition entitled "*Sri Sai Satcharita*" are relevant for discussion. According to the learned authoress, what appeared to the people of Shirdi as Baba shedding His mortal coil in the year 1886 for a period of three days, was His transmigration to the Muttal at Dakshineswar of Sri Ramakrishna Paramahamsa to commune with him another saint or godman almost of the same status or distinction as Baba of Shirdi and to gain from him additional spiritual strength from him before his passing away from the earth in that year. In the opinion of this writer this interpretation goes counter to verisimilitude, for the simple and obvious reason that before his passing away the sage Ramakrishna had bequeathed his entire spiritual power to his disciple Narendranath to be afterwards Swamy Vivekananda of world fame. In the words of the sage himself, all his wonderful spiritual powers were then embodied in Naren (the saint's name of Vivekananda) and in the course of a short time to come out from Naren to shake the world in the realm of religion and spirituality. So there was little to gain for Baba of Shirdi from Ramakrishna Paramahamsa. What was there to gain from an already spent force which the Paramahamsa was 1886?

The other miracle of Baba is concerned with the goldsmith Mahalaspathy and his worship of the living Baba, a phenomenon or process extremely simple but later to blaze into the mass idolatry of Baba in the flesh. To many of Baba's worshippers the Baba Mahalsapathy event will cause an exhiliration of the spirits even by repeated recollection of the same. What was this worship of Baba by Mahalsapa and what must have been the cause behind ? The light lit by Baba inside Mahalaspathy must have been the cause and the worship was in the form of smearing the neck of Baba with sandal paste and the offering of flowers at His feet by Mahalaspathy. To Mahalsapathy Baba was a living god to whom he was compelled to offer his worship in a most simple form though it was. And the more interesting aspect of the worship was Baba appearing like a Muslim accepting the worship from a Hindu. This is the crux of the problem as will he seen below.

Sai Baba of Shirdi had many Muslim followers both in Shirdi and outside. According to Islamic tenets the Muslims looked upon Baba as a "Saint" or 'Aulia' and so did unto him respect and honour as a Hindu does to his "Guru", but offered not unlike the Hindu, worship to his Guru as to deity in a temple, because Islam forbids idolatry of any type. What Mahalsapathy was doing was worship of Baba in the Hindu fashion with no dividing line between God and Guru and this the Muslims in Shirdi could not stomach, as to them Baba was only a Muslim Aulia and what more His abode was a mosque or masjid. The Muslims wanted to nip in the bid such an idolatry of one who in their view was a Muslim saint. A plot was hatched with the local Kazi and that was the Muslims to station themselves at the entrance of the masjid to prevent the entry of Mahalsapathy into it to his daily worship of Baba.

So one day when as usual Mahalsapathy came to do his usual *"Puja"* of Baba, he was started to find his way barred by a few stalwart Muslims. Being meek and gentle by disposition Mahalsapathy retired to the wall of the masjid and from there started his worship of Baba seated in the masjid. When Baba saw this He asked His *bhakta* as to why he offered his worship from a distance. The masjid being small was visible and audible from anywhere Mahalasapathy pointed out to the Muslims guarding the entrance of the masjid to prevent his moving in.

Now let the reader prepare himself or herself for another *"Chamatkar"* from that God presideing over in Shirdi. His eyes flashed fire and taking His *satka* dashed it on the floor, and addressing Mahalaspathy asked him to walk into the masjid, do his puja even to the extent of annoting His entire body with sandal to are anyone against it. The sound of Baba's *satka* was like a peal of thunder to the Muslims who trembled at its sound and were made mute by Baba's words. The gentle devotee Mahalsapathy walked majestically into the masjid and did his usual worship of his living God.

Here is the actual miracle of Baba or His *"Leela"*. The beef-eating Muslims could have over-powered the little gold smith ... just by a whiff from their mouths. The same Muslims could have overlooked the person of Baba sitting in the masjid. Why did these not happen ? It was because of the mystic power of God Baba was seen at its zenith. The walking in of Mahlasapathy into the masjid is a scene worthy of being recorded by a Poet Laureate. The Muslims designed to bar him, were reduced to pitiable objects and Baba of Shirdi shone like the sun in all its splendour.

Hence forth the worship of Baba in the flesh, an unheard of phenomenon in the histroy of any religion, developed into a congregational turn, a daily mass worship of Him at midday in the masjid and an elegant *aagamic* submission to Him in the Chavadi on alternate nights to be preceeded by a procession from the masjid to the Chavadi. Both these phenomena were supremely unique. Baba walking and not riding a vehicle as in the case of Hindu gods and Baba enthroned in the chavadi and the common folks along with the elite showering their adoration on His living person. The self-inposed death and the rescurrection of Baba of Shirdi is a miracle number one and the worship of Him in the flesh as a deity in a temple beginning from the simple offering of sandal paste and flowers by Mahlsapathy to its culmination in the mass worship of in the traditional Hindu way is miracle number two.

      Baba of Shirdi is thus our Avatar Supreme and God unique. SAI RAM!

Prof. C.R. Narayanan\
Resident (12),\
Sri P. Reddy Citizens Home\
Andhra Mahila Sabha\
Madras - 600028

8

SAI BABA AS I SAW HIM

Mrs. Manager

(*Mrs. Manager, a Parsee devotee from Bombay had visited Sri Shirdi Sai Baba many times during 1910-1915. In her thrilling memories she has presented a first-hand account of her impressions of her face to face interactions with the divine charismatic personality of Baba*).

–Sri Shirdi Sai Baba

One's first impression of Sai Baba was derived from his eyes. There was such power and penetration in his glance that none could continue to look at his eyes. One felt that Sai Baba was reading him or her, through and through. Soon one lowered one's eyes and bowed down. One felt that He was not only in one's heart, but in every atom of one's body. A few words, a gesture would reveal to one that Sai Baba knew all about the past, present and even future and about everything else. There was nothing else to do for one, except to submit trustfully and to surrender oneself to Him. And there He was to look after every minute detail, and guide one safe through every turn and every vicissitude of life. He was the *Antaryami*, call Him God or *Satpurusha* in *Sahaja Sthithi* or what you like. But the overpowering personality was there, and in his presence no doubts, no fears, no questioning had any place and one resigned oneself and found that was the only course, the safest and best course. From one's first entry into His presence, one went on getting experience of His power, His all-knowing and all-pervasive personality. His protecting care that shielded one, wherever one went and at any time whatsoever.

I shall give some instances of his *Antaryamitva* that I

personally got or learnt of in the early days of my stay at Shirdi.

Shirdi in those days was a neglected hamlet without any lighting, and other conveniences of civilization. It has had some improvement since. But when I was there, the streets and passages were all dark and unlit at night. One night I was walking about. But suddenly and abruptly I stopped. There was no sound or sight to account for my stopping. For some unknown reason I felt I must stop and I did. A little time passed and a light was brought by some one and there lo, and behold! at the very place where I was to have placed my foot at the next step, there was a serpent lying quiet. Of course, if I had put my foot, the consequences might have been very serious, if not fatal. The light showed what the danger was that I escaped. But I could not have guessed of its existence so near me by the use of my own powers, in the absence of the light. Why and how had I stopped so abruptly and how did the light come in so opportune a moment to show me the danger? The only answer is the all-seeing and ever watchful power and protective grace of Sai Baba. He has saved this body of mine from death on many occasions. But these or some of these will be mentioned later on.

To take another instance. We used to go and sit near Sai Baba at his Mosque. Any one could go up at the usual time, without permission asked of or introduction taken to Sai Baba and bow before him and all there. On one occasion, as I was seated at a short distance from Sai Baba, there came a leper to the Mosque. His disease was far advanced. He was stinking and he had little strength left in him, so that it was with much difficulty and very slowly, he clambered up the three steps of the Mosque, moved on to the *Dhuni* (fire) and then to Sai Baba and placed his head on Baba's feet. It took so much time for him to take his *Darsana*, and I feeling the strench from him intensely, hoped he would clear off. At last when he got down slowly carrying a small parcel wrapped up in a dirty cloth, I felt relief and said within myself, "Thank God. He is off". Sai Baba at once darted a piercing glace at me, and I knew that he read my thought. Before the leper had gone far, Sai Baba called out and sent some one to fetch him back. The man came. It was again the slow process of his clambering up, emitting foul strench all the time; and as the man bowed to Baba, Baba picked up that parcel saying "What is this?" and opened it. It contained some *"Pedas"* (i.e., milk sweets) and Sai Baba took up a piece and gave it to me alone of all present and asked me to eat it. What horror! To eat up a thing brought by the stinking leper! But it was Sai Baba's order, and there was no option but to obey. So I ate it up. Sai Baba took another piece and himself swallowed it and then sent the man away with the remainder. Why he was recalled and I alone was the chosen recipient of his *peda*, none then understood. But I knew full well that Sai Baba had read my heart and was teaching me valuable lessons, e.g., in humility, fraternity, sympathy, endurance and trust in His Supreme wisdom rather than in my own notions of hygiene and sanitation for saving me from diseases.

When we had difficulties to get over, we never had to speak we had merely to go and sit or stand in his presence. He at once knew what the matter was and gave a direction exactly meeting our requirements. We had our servant with us at Shirdi. He had acute pain in his lumber region. My husband went to Sai Baba and was standing. Some others were also present before Sai Baba. Baba suddenly said "Hallo, my leg is paining. Great is the pain." Some one suggested that something should be done to relieve the pain. "Yes", said Baba, "if green leaves are heated and applied over it, it will go away." "What leaves, Baba?" was the query by some one. Baba said, "These green leaves near the Lendi" (i.e., streamlet.) One suggested one leaf and another a different leaf. One finally asked if it was *Korphad*. "Yes" Baba said, "that is it. The leaf has to be brought, split into two, slightly heated over the fire and applied. That is all." At once, my husband knew that this was Baba's kind prescription for our servant. We fetched the leaf and applied it as directed, and the servant was relieved of his pain.

Not only was he present at all places when his physical body was in one place, say the mosque, but he was also able to do various things with his invisible body.

My eyes have been giving me trouble constantly. On one occasion while I was at Shirdi, they were greatly paining me and water was freely flowing from them. In such a condition I went and sat up before Baba. He looked at me. My eyes ceased to pain and water. But his eyes were dropping tears. The accurate diagnosis of the disease at a glance was wondrous enough. Still more wondrous was his curing deep seated organic disease abruptly and suddenly without any visible application of remedy or treatment. Scientists or medical men may disbelieve this. But having actually experienced it in my own case and in that of others who came before Sai Baba,

I cannot disbelieve such cases and what is most peculiar the drawing of diseases on to himself by pure willpower.

These wonderful powers and especially this wonderful nature of Sri Sai Baba with his *Antaryamitva*, i.e., his being inside every creature and every object animate or inanimate so as to control all voluntary and involuntary movements of creatures and objects, throw light on what He occasionally said of himself. "I am not at Shirdi", he would say, while he was at Shirdi. As was frequently said, he was not confined within the three cubits length of flesh, bone and blood that people called Sri Baba. He was in every dog, cat, pig, man and woman. While we cannot shake off the idea that we are this physical sheath or the attachment we feel to things connected with it, he was ever free from such narrow ideas or attachments. He seemed to be in or to be the oversoul, the Super-consciousness, *Sahaj Samadhi*, or *Jnanamaya Shariri* by whatever name we choose to refer to that higher state of his.

One noticeable difference between Sri Sai Baba and other saints struck me. I have moved with other notable saints also. I have seen them in high Samadhi or trance condition entirely forgetting their body and course) effacing the narrow notion of the self confined to the body; and I have seen them later getting conscious of their surroundings, knowing what is in our hearts and replying to us. But with Sri Sai Baba, there was this peculiar feature. He had not to go into trance to achieve anything or to reach any higher position or knowledge. He was every moment exercising a double consciousness, one actively utilizing the Ego called Sri Sai Baba and dealing with other Egos in temporal or spiritual affairs, and the other entirely superseding all Egos and resting in the position of the Universal Soul or Ego; he was exercising and manifesting all the powers and features incidental to both the states of consciousness. Other saints would forget their body and surroundings and then return to it. But Sri Sai Baba always was in and outside the material world. Others seemed to take pains and by efforts to trace the contents of others' minds and read their past history. But with Sri Sai Baba this was not a matter of effort. He was in the all knowing state always.

Sai Baba was one whom some people could not understand at all. He would talk, e.g., to a hawker about some cloth brought for making *kafnis*, higgle and haggle like the most inveterate shopper at a bazaar, and beat down the price of the cloth, say from Annas.

8 a yard to Annas 5 a yard and take say 40 yards. This would make the lastly onlooker conclude that Sai Baba was parsimonious, and avaricious or at any rate attached to wealth. A little later, he (i.e., Sai Baba) would pay the hawker, and then he would sometimes pay four times the price settled. Again the hasty onlooker would conclude that Baba was crazy, touched in the brain, or needlessly ostentatious in his misplaced charity. In both cases, the hasty judgments would be wide off the mark and the real reasons for Sai Baba's conduct would remain mysterious to all except those whom he meant to enlighten.

It is not merely his power that endeared him to his devotees. His loving care combined with those powers made Shirdi, a veritable paradise to the devotees who went there. Directly we went there, we felt safe, that nothing could harm us. When I went and sat in his presence, I always forgot my pain — nay the body itself with all mundane concerns and anxieties. Hours would pass and I would be in blissful uncosciousness of their passing. That was a unique experience shared, I believe, by, all his real devotees. He was all in all and the All for us.

We never could think of his having limitations. Now that he has passed away, I feel what a terrible loss it is as I can no longer pass hours together in blissful unconsciousness of time and affairs at his feet. We feel we have lost our soul; our bodies alone are left to us now. Yet it would not be true to say that he has altogether vanished. He is still living now and we have ample proof of his powers and protecting care in many matters of and on; though the assurance we derive from these about his continuance can never compare with the bliss we felt in his presence when he was in the active care for us and of the help he has rendered to us after dropping his physical sheath.

I was suffering for over a month during summer of 1915 with a splitting neuralgic headache; we were at Panchgani, a sanatorium, and we tried a number of remedies. It was all to no purpose. I felt I must die, with that feeling, I resolved to go to Shirdi, so that I may have the privilege of dying at Baba's feet; and in spite of some objections raised by my husband at first, we moved on to Kopergaon and came to the river Godavari which we had to cross. It struck me at once that I should bathe in the holy river as anyhow I was going to die soon. A cold bath might increase my pain and accelerate death. Well, so much the better, I had my bath. Well?

Judge of our surprise! The bath over, I came out and the headache instead of getting aggravated, left me at once and for ever. That long standing scourge left me for good by that bath, even though a cold bath when the headache was on was previously totally practicable and a terror to me. This cure was surely due to Sri Sai.

Sri Sai Baba did not found any *Math* or Institution and therefore left no one to occupy the *Gadi* (seat) he sat on.

Sri Sai Baba's qualities shine out of his own conduct and his virtues are worthy of mention. His kindness would be amply borne out by the incidents already mentioned. Many other incidents known to and experienced by all who came to him can be mentioned which show that it extended far beyond Shirdi thousands of miles away even to Europe, when his devotees were facing danger in the Great World War I in 1914-19. But he was also just and impartial, while he was kind. If the occasion called for it, he said, one should sacrifice one's own child. His serene impartiality knew no difference between the king and a beggar. All were equal in his eyes. He was never obsequious to the rich and high placed, nor supercilious and contemptuous to the lowly. Revenue Commissioners and Collectors have called to see him, and lower officials in numbers, e.g., D.Os, D.Cs, Mamlatdars, etc. But wealth and position were no special grounds of preference or differential treatment with him. His accessibility to all and at all hours practically was a remarkable features of his. "My Darbar is always open", he used to say - "at all hours". He had nothing to fear from scrutiny, and nothing shameful to conceal. All his actions were open and above board.

Another distinguishing feature of his life was Freedom from care and anxiety. He had no interests to serve or protect, no institution to seek support for or maintain; no acquisitions to safeguard; no private property to feel anxious about. Everything got was quickly disposed of. He lived on the begged and freely offered food. He daily collected *Dakshina* of that a further detail may be given later on. But he spent it. During the last nine years or so of his life, he was daily giving Rs. 110 away to Tatya and Bade Baba. Each day's earning were depleted in no time. And when he died, he left in his pocket just the amount needed to cover his funeral expenses. His self-control and equanimity may be mentioned in this connection. He was far too lofty to care for trivial things. His palate, like his other senses, was so strictly under his control that none ever found him show any trace of desire for anything, so far as I know.

His generosity may next be mentioned. Besides Rs. 110 daily paid to some, he would scatter money and gifts. Some would say it was Rs. 300 daily - fancying that untruth or exaggeration is needed to set out Baba's glory. But his greatness needed no such untruth or exaggeration to set it off. A few actual facts would suffice to establish his greatness beyond question. Coming to the question of his generosity, we may state what we have seen Bhajan parties (Hindus) and Fakirs would come and would be liberally supplied.

His methods of imparting spiritual benefit and his religious ideas were hardly brought to others' notice. He would speak of God as any other religious and pious man might i.e., rarely, and with feeling. His religious practice was hardly noticeable. He would sit in the mornings near his *Dhuni* i.e., fire and wave his arms and fingers about, making gestures which conveyed no meaning to us, and saying ... "*Haq*", i.e., God.

Purity, Strength, Regularity and Self-denial one noticed about him always. He would always beg his food. Even during his illness, he never lay bedridden, but would get up and go round to beg his food. He would beg for food only in the accustomed quarters and to a limited extent. And out of his begged food, he ate only a little and the rest he would give away.

There may be some who complain that even the ordinary talk of Sai Baba was meaningless jargon. So it was no doubt to them and was intended to be that. "*Jaya Mani Jaisa Bhav, Taya Taisa Anubhav*". But those who were intended to be benefitted by that talk would find their full and vast significance. He did not want comforts to be provided for him. When the Mosque was sought to be repaired - it was first a rumbling old dirty dilapidated building needing repairs he objected and put it off. It was by the devotees' insistence and by their conducting the repairs at night when he was sleeping in the Chavadi, that the reconstruction was pushed through.

Sri Sai Baba's methods of giving spiritual help to visitors were not usual once. There was no Upadesh Mantra given. He never talked of Yoga, Pranayam and Kundalini. But when anything went wrong to one pursuing some Marga, he would come to Sri Sai Baba and would be helped. There was a man who had practiced *Asan* and *Pranayam* and the poor man's system broke down. He was passing blood in his motions. So he came to Sri Sai Baba and stayed. After a while his health was restored during his stay at Shirdi.

Section III

Spiritual Significance and Social Relevance of Sri Shirdi Sai Baba.

"If My Name is chanted with loved and reverence, you get the results far more expected by you, than the mechanical repetition while the mind wanders."

Section I

Sri Shirdi Sai Baba's Avataric Career

"I am immortal. The primary duty of My Avatar is to provide My devotees all their requirements in this world and that beyond. If you worship Me, I will make you unambitious."

9

SAI IS UNIVERSAL TRUTH

Sai Bindu

> "If one meditates on Me with truthful urge, he can know Me. To such a person, I shall grant not only the vision of My physical body but also take him to greater spiritual heights and make him eligible to receive the vision and blessings of 'Siddha Purusha' (God - realiased soul)."
>
> —Sri Shirdi Sai Baba

A : Almighty S : Self S : Silence B : Bounty

U : Ultimate R : Realisation A : Awareness A : Abound

M : Mystery I : Insight I : Illumination B : Bliss A : All Round.

Sai is Universal Truth. Sai is Cosmic Trinity (of creation, preservation and inhalation). Sai is *Parabrahma*. Sai is Father, Mother and every thing. Sai is *Shivashakti Swarup*. He is that space. he is that Nature-force. He is *Purusha* and *Prakriti*. Sai is *Nirakar* in reality. Sai is *Adhar* in relation. He is *Ajanma Bandhu* - until He takes us into Him. There is no retrace, but it is all "Onward March" in the process of Evolution. Sai is Nirgun of the meaningful sense. Sai is *Sagun* of the purposeful essence. Sai is the Fountain Head of Bliss. The Kingdom of Peace is His, where all subjecs are blessed. Sitting under the shelter of neem, He is the Protector and Nectar to all who come to his abode. The Omnipresent, Omnipotent and Omniscient, *Sat-Chit-Anand* descends in the *Swarup* from time to time. The time immemorial, to guard and guide the humanity towards the Goal, He is the path and the Goal. Let the attempts and efforts to see Him as the Universal Principle, gradually unfold and unveil the unfathomable secrets and subtleties of nature, paving the way towards journeying into the merger. The process of creativity and compassion springs from the zone of silence, the unlimited kingdom of Sai, where all are within, but the ruler is yet unseen. The Mineral Kingdom, Vegetable Kingdom, Animal Kingdom and Human Kingdom and all the known and the unknown, the three worlds of past, present and future, the three states of sleepy, dreamy and wakeful existences, the set boundaries of milky ways, the galaxies and the planetary objects of the matter and the mind, the beginningless and endless source of energy and space are within Him.

Sai Baba comes as personality from the stand point of time as an outward expression to set the universal house of cause and effect in certain order. Since He is beyond the time-scale, He in reality is not the personality, but the infinity. How can any entity comprehend the infinity? Rather, one can just identify Himself with that force and immerse in it. He comes down to reveal His infinity to be our own true nature, presently being eclipsed by the finite relationships. He sings the eternal musical tunes of melody to reveal the truth for magical illusions of the world. When we see him as the finite point, we capture the distance between a Me and Him and place Him in the law of motion and relativity. The *Ghatakash* is the space in the pot and the *Mahakash* is the space of the cosmos. When the pot is moved, the matter moves and not the space. It exists. When we establish the relationship, we formulate the entities, one to be greater and other to be smaller. How can the Infinity be compressed into Entity? Our limited minds corner Him into a certain mould, who is beyond all moulds and yet, He accepts all moulds. He is *Virat*. He is Self of all self. There is no Action-Thought-Mould without Him. He is fullness. He is Absolute. Why to condense the person, group, sect, region or religion of the parochial moulds? Why to isolate Him into misconceived narrowness of petty thinking and miserly actions? Why to imprison Him always into the four walls of the earthen temples outside me as if a separate, different and distinct entity is being forbids the entry into the vast inward empire of self, which is His? Why not also try to visualise Him, within Myself, as the all pervading reality? Did He not demonstrate of a dog fed of food having reached Him? Did he not suffer of a dog beaten by the stick, having reached Him? He is all-awareness, He is all-powerful and yet He is all-merciful. He is the witness and nothing can escape His attention. He is everybody, every thing, every-where including myself.

The adoration of that great glory is to gain that greater knowledge to be capable of seeing everything with ripen love, compassion and the reality as He saw. We may see all in all as Sri Sai. We may see nothing without Him and every thing within Him, the absolute and the whole, the name and form in the time frame and the Cosmic force in the infinity.

Like the salt idol venturing to measure the depth of ocean, the longing for the vision is hoped to be certainly graced in the Sai darbar of fair play and justice of the cosmic equilibrium. Pray that Akilanandakoti Brahmananda Nayaka Rajadiraja Yogiraja Parabrahma Sri Sri Sri Sat-Chit-Ananda Sadguru Sai Nath Maharaj. Surrender to this Root of all roots, the Glorious Feet of the Cosmic Lord through the Cosmic Guru.

It is for that vision which is scintillating and enchanting. It is for that vision, which is accelerating, astounding and accomplishing.

Yes, with the celestial offering of faith and patience (the *Shradda* and *Saburi* sought by Sai) it will be completed.

Aum Sri Sai Baba.
-Sai Bindu, C-26, 52(2), Colaco House,
Near Power House, Aguem,
Margao - 403 601, Goa.
(*Shri Sai Leela*, Nov., 1988)

10

SHIRDI SAI BABA AND HIS DIVINE GRACE

Jal M. Chinoy

"Believe Me, though I pass away, My bones in My tomb will give you hope and confidence. Not only Myself but My Tomb would be Speaking, moving and communicating with those who would surrender themselves wholeheartedly to Me. But remember My always, believe in Me heart and soul and then you will be most benefitted."

—*Sri Shirdi Sai Baba*

To state anything about the great Saint of Shirdi, the Greatest Universal Spiritual Master of this era, is just equivalent to showing a small torch against the Sun. Truly confessing, to realise HIM and his spiritual powers only one birth is certainly not enough. A number of births with the same carried over mission or purpose of life are essential.

Remember one thing once for all: the Saint is one but the followers are in thousands seeking HIS divine grace. But how many ultimately succeed? How many are rewarded? Those making half-hearted attempt totally lacking in strong determination, are, automatically, weeded out. Only a few headstrong, obstinate, staunch of purpose, cling to his feet. They are kicked off number of times, but again and again they promptly rush back to kiss the Lotus feet of Sai Baba. Thus subsequently filtered, tested, moulded, they finally earn the real divine grace of Sri Shirdi Sai. Astonishingly, at times

Sri Sai Himself on his own picks up some out of the millions and showers His divine grace on them, which is known to us all in this world.

No country in the world is so famous for Saints, Sadhus and Sages as our country Bharat. We are the inheritors of the richest cultural inheritance in the world. When the westernees were moving with arrows and guns and indulging only in hunting, drinking and merry-making we had the oldest and the richest sacred civilization in our land. Top class scholars, writers, saints and sages occupied golden pages of our Indian History. A lineage of them and Avatars are studded as gems in the recorded pages of our land.

Sri Sai Baba of Shirdi is one Avatar singled out above all the various Avatars whose name, fame and popularity reigns supreme not only in our Bharat, but practically in all parts of the world. While many others shone, glittered and faded away in public minds, one Supreme power, one divine power, one Universal force, outlived all and that is our beloved Shirdi Sai Baba. Sri Sai is a live spiritual force. He, Himself, had said, when living, "I shall speak to My devotees through My tomb." He has withstood the test of time and tides of this era.

Every human being surviving today is banking upon one spiritual power or the other. Our living is such that some day or the other we step into some difficulty. At such juncture, the mortals remember a spiritual force and his assistance. Sri Sai is one unique force who is approached at the time of difficulties. One cardinal point of his functioning is his promptness of response. With those who have built up their links with Him, his response comes like a flash. Believe it, I am one who has well experienced it not once but a number of times in my life. You have only to go through my related experiences with Sri Sai to convince yourself.

Now you will ask me how to build up link with Sri Sai. The only thing required between Him and us is a strong building up of Supreme Faith in his unseen powers, total surrender at his Lotus Feet. Nothing can convince you better than your personal experiences with Sri Sai Baba, which I had the fortune of having not once but a dozen times. If you go through my experiences of Sai leelas showered on me, you will understand him better. The same are incorporated elsewhere in this book. I can thoughtfully assert that no amount of money, no frequent visits to any Sai Mandir, no amount of flowery offerings can bring Sri Sai close to you. Your total, absolute faith in him, your absolute surrender unto him, your deep concentration, remembering his immortal spirit are a few very effective ways and essential requirements and you can find the Sai spirit in front of you, any time you want.

This is my personal experience and this can be the experience of anybody else. We must have that much of power intrinsically in you first. He is our caretaker, our mother and our protector. He forms a ring around us which no evil force can pierce. He develop an aura around our personality, which goes a long way in every walk of life in this world. His flash point response, protecting us from accidents, steering us out of our difficulties or difficult situations, and granting us exactly what we have in our own minds, is so singularly unique that no power on earth today matches his might. Today, he is the Universal Master with lakhs and lakhs of devotees visiting His Shirdi shrine and his Mandirs not only everywhere in India but throughout the world, seeking his blessings and his divine response.

For the benefit of those who desire to seek him and his power, I have certain points in mind which if you apply will help you to get close to that Supreme Power. First convince yourself throughly well, beyond any doubt, that Sri Sai is a responsive spirit which can be contacted by you. Inculcate absolute faith in him. Surrender yourself totally to him. Tell him "I am at your feet, Baba. Everything of mine is yours. You are my Saviour and you are my God and beneficiary. You take care of me, my activities, my family and children, my service or business." One thing is very sure. You are under his umbrella his protective powers. From this day he will have an unseen hand in manipulating your entire affairs. He has the sole power to reduce the impact of any damage or injury caused in your sphere.

Out of personal experience, I have no hesitation to apprise you that whenever he comes in your home, when he personally welcomes you, he will make you cry, you will cry like a babe. That feeling will be so imperative that you will not be able to suppress it in any way. This is one concrete indication that his divine Soul, or Spirit you may call, is in contact with yours. Be assured of that, I am speaking out of my intimate experience, not once but numerous times any day outside or within my own house. Meditation on his name is yet another approach to him, but it requires life-long practice and time also. Morning hours from 3 A.M. to 5 A.M. are most suitable for meditation on his name.

Sri Sai Baba has himself said that "With good faith if you come to Me one step, I come to you ten steps". He has also said "Why fear when I am near". This one assurance imbibed in me has given me personally one confidence that I do not fear anybody. It has granted me this psychology. I always move with my head up in the world. This is not conceit. Do not misunderstand. It is my strong point. He also rightly said, "You will never look to me in vain". He is ever merciful, ready to pardon our ill-doings if only we sincerely pray and acknowledge our mistakes. Assure him that such mistakes will not be repeated. He pardons us. Its indication is that you at once start feeling light. That obsession of error is erased in full. Your life and living must be on pure lines. Your intentions must be good. Your bad karmas are burnt up by unseen spiritual power which He, Shirdi Sai Baba, himself possesses. Inspite of his warnings, if you indulge in bad Karmas, ignoring Sri Sai Baba, then he feels quite helpless. He has to unwillingly witness you go into a ditch. Death and birth are predestined by the Providence.

Our Sri Sai has on record cases where he has given new lease of life to the ones already departed. *Sri Sai Satcharita* gives us many examples of this type, and his unseen and unlimited powers. One who has realised him with all his powers, has realised God-powers. Just imagine that you are facing some impossible task and you are entrusted to make it achievable. Do not feel despair. Impossible situations have been converted into possible one. Just refer to my personal experience with him. How I had converted an impossible task into a possible one. None, other the unseen power of Sri Shirdi Sai had come to my rescue. Another narration of his powers is that he had total control over the five elements on this earth. While at Shirdi he had to give sermons to a congregation of his devotees. It was very rainy as if the whole Shirdi village would be washed out. But they had one protector. Those who did not have full faith in the powers of Baba got up and walked away from that area and were badly caught in rains and storm. Those who stuck to their ground were saved as it did not rain a drop in the mosque where Sai's devotees were seated. It is on record that he had stopped a storm, he had lighted *divas* by using water when oil was not given to him, he had saved Shirdi village from epidemic of plague by grinding wheat flour and spraying it around Shirdi village. He was God descended in physical human form. He was the full incarnation of Lord Shiva, and also of Lord Dattatreya.

If we look back in the annals Indian history we learn that a 'Miya' and 'Madhav' never lived in harmony but that discord was purely political. Muslims and Hindus were always kept fighting among themselves. This was the design and style of the British rule. Sri Sai of Shirdi never indulged in the political life in Shirdi or elsewhere, but he well realised that he should work for good harmony between Muslims and Hindus. In his mosque and Muslims sat together at one place with Baba, dined together and prayed together. Sri Sai Baba had as many Hindu disciples as Muslims. He treated all very lovingly. Baba also gave medicines to the sick. He used the udhi of the Dhuni at his Dwarkamai as medicine. Whoever used it with full faith was invariably cured of his sickness. I myself apply his Udi received from His Mandir every time on the forehead before I step out of my house. I also put on his ring, and his small photo around my neck when I move out. Fortunate are we, the readers and the listeners who have developed this interest and link with such a great Spiritual Master of the century. Under the umbrella of his blessings everywhere, every time we are protected by him.

11

SAI BABA ··· GOD'S PRICELESS GIFT TO INDIA

Acharya E. Bharadwaja

A nation which is cursed with almost a daily occurence of communal riots, the *Vijayadasami* (October) has a special message. For it is also the day which Sri Sai Baba of Shirdi cast off his normal coil to live forth in the hearts of his devotees in a spirit of love for all creatures and the brotherhood of all religions.

Whatever be one's religion e.g. killing of fellowmen is the sin. Hatred in the name of religion is a blasphemy. It is classic instance of quoting the scriptures.

Baba appeared as a handsome boy of 16, seated under a *neem* on the outskirts of Shirdi and lived there for 60 years. He took Samadhi on October 15, 1918. During this period countless devotees came from far and near which healed their minds and souls.

Revered by Hindus & Muslims alike

Devout Moslem like one of Kanad (Behar), Anwar Khan of Varhad got his guidance. Baba initiated them with Arabic prayer from the Holy Quran and sent the former to Cantonment at Kanad householders (near Aurangabad) and the latter to live as perfect householder.

Hence Moslems like Yakul of Delhi stayed on his holy place and recited the Quran in the mosque in which he lived. Several Moslems like Hazrat Darvesh of Aurangabad and Amiruddin of Nanded used to send their devotees for Spiritual training and blessings.

The Hindus like Sri Kasi Upasani Sastry, Nanasaheb Borkar and others visited Baba and guided them along Hindu spiritual tradition. Saheb was proud of his edge of the Bhagavad Gita and principal commentaries. He went on putting questions to him on one of the Gita verses (No. 34 of chapter IV). Nanasaheb had to shed his pride of learning and then Baba gave an exposition of the verse which is unparalled.

Baba encouraged Hindu devotees to celebrate festivals like Ramnavami and Guru-Purnima at the Masjid while he encouraged Moslem devotee to celebrate their festivals like Muhurram. The unique feature of these celebrations was that both Hindus and Moslem joined heartily together. How did he do it?

To Moslems, he was a Moslem, fakir who lived in the dilapidated mosque on alms always uttering *"Allah Malik"* or assuring his devotees *'Allah Accha Karega'*. He told them that one of his gurus was one Roshan Shah. To an orthodox Moslem who asked him why he tolerated Hindu ways of worship, he said *'Jaisa desh taisa vesh'* ('Be a Roman while in Rome').

To Hindus he is a Sadguru, an Avatar of Lord Dattareya. He named the Mosque as Dwarakamayi. He kept a perpetual holy fire *dhuni* burning in front of him. He told them that his guru was one Venkusa, that he kept repeating the name of Lord Hari till he became one with Him. He assured a sceptic that Rama and Krishna did exist in flesh and blood. He told them to study holy books like the *Bhagavadgita*, the *Bhagavata. Vishnu Sahasranamam* and the *'Guru Charitra'*.

Baba's zeal for religious harmony had to manifest itself in a sterner vein some times. A bigoted Moslem once said he would do away with a group of Hindus sleeping there as he thought they were desecrating the Mosque through their heretical religious practices. Baba calmly said that it would be better to do away with him rather, for if he had not permitted them to do so, such a situation would not have arisen.

So too when a Moslem devotee once brought a young man to him and proudly declared that he had changed his religion to Islam. Baba slapped the convert saying *'Did you change your father'*?

This reminds us of what Bhagwan Ramana Maharshi said, "One who considers himself as a Jnani and as a guru to some others is not worth the name". For, he explained "A Jnani will find that

Jnana or Enlightenment is the essential being of all". To the fakes who want to believed as special apostles by the devout masses, his words are : "take a portherd and regard it as your guru and see if your goal is reached or not. What a shattering and revealing asseveration for self imposing gurus.

The unostentatious, mode of living of Baba exemplifies the wisdom of mystics down the ages. "Take no thought for the morrow" said Christ. Hindu, Buddhist and Jain scriptures enjoin a houseless, wandering life of a beggar to a renunciate, a true sadhu. That is what Baba is. This ageless wisdom has some caustic words for those who, while claiming to be sadhus and swamis, live far more luxuriously than common worldlings.

A seeker after enlightenment

It is said for instance that a seeker after enlightenment and a enlightened sage who side back into luxurious of such a one how ever sublime they might sound are unworthy of acceptance. For, even the water of the sacred Ganges falling into a stinking cases pool, is unift for drinking.

Four things were prohibited for the truly enlightened and for seekers after enlightenment.

(1) Raising a mandir, ashram, house or a mutt be live in; instead, such a one should live under a tree, in the cremation or burial ground or in a dilapidated house or shrine; (2) Gathering of disciples (as different from devotees); (3) Accumulation of things and wealth for worldly or holy needs; (4) Acceptance of honour and pomp.

Sai Baba's life is one of those which hearten mankind that this world is not as yet completely a waste land of hollow men.

Sai Baba is a priceless gift to the modern society in yet another way. His life and conduct were an object lesson to all sadhus and mahatmas. And account of his life would go a long way in educating the credulous masses all over the world against their cynical exploitation by self-styled fake Gurus, Bhagavans and Acharyas. Four aspects of his life deserve special mention:

1. Devout Hindus had in him the darshan of their chosen deities like Rama, Vithoba, Dattatreya and Hanuman. Devotees of other mahatmas had darshan of their chosen mahatmas in him.

Devotees had unmistakable experiences of his mysterious presence in all peoples and creatures. Yet he considered himself a poor begging fakir whose biography or portrait did not deserve to be preserved before posterity; how different from those sadhus who, as Bhagavath Gita cautions us, declare "I am the Lord Supreme" (*Ishwaram*, Shambhogi etc.")

2. He gave away all gifts of money (amounting to 3 or 4 hundred rupees a day) rich clothes, food and delicacies he received from his wealthy devotees every day to the poor by sunset the same day, and he again begged for food at five houses in the village! Indeed, how different and divine he is from some other modern millionaire "swamis".

3. Even though he was presented with a palanquin, a horse and procession car or chariot by his devotees, not once in 60 years did he allow himself to be taken in a procession around the village. He went about the village barefooted in rags. Again how different from a modern mahatma who can not walk from his AC hermitage!

4. Now-a-days we fine almost every popular brand of Mahatama, Bhagavan, Acharya or Swami vehemently vilifying every other as a fake, a hypnotist etc. as though that is enough to confirm his claims of being a true guru. We hardly find one among them humble and decent enough to respect other Mahatma. Baba, if he exposed any fake guru, did so in dignified, tacit and austere manner. When devotees sang the aratis of saints like Jnaneswar and Tukaram, Baba sat straight with folded hands in obeisance.

The stock-in-trade of almost every 'popular' guru today is 'follow me and none other, Baba's standard teaching was 'stick to your own guru with unabated faith, whatever the merits of other gurus and however little the merit of your own'. While the unabated advertisement of some popular gurus tries to project them as the best, Baba tells us, "it is not the guru, it is you that must regard him as your guru, i.e., place your entire faith in him.

.... The unostentatious simple living of Baba exemplifies the wisdom of the mystics down the ages. "Take no thought for the morrow" said Baba. Christian, Hindus, Bhddhist and Jain scriptures enjoin a householder, wandering life of a beggar to the renunciate, a true Sadhu. That is what Baba is. This ageless wisdom has some cuastic words for those who while claiming to be sadhus, and swamis live far more luxuriously than common worldlings.

...Four things were prohibited for the truly enlightenend and for seekers after enlightenment:

(1) Raising a mandir, ashram, house or muth to live in; instead such a one should live under a tree, in the remation or burial ground in a dilapidated house or shrine;

(2) Gathering of disciples (as different from devotees);

(3) Accumulation of things and wealth for worldly or holy needs;

(4) Acceptance of honour and pomp.

How many do we have of such?

Sai Baba's life is one of those which heartens mankind that this world is not yet completely a wasteland of holymen.

12

SRI SHIRDI SAI BABA'S MISSION

Sri Saipadananda Radha Krishna Swamiji

"Love is the highest. Love and devotion make one forgetful of every thing else. Love unites the lover with Me. What ineffable joy does one find though love of Me, the Blissful Self. Once that joy is realized, all earthly pleasure fade into nothingness."

—Sri Shirdi Sai Baba

Mysticism denotes that attitude of mind which involves a direct, immediate, intuitive apprehension of God. It signifies the highest attitude of which man is capable, namely, a beatific contemplation of God and its dissemination in the society and the world.

All roads led to Rome. All paths (*margas*) lead to the divinely gifted or perfect souls which transform every one who comes into contact witth their divine personality - especially those who are drawn through *Rinanubandha* by their divinity and that is the purpose or mission of their lives. So, Baba has not one mission, but a hundred missions. Protecting the good and virtuous, punishing or reforming the wicked, establishing *Dharma* or its hold on the people, are the functions of divine personalities and Baba was performing all these functions. A mission may come in as a part of these functions.

Saints expound all the *margas* and find out which *marga* or the combination of which *margas* would suit each approaching devotee and give the same to him. Thus Baba adopted every *marga* but in particular one may not know that predominance in his methods was neither for ritual nor for Vedic study, but for living in consonance with the supreme manifestation of Divinity in himself. His mission is to help every one; that means, of course, every one capable of benefiting - not persons who come in an unreceptive mood. Baba was distributing not merely wealth, worldly relief and comforts but also spiritual blessings to all and sundry who were capable of receiving those benefits.

To us, Sai devotees, Baba is not only a teacher but a controller from within the everwatching Guardian Angel. He regulated the lives of those who wholly surrendered to him. While doing service, incidentally the work of conveying moral teachings was carried on by Baba and he gave occasional talks about morality.

'Behave properly', 'Behave with integrity and probity'. 'Hurting others is sinful', such were the words of advice given by Baba to Shama and Rao Sahib Galwanker. Baba expected people to act upon this teaching.

When a great saint like Baba, leading a perfectly pure life as a *Samartha Sadguru* and helping thousands comes, his utterance are full of ethics and spiritually; it is neither possible nor desirable to make anattempt to give a full account of his moral teachings. Baba was moulding his devotees from inside and he used not merely words but also his gaze, his touch and even his aura or the will power to remove undesirable tendencies and influences and replace them by useful and holy ones.

Even today it is his inner working that counts in the improvement and building up of the devotee. His presence, his glance, his touch all have their effect. Each of these has its own peculiar effect. Baba in many ways sowed seeds of morality and spirituality in the hearts of those approaching him, and sometimes almost imperceptibly. Whenever he rendered any worldly help, that help was accompanied by a spiritual seed sowing and the beneficiary remembered Baba with faith, love and admiration for his power, guidance and kindness. These thoughts were the seeds from which a gigantic tree of faith would grow up later on and Baba who sowed the seeds mostly watered and manured his plant and in many a case, beginning with worldly benefit, the devotee got on to higher and higher spiritual levels.

Baba's teachings are so common that they may look like copy book maxims and one may wonder why these should be set out at all, as everyone knows these moral teachings. What Baba taught was not something new and strange. It is the set of old truths of morality and spirituality that have to be rubbed into each self and lived upto. In curious readers want case to know what sort of teachings Baba's were, we shall give below a few of his teachings. Baba occasionally said 'How great is God? No one can compare with him. God creates, supports and destroys. "His *leela* (sport) is inscrutable. Let us be content to remain as he makes us, to submit our wills to His." This is the most important doctrine, a doctrine of submission and surrender. Baba said "As God places us, let us remain. Take what comes. Be contented and cheerful. Never worry. Not a leaf moves but by His consent and will. We should be honest, upright and virtuous. We must distinguish right from wrong. We must each attend to our own duty. But we must not be obsessed by egotism and fancy that we are the independent causes of action. God is the Actor. We must recognise his independence and our dependence on Him and see all acts as His. If we do so, we shall be unattached and free from Karmic bondage."

Another important prerequisite for peace and happiness is love for all creation. Baba's moral teachings were conveyed by his own life and activity. Baba loved all creatures and the underlying motive of every act of his was love towards all human being and all creatures. Baba said "Love all creatures. Do not fight with any one. Do not retaliate nor scandalise any. When any one talks ill of you, that is, against you, pass on unperturbed. His words cannot pierce into your body. Others acts will affect them alone and not you."

As for activity, Baba was ever active and never idle. And his advice was 'Do not be idle. Work. Utter God's name. Read scriptures. Do not harbour envy, rivalry or combative disposition towards others. If others hate you, simply take to '*Nama Japa*' and avoid their company."

Baba has assured us;

"I am Divinity personfied and all-pervasive. According to the needs of My devotees, I grant them the visions of Myself in different physical forms. For this, spiritual practice (Sadhana) is essential.

Baba said once "God has agents everywhere and they have vast powers and I also have vast powers. But *abhimana* the idea that I am doing has to be completely suppressed in order that one may really have spiritual elevation, peace and happiness."

All these teachings form part and parcel of the most essential teachings of all religions.

13

SAI BABA'S UNIQUE MISSION

Mitta Sri Lakshminarsiah

> "All the world lives in Me. My order is the law everywhere. All forms are Mine. I am the saviour of all beings from ant to Brahman. I am the protector of all lives. I am present event before the creation. I am prime God. Those who possess bad ideas, sense desires, false ego, and those who are in the darkness of ignorance, are not fit to see My face."
>
> — Sri Shirdi Sai Baba

The life of Sri Sai Baba of Shirdi is purely the life of a Spiritual Saint. Among the spiritual luminaries of recent times he may be counted as the most widely worshipped in the country. He is an embodiment of all the religions of the world and had high respect for each and every religion. According to him every religion - Hinduism, Islam, Christianity and Zorastrianism - are different roads leading to the same goal of the realisation of God. There cannot be any difference in the fundamental and basic principles of any religion. He was extremely simple in his habits and highly sincere in his words and deeds. It is his utmost simplicity and sincerity that attracted milions of people - men, women and children - towards him. Shirdi, where Sri Sai Baba took his abode is a place of pilgrimage where the young and the old, the able and the disabled, the rich and the poor, the learned and the illiterate, go with implicit faith in Sri Sai Baba all round the year. Even during the life time of Sri Sai Baba, when his name began to reach and ring the others of the people, the scholars and administrators, the lawyers and doctors, pupils and professors, the high and the low, dacoits and devotees - went to Shirdi for His 'Darshan' and poured forth all their difficulties an ddesires at His lotus feet. Those who had no faith in him and mocked at him also went to him and when Sri Sai Baba read their thought and advised them, they at once became his disciples with unfailing faith in Him. Sri Bal Gangadhar Tilak the eminent Philosopher and Politician went to Him to have his Darshan, before his going to England in the company of Yogi Sudananda Bharathiar and Karandikar. Sri Sai Baba afterHis blessings, advised him to win Swaraj by spiritual force.

One Anand Maharaj who came into contact with Sri Sai Baba said about Him "He is a diamond. You donot know his real worth. Although he may be on a dunghill, still remember that he is a real diamond". Similarly, one Sadhu Gangagir, on seeing Sri Sai Baba said " He is a precious jewel. His worth is very high. It is the greatest good luck of this village that you should have such a gem here". His Holiness Swami Sivananda of Rishikesh in his Foreward to the Book "Life of Sai Baba" by H. H. Narasimha Swamiji Vol. I says: "Glory be to the blessed Saint of Shirdi in whom the Light of Divinity was fully manifested in all resplendence. I deem it a great joy and a unique 'Sowbhagya' to write something about this great Mahapursha, who illumined this holy land with His radian presence and lived a life of a Divine absorption, love of mankind and compassion to all creatures (Bhoota-daya) solely for the welfare and benefit of humanity. To think about such great souls, to speak about such great souls, to write about their glories and to remember their lofty lives - this in itself is an act that is purifying and elevating and a devout exercise that draws down upon all, their divine blessings. It is equal to Sravan, Manan, and Nidhidhyasan. It will elevate the man of faith and the sincere seeker to sublime heights of joy and spiritual felicity. Blessed indeed is one who narrates such Sant-Lilas and equally blessed are they that listen to such holy narration ... ".

It is not His disciples, devotees and the general public that highly appreciated Sri Sai Baba and His mission to serve humanity at large in various ways, but several other Saints and Sages with their spiritual insight recognised in Sri Sai Baba a spiritual saint of a very high order and an ardent worker for humanity at large.

Sri Sai Baba possessed within him Lilas of Krishna, the compassion of Buddha, the love of Christ, the vision of Mohammed, the Prophet, the philosophy of Sankara and the intellect and Bhakti Marg of Ramanuja who guided humanity by different roads to reach the final goal of God-realisation.

Sri Sai Baba always discouraged change of religion. On the other hand he insisted upon sticking upto one's own religion and act according to the rituals of one's own religion he belonged to. He taught people to continue their respective religion and never to change it.

Though Sri Sai Baba lived in a Mosque at Shirdi which He called Dwarkamayi also called the Brahmin Masjid - He fully believed in almost all the essential principles of Hinduism. Hinduism is a conglomeration of religions and faiths. Other religions are based on different grounds and are greatly regimented with the result that owing to the regimentation of principles and the rituals of the other religions the acts and movements of the followers of other religions are circumscribed. Great stress has been laid upon the respective prophets of all the religions except Hinduism. Swami Vivekananda says: "... It is to be Christianity cannot stand without Christ, Mohammadanism without Mohammad and Budhism without Buddha; but Hinduism stand indepent of any man ...". Hinduism is the way of life; it is a sponge-like religion. It affords greatest freedom for a man to liberalise his mind in his own way. It is a synthetic religion without much regimentation. It answers every individual according to his capacity of understanding. A characteristics of Hinduism is the receptivity and all comprehensiveness. It claims to be the one religion of humanity of the entire world. Hinduism has no difficulty in including all other religious within its all embracing arms and ever widening fold.

Sri Sai Baba believed in the transmigration of soul - the references of which are to be found in his sermons and talks on various occasions. He emphasised on the elevation of soul by good and virtuous deeds which ultimately would lead to spiritual development. The acts and doings of one's present life are responsible to and would accout for one's next birth.

He always served the poor people by personally grinding jawar etc. in the mosque and feeding them. He was generally insisting upon his devotees and sometimes on the visitors to play him money which was called 'Dakshana'. Sometimes He would ask the same person for money several times on the same day, with the result that he would have nothing left. Others who did not know Sri Sai Baba would feel that He was greedy and exacting money. But the fact is that He used to test his devotees far they would stand the test of the worldly temptations. In later period of His life Sri Sai Baba used to get good deal of money, thousands of rupees a day which he used to distribute on that very day among the poor and next morning Baba was a beggar again, having no money in His hands. This went on for several years. Thus every day Baba was a beggar in the morning and evening, a rich man during the day time. He was highly popular and people used to love him for us simplicity, sincerity and unfailing serves to the poor in particular.

Sri Sai Baba's way of attracting people and the way of approaching them with his mission of service to humanity for elevating them spiritually, was both novel and interesting. He always granted people temporal gainst and fulfilled their worldly desires which in turn created in them a desire for spiritual development and elevation of soul, in frequent contact with Sri Sai Baba. He thus succeeded in his mission of spreading the spiritual aspect of life in a great measure. He was of the opinion that the problems of spiritualims would not create any interest in the minds of the people, unless and until they were benefited by the temporal gains which would prepare the ground for spiritual development.

One of the greatest object of his mission was to bring all mankind into one fold and to teach Hindus and Muslims to live together as brothers since both are born and bred up on the same soil. Even today afte His Mahasamadhi on 15th October 1918-Vijaya Dasami Day, both the Hindus and the Muslims go to His Mahasamadhi at Shirdi and worship in their own way simultaneously. This is His Mission, the essence of his teachings and the very object of his life.

14

SOME REFLECTIONS ON SAI BABA

V.V.Giri

"I am the sustainer of all. I am the wisdom of the wise. No creation exists in this universe without Me. Every creature is a manifestation of a divine spark of my effulgence."

—Sri Shirdi Sai Baba

The life and teachings of Sai Baba are indeed greatly inspiring, helping the individual to progress in his spiritual path. I had the privilege of visiting Shirdi some six years ago, along with Mrs. Giri and children when I could have the darshan of the Samadhi. During his lifetime, Baba performed many miracles and whosoever thought of him was helped by Baba. Today all over the country a large number of Samaj's and Societies have sprung up with a lot of devotees who are trying to imbibe in their own way the messages and teaching of Baba. Many people prayed for material and spiritual upliftment and received the blessings of Sri Sai Baba in full measure. Sri Sai Baba always used to say 'Why fear when I am here', and advised the devotees 'to cast all their burdens upon him'. He stressed that everyone should surrender himself to the great Almighty by whatever name and in whatever from one might worship him. In fact, it is stated that Sri Sai Baba himself was born a Hindu, who was brought up by a Muslim Fakir, and to him all religions were one and the same. What he essentially preached and propagated was love, goodness, tolerance and a feeling of fellowship and brotherhood to all living creatures.

The All India Sai Samaj which has its Head-quarters at madras is doing considerable good work not only for the spiritual but also for the material upliftment of the people. the hospital they run and the library they have is a boon to the residents of the area. Apart from that every Thursday and on important festival days, a large number of devotees throng to the temple to attend the religious discourses and Bhajans held there. In this connection, I would like to mention about the foremost disciple of Sri Sai Baba, Shri Narasimhaswamy whose friendship I had the privilege to enjoy. He was one of God's own men. In his poo'vashrama he was an able lawyer and a patriot who renounced everything worldly and completely surrendered himself to Sri Sai Baba. It was he who was primarily responsible for the establishment and nurturing of Sai Samajam in Madras.

Baba preached a catholicity of outlook and to him all religions are the same. All of them are like streams from different directions leading to the mighty ocean of Brahman. Devotion, faith and surrender form the basic principles on which Baba's philosophy rests. Anyone sincerely bearing to reach the goal will easily find solace and the solution.

It is great personages like Sri Sai Baba who are responsible for shaping the thoughts and ideals of the people of India. Our emphasis on secularism is founded not only on the national thought that all men are created equal but is the outcome of the deep spirituality embedded in our blood from the earliest times.

The followers of Baba should work with the motto of *service above self.* They should propagate religious tolerance and communal harmony and also render assistance and succour to those that are in need.

15

PRECIOUS TEACHINGS OF SRI SHIRDI SAI AVATAR

Compiled by: Dr. S.P. Ruhela

"I am present in all beings. I have neither dislike nor liking for any one. Whosoever devotedly worships Me, I stand revealed in him wholeheartedly. Even if the worst sinner worships Me with complete faith, he will become virtuous and secure lasting peace. Even those that are born in sin, if they take refuge in Me, they will obtain supreme peace and the eternal abode."

—Sri Shirdi Sai Baba

ACTIONS

"The present fate (*Deha Prarabdha*) is the result of the actions (*Karma*) of our former births".

ACTIONS

"In the less-ego shape, all actions are joyous, effortless and spontaneous".

ASSURANCE

"If a man utters My Name with love, I shall fulfil all his wishes, increase his devotion. If he sings earnestly of My life and deeds. I shall surround him on all sides".

ATTACHMENT

"How can he whose mind is engrossed in wealth, progeny and prosperity, expect to know Brahma?"

AUSPICIOUS SIGNS

"Offers of bread and food should be regarded as auspicious signs of success".

BATTLE OF LIFE

"Do not fight the battles of life yourself. Surrender. Let God fight them for you. When God himself fights, there will definitely be results".

BEAUTY

"We do not have to bother about the beauty or ugliness of a person, but concentrate solely on the God underlying that form".

BORROWING

"Do not borrow for celebrating a feast or a festival, for a pilgrimage or any other journey".

CHARITY

"The donor gives, that is, sows his seeds, only to reap a rich harvest in future. Wealth should be the means to work out *Dharma*. If it is not given before, you do not get it now. So the best way to receive is to give".

CLEVERNESS

"Leave off all cleverness and always remember *Sai-Sai*. If you do so, all your shackles will be removed and you will be free".

CONTENTMENT

"One must rest content with one's lot".

DAKSHINA

"The giving of a reverential gift (*Dakshina*) advances non-attachment (*Vairagya*) and thereby devotion (*Bhakti*)".

DEATH

"None dies; see with your inner eyes. Then you will realize that you are God and not different from Him. Like worn out garments, the body is cast away on death".

DEATH

"At the time of death, have no desire at all. Concentrate on God, i.e. your *Ista Devata*. If death comes when your mind merges in the *Ista Devata*, Salvation (*Mukti*) is attained".

DESTINY

"Whosoever is destined to be struck will be struck; whosoever is to die will die".

DEVOTEE

"He who withdraws his heart from wife, child and parents and loves me, is My real lover or devotee and he merges in Me like a river in the sea".

DEVOTION

"Knowledge of the Vedas or fame as a great scholar (*jinani*) or formal worship are of no avail unless they are accompanied by devotion".

DIFFERENCES

"All creatures differ from each other because of their deeds in previous births".

DISCRIMINATION

"There are two sorts of things—the good and the pleasant. A man has to think and choose one of them. The wise man prefers the good to the pleasant, but the unwise, through greed and attachment, chooses the pleasant and thereby cannot get self realization *Brahma Gyana*.

DISILLUSION

"Whenever any idea of joy or sorrow arises in your mind, resist it. Do not give room to it. It is pure illusion".

DOERSHIP

"Renounce the idea of doership. God alone is the real doer. If you accept doership of actions you shall be bound by the bondage of action (*Karma bandhan*). You shall thereby be caught in the unending transmigration of soul".

DUTY

"Unless a man discharges his duties satisfactorily and dispassionately, his mind will not be purified".

EGOISM

"The teachings of a Guru are of no use to a man who is full of egoism and who always thinks about sense-objects".

END

"Sit quiet *Uge Muge*. I will do the needful. I will take you to the end. I will not desert men before the end".

ENEMY

Do not say of any one that he is your enemy. All are one and the same".

EQUANIMITY

"Let the world go topsy-turvy, remain where you are. Staying at your own place, look calmly at the show of all things passing before you".

EXPLOITATION

"Nobody should take the labour of others' gratis. The worker should be paid his dues promptly and liberally".

FAITH

"Nobody who has a firm faith in God craves for anything".

FEEDING

"Know for certain that he who feeds the hungry, really serves Me with food".

FOOD

"Sitting in the mosque I shall never, never speak an untruth. Take pity on Me like this: first give bread to the hungry and then eat yourself".

FOREBEARANCE

"Our *Karma* is the reason behind happiness and sorrow. Therefore put up with whatever comes to you".

GOD

"Allah (God) is the sole dispenser and protector. Think of him always. He will take care of you. Surender at his feet with body, mind, wealth and speech, completely and then see what He does".

GOD

"God lives in all beings. He is the greatest wirepuller of the world and all beings, serpents, scorpions etc. obey His command".

GOD'S GIFTS

"What a man gives does not last long, and is always imperfect. But what my God (*Sircar*) gives, lasts lifetime. No other gift from any man can be compared to His".

GOD'S GRACE

"You must always adhere to truth and fulfil all the promises you make. Have faith (*Shraddha*) and patience (*Saburi*). Then I will always be with you wherever you are".

GOD'S WILL

"Unless God wills it, nobody meets us on the way; unless the God wills, nobody can do any harm to others".

GOODNESS

"If you act in a good way, good will really follow".

GREED

"Greed and spirituality are poles apart; they are eternally opposed to each other. Where there is greed, there is no room for meditation of the God (*Brahma*)".

GURU

"Stick to your own Guru with unabated faith, whatever be the merits of other gurus and however little the merits of your own".

GURU'S GRACE

"The mother tortoise is on one bank of the river and her younger ones are on the other. She gives neither milk nor warmth to them. Her mere glance gives them warmth. The young ones do nothing but remember (mediating upon) their mother. The tortoise glance is to the young ones, a downpour of nectar, the only source of sustenance and happiness. Similar is the relationship between the Guru and the disciples".

HAPPINESS

"If others hate us, let us take to the chanting of God's Name and avoid them. Do not speak rudely to people; do not be pugnacious. Bear with reproach. This is the way to happiness".

HARM

"I will not allow my devotees to come to harm. I have to care for my devotees. If a devotee is about to fall, I stretch out my hands to support him. I will not let him fall".

HELP

"If someone begs for anything, and if it's in your hands or within your power and you can grant the request, do not say 'no'. If you have nothing to give them, give a polite negative reply but do not mock or ridicule the man, nor get angry with him".

HOSPITALITY

"No one comes to us without *Rinanubandha* (some previous bond of give and take). So when a dog, cat, pig, fly or person approaches you, do not drive it or him away".

HUMILITY

"Humility should not be towards all. Severity is necessary in dealing with the wicked".

IGNORANCE

"People are ignorant. When they do not see My physical body, they think I am absent".

INQUIRY

"Inquire always: 'Who am I?"

INTROSPECTION

"We must see things for ourselves. What good is there in going about asking for this man of that, for his views and experiences? It is no good asking for others' views and experiences".

KARMA

"If one meditates on Me repeating my name, sings my deeds, and is thus transformed in to me his *karma* is destroyed. I stay by his side always".

LIBERATION

"Service at the feet of the Master (Guru) is essential to attain Liberation".

LUST

"A person who has not overcome lust cannot realise God".

LUST

"Enjoyment of marital pleasure is permissible, but do not be enslaved by it. Liberation is impossible for persons addicted to lust. Lust ruins mental balance and strength or firmness. It effects the learned also".

MEALS

"Always take your meals before you start for a journey".

MEDITATION

"Real meditation is to merge one's false individuality into the Divine Personality".

NAME-CHANTING

"If you just chant "Raja Ram, Raja Ram", your mind will attain peace and you will be immensely benefited".

NON-POSSESSION

"Everything belongs to us for use. Nothing is for us to possess".

OFFERING

"Am I not always with you? Then do you offer Me anything before you eat?"

OMNISCIENCE

"My eye (of vigilance) is always on those who love Me. Wherever you do, wherever you may be, ever bear this in mind that I am always aware of everything you do".

ONENESS

"The dog to which you gave a piece of bread before your meal is one with Me, so are other creatures. I am roaming in their forms. So abandon the sense of duality and serve Me as you did today (by feeding that dog)".

POVERTY

"Poverty is the highest riches and superior in Lord's position. God is brother of the poor. A *Faqir* is the real emperor. Faqirship does not perish, but an empire is soon lost".

PRESENT

"Do not think of the past nor delve into the future. Live, live intensely in the present".

QUARREL

"If anybody comes and abuses you or punishes you, do not quarrel with him. If you cannot endure it, speak a simple word or two, or else go away from that place".

QUESTIONING

"Mere questioning is not enough. The question must not be asked with an improper motive or attitude to trap the Guru and catch his mistakes in the answer, or out of idle curiosity. It must be asked with a view to achieve spiritual progress or *moksha*".

REALITY

"God is the only 'Reality' and the Universe is ephemeral, and no one in this world, be he son, father or wife, is really ours".

REALIZATION

"People think that they are different from each other. But in this, they are wrong. I am inside you, you are inside Me. If you continue to think like this, then you will have realization".

RINANUBANDH

"It is on account of former relationship (*Rinanubandh*) that we have come together; let us love and serve each other and be happy".

SAI

"I am not confined within this body of 3½ cubits, I am everywhere. See Me in every place".

SAI NAME

"The simple remembrance of My name as 'Sai Sai' will burn all the bad thoughts it will remove all sins of speech and hearing".

SELF-REALIZATION

"The idea that "I am the body" is a great illusion and attachment to this idea is the cause of bondage. Leave this idea and the resultant attachment, if you want to reach the goal of Self - realization".

SELF-REALIZATION

"He who turns to Me entirely, hears and expends my divine activities (*Leelas*) and does not think of anything else, is sure to attain self-realization".

SERVICE

"*Seva* is not rendering service while retaining still the feeling that one is free to offer or refuse service. One must feel that he is not the master of the body, that the body is Guru's and exists merely to render service to him".

SIN

"Inflicting pain on others by body, mind and speech is sin; the reverse is Merit (*punya*)".

SPIRITUALITY

"The spiritual plant flowers silently in humility and egolessness".

SPIRITUAL GOAL

"Do not try to take any *Mantra* or *Upadesh* from anybody. Make Me the sole object of your thoughts and actions and you will, no doubt, attain the spiritual goal of life".

SUFFERING

"Suffering willingly for one's past actions *(Karmas)* with self-surrender in mind attracts the Divine Grace".

SUPPORT

"Come what may, stick to your support, i.e., Guru, and ever remain steady, always in union with him".

SURRENDER

"It is My special characteristic that I free any person who surrenders completely to Me, worships Me faithfully and, who remembers Me, and mediates on Me constantly".

TRUTH

"You should always have truth with you. Then I will be with you always, wherever you are and at all times".

TRUTH

"He who surrenders to Truth whole-heartedly, ultimately wins the race".

UNITY

"Rama and Rahim are one and the same; there is not the least difference between them; then why should their devotees fall out and quarrel among themselves? You ignorant folks, join hands and bring both communities together, act sanely and you will gain your object of national unity".

VISSITUDES OF LIFE

"Gain and loss, birth and death, are in the hand of God. But how blindly people forget that God looks after life as long as it lasts".

WISDOM

"True wisdom is the inner experience of oneness of all life".

WISE

"The wise should be cheerful and contented with their lot as it is the result of past actions".

WORLD

"This world is funny. All are my subjects. I look upon all equally, but some become thieves and what can I do for them? People who are themselves very near death desire and make preparations for the death of others. They offend Me a great deal".

WORLDLY HONOUR

"Do not be deluded by worldly honour. The form of the deity should be firmly fixed in the mind. Let all the senses and mind be ever devoted to the worship of the Lord".

16

SAI BABA'S SAYINGS AND TEACHINGS

K. Venkataramiah

"I am the minutest particle of the minute atoms. I am the greatest of all the great things. I am neither small nor big. I am the witness and also the player. In your darkness of ignorance, you are driven away and not able to understand who I am? You are filled with worldly desires and are heading towards your downfall. I am in you. I am present in the whole Universe. I am shining in all your minds and I am pulsating in you blood vessels."

–Sri Shirdi Sai Baba

    This is one of the problems discussed by intellectuals on purely rationalistic lines. The author of *'Thirukkural'* says that it is only true knowledge, which enables you to see the reality behind the final outward forms of things, which means the truth, which remains after the analysis of the entire Triad, namely, Self, World, and God; that is Brahman. We need not enter into questions of Dvaita or Advaita, though there are people, who say that to deny the separate existence of a human soul, is to commit suicide, that on ultimate analysis two things remain namely, the self undestroyed and the God, whom the self reaches. There are also many other divergent views. The ultimate is complex and not capable of a simple statement, and thus intellect also go on contradicting and fighting. How does Baba deal with devotees, when they are faced with this problem ? Chandorkar and other graduates, who had studied philosophy, Sankara's commentary on the Gita, and other works, were confronted with these problems, and sometimes they discussed these at the wada at Shirdi. Baba did not profess to be a University professor offering solutions for problems to be published to the world, but dealt with each man individually as he approached Him as Guru. Baba's solution was always on the lines of getting over theoretical difficulties by adherence to practical methods. By sticking to Baba with full faith, these problems could be solved. Unless there was the proper approach, there was no solution. Baba indicated this view in the way, in which He dealt with a sceptic like the Station Master of the Valambi railway station. That man had no belief in Baba. But having been persuaded by Das Ganu, that Baba was a great soul with wonderful powers, he just prepared to accept Das Ganu's invitation, so that he might go and see Baba for himself before he judged about Him. When the Valambi Station Master and Das Ganu came to Shirdi, the all-knowing Baba was behaving peculiarly. He took up a number of pots, washed them one after another, and placed them mouth downwards, which seemed to be quite the reverse of what one should do, and what one does usually. The Valambi Station Master was impatient and asked Das Ganu, "What is the meaning of all this procedure of Baba?" Das Ganu asked Baba, and Baba's reply was, "This is the way, in which people approach Me, only when the vessel is placed with mouth upwards, it can receive anything; but this is the way, in which people approach Me, with mouth downwards". The hit was not quite intelligible to the Valambi Station Master. Receptivity meant some degree of faith and respect for the person approached, so that the person approached, could pour into the approaching person some seeds of instruction, edification or other useful teaching. But, the Valambi Station Master was quite innocent of any faith or regard for Baba, and could not derive any benefit from Baba. But, Baba's point was quite clear, to solve any problem, connected with one's spiritual progress, one must be in dead earnest and approach some person, whom he has got regard for, or faith in, and then patiently wait for the solution of his intellectual or other problems. Baba ocassionally used even accidental chances to furnish further illumination on this matter. After 1910, Dixit and some other friends wanted to leave Shirdi, and asked permission of Baba to go; Baba said "You may go". Then a devotee asked, "Baba, where is one to go ?". Baba at once gave a new turn to the talk, and made it educative. Baba's answer was "There are plenty of ways proceeding from each place. For you here, there is a way leading from here. But the way is rugged. There are tigers and bears on the route." Baba was talking in symbolic language. There were no bears at Shirdi nor tigers. But, what he meant was, 'There were obstructions on the way to one's spiritual progress, which are as fierce and terrible as tigers and bears !'

It was just then the H.S. Dixit intervened and said, "But Baba, if one has a guide with him ?". Baba answered: "If one has a guide with him, then there is no difficulty. Then, the tigers and bears move aside. If there is not guide, there is also a deep yawning pit on the way, and there is the danger of falling into it". During the discourse, Annasaheb Dabholkar was present, and he had been debating once, whether a Guru was necessary at all for one's spiritual progress. Dabholkar felt that this was the instruction given to him, that a Guru was essential and useful to overcome obstacles, that would otherwise hamper one's spirtitual progress. The word 'Guide' here meant 'Guru'. Baba's reference to the deep yawning pit meant 'hell'. So, Baba drove once again the much needed lesson, that unless one got a Guru, one would make no progress at all, or in the language of Kabir. *Guru, Vin Kene Bhavave Vat* that is, 'Unless there is a Guru, who is to show the way?". Baba again and again pointed out that the solution to one's intellectual riddles, conundrums and mazes, lies in the practical step of summoning up faith and reverence and love to a Guru, who will himself thereafter solve all problems, remove all difficulties, and drive off all tigers and bears from the route, and save one from falling into the yawning pit. Baba's metaphors must have been reported or in any case had far reaching results. Upasani Baba, who came to Shirdi in 1911, took Baba for his Guide and got his help, especially, by silent instruction through visions. In one of the visions, Upasani found that as he was passing on there was deep pit, which afterwards he learnt was hell, and that when he approached it, hands came out of that hell, and clutched at his feet, and tried to pull him down. He had sufficient grace to remember his Guru, and said, "Let go, let go, If you don't let go, I will tell Sai Baba". The remembrance of the Guru knocks off all Vasanas and tendencies. which lead to hell, Thus, Upasani's feet were released from the clutches of the hands of that hell was then told that it was a mistake to go very near the brink of that pit. It was the Guru's grace, that saved him from that pit. This is allegorical or symbolical, but, in point of fact, it was this same Guru Sai Baba's grace, that saved Rao Bahadur H. V. Sathe from the brink of hell, the sin of immorality with a lady of doubtful reputation at the Shala at Shirdi. On that occasion Sathe felt like a thief caught red-handed. He repented immediately his stupidity and he resolved never again to call at that woman's place or to ommit such a sin. So, Baba did really save this devotee of His from falling into the yawning pit, and thus showed that He was the Guru, who would take a man on to the goal of his life. If a man commits such mortal as adultery or debauchery, he can never be fit to receive the higher truths, which alone can take him on to the purity, detachment, and love of God, that ensure salvation and liberation. Thus, what Baba spoke to Dabholkar was illustrated in the case of Sathe. But, this was not the only instance, in which Baba helped either Sathe or others. It is not merely Kama, that degrades the soul and takes it to hell. Krodha, anger, or hatred does the same. Baba in the case of Sathe, did another piece of signal service. Sathe had purchased a plot of land at or near Shirdi and wanted to go and see the place. He brought a cart and wanted his wife to get into it, so that they might go and see the place. But, Dada Kelkar, his father-in-law, who arranged the sale, was anxious that claims to that land should not be put forward by Sathe's *Jnytis* or next of kin, as they would claim it if they came to know, that the land was purchased by him. So, he had told his daughter not to go with her husband to see the land. So, when Sathe wanted his wife to get into the cart, she would not come. Then, at once Sathe got angry, and took the horse whip in his hand, and wanted to whip his wife, for her impertinent refusal. He had lifed his hand, when Sai Baba, Who was watching the whole-scene, unscene, from his own Mosque, sent up Megha to hurry up and bring Sathe to Baba. So, as the whip was lifted, Megha said: "Baba wants you", and down fell the whip, Sathe went to Baba. Baba there softened Sathe, and told him that there was no necessitly for him to see the land for the land was there all the time. Sathe found how Baba had saved him once again from an act of gross cruelty to his wife, which would also be one of the sins leading to hell. Conquest of temper is essential for one's religious progress.

–K. Venkatramaiah,
D.R. of Co-op. Societies (Rtd.)
Sudarshan, Krishna Nagar, II Line,
Guntur - 522 006 (A.P.)
(Shri Sai Leela, Jan. 1990)

17

TEACHINGS OF SAI BABA AND DATTATREYA

R. K. Kapoor

> *"Worship Me with determination. I am the giver of fruits of all. (Sarva Karma Phala Data). Learn that I am beyond old age and death. Those who worship Me with one-pointed devotion (Ananya Bhakti) shall attain the Supreme state (Para Brahma Sthiti). Those who are devoted to Me with a pure heart, submerge in Me after death."*
>
> —Sri Shirdi Sai Baba

Sai Baba, when he was in flesh and blood, assured his devotees that he would be active even from his tomb after His Mahasamadhi. The experiences of his devotees everywhere in the country prove it. Sai Baba is Dattatreya to his devotees as he is belssing and directly guiding those earnest seekers who accept him and surrender to him without any reservation.

Sai devotees who accept '*Shri Sai sat charita*' as their authoritative scripture, accept with equal reverence that Sai Baba is Dattatreya, who is a full incarnation of God and accept him as their greatest teacher. They accord the same posititon and importance to '*Avadhootagita*' attributed to Dattatreya as they do to '*Shri Sai-Sat-charitra*'. Indeed both are celestial like Gita; since they shower infinite compassion and eternal wisdom on the suffering humanity.

The essence of Sai - Datta philosophy is the 'oneness of the individual soul with the universal soul'. This is explained briefly as follows:

DATTA PHILOSOPHY

1. **World of Plurality:** The world of objects is jugglery akin to a mirage in the desert and the one immutable and auspicious alone is real.

2. The sages declare in many ways that all is God and that one is never the body and, therefore, one has neither birth nor death.

3. That individual who neglects his immortal self which is his real nature, like the despicable crow is speeding towards hell.

4. **Means to attain *Mukti*:** Know form to be unreal and the formless alone to be eternal. By absorbing this instructionrebirth is destroyed.

5. **Advice to the mind:** O mind, give up finitude, abandon it; give up even the notion that 'I have renounced'. The pure and immortal principle will destroy, like poison both renunciation and non-renunciation.

6. **Facing challenges of life:** What I do, what I eat, what oblation I offer, what I give - they do not concern me because I am the ever pure, unborn and immaculate one.

7. **Concept of '*Jevanmukti*':** The state of liberation while still living in this body, is alone "*Jeevanmukti*". If it is a state that is attained after the fall of the body, then even dogs and pigs will attain it.

8. Even now Dattatreya is blessing and guiding those earnest seekers who accept Him and surrender to Him.

SAI PHILOSOPHY

1. Look to me and I will look after you. Trust in the Guru fully. This is the only *sadhana*. Guru is all the Gods.

2. If one meditates on Me, repeats My name, sings My deeds, and is thus transformed into Me, his *Karma* is destroyed. I will stay by his side always.

3. Give up all desires and dwell upon GOD-IN-ALL. If the mind is thus concentrated, the goal is achieved.

4. If you make me the sole object of your thoughts and aims, you will attain '*Paramartha*' the supreme goal.

5. Meditate on Me either as with form or as formless. And the latter is hard, then think of my form, just as you see it here. Think of it day and night. With such meditation the mind dissolves into unity.

6. My Guru asked me for two pice: I gave them to him. What he asked for was (i) Faith (*Shraddha*) (ii) Patience (*Saburi*), i.e., cheerful endurance.

7. Be the real and true sons of Dwarakamayi. What is to become of us? Earth will return to earth and breath will return to the air. This opportunity will not return. Sit quiet. I will do the needful. I will take you to the goal.

8. My tomb will speak and move with those who make Me their sole refuge. I shall be active and vigorous from the tomb also.

Salutation to Lord Sainath, who is Dattatreya Himself incarnated to bless us. He is bound to His devotees. He, the indivisible and mighty, and the embodiment of the greatest bliss, is ever calm and composed. He is a promoter of good fortune. He is beyond the worlds and incomprehensive; yet He is the warder of all fears of '*samasara*'. Lord Sainath is a veritable sea of kindness. He is the supreme God; He is absolute Bliss.

(*Shri Sai Leela, Shirdi*))
March 1988, pp.28-29

18

SRI SHIRDI SAI THE UNIVERSAL MASTER

Dr. S.P. Ruhela

"I am the permanent seal of the whole Universe. I do not have like and dislikes. I am the Father of Saints and sinners, Jnanis and Ajnanis (nesciences) also."

–Sri Shirdi Sai Baba

Sai Baba (1838-1918) lived for 60 years at Shirdi during which period He did not move out physically to any other town or city. He never saw a railway train. He was never seen by anyone reading a book or writing anything He never signed. He did not give long scholarly discourses on philosophy or spirituality. He did not start any new religious school of philosophy or sect. He did not make anyone His disciple or spiritual heir. Although thousands of people rushed towards Him to seek divine grace and protection, only a few names of His close devotees, most of whom belonged to Shirdi village, are heard.

How can such a simple and humble *faqir* living in a small mosque be called a 'Universal Master'? In His own days, the villagers of Shirdi and the visitors thereto thought of Him as their local *chamatkari* (miracle maker) *faqir* having extraordinary divine powers. How more and more people in the world during the last eight decades have come to recognize His stature as a great Universal Master is indeed a topic of great importance.

Although He was born a Brahmin, yet He did not consider it worthwhile to emphasize this fact all His life. He kept people ignorant about His caste, community and parental family. He did not choose to take up the propagation of Hindu religion as His life mission. He was an ideal secularist in the best traditions of religious harmony and unity. He treated all religions with equal respect and strove to bring about followers of different religions. Only a genuine Universal Master such as Sri Sai Baba of Shirdi could bring Hindus, Muslims, Parsees, Christians and followers of other religions to such an ultimate and supreme realisation that all are essentially one and that is the very basis of intrinsic unity and integration among all people. Instead of merely teaching, preaching or forcing the ideals of secularism, communal harmony and integration, He actually lived these ideals and His unique living example as such is the first testimony of His being considered as the 'Universal Master.

These days, all kinds of religious, political and social leaders profess grand ideals of secularism, communal harmony and national integration, yet everyone knows how weak is the commitment of most of them to these ideals and what a fragile and pseudo kind of secularism, unity and integration they have been promoting in society. Even the best known among them are, at critical times, found to be exposed as the prisoners of their own parochial religious or beliefs, merely paying lipservice to these ideals. They remain Hindu, Muslim, Sikh, Jain, Christian, etc. refusing to come out of the shells of their own religious beliefs or to treat other religions on equal footing. Their tolerance is superficial, not genuine. Which Hindu religious saint or temple would allow Muslims to read the *Quran* in their temple or *ashram*, and which Muslim saint or mosque would allow the Hindus, Christians and others to read their scriptures in their mosque? Only a *Mahapurush*, the Universal Master, of the stature of Sri Shirdi Sai Baba could do so, as He did at His Dwarka Mai Masjid at Shirdi with such perfect neutrality, poise and case that has no parallel in the history of human civilisations. Any one can read *Shri Sai Sat Charita, 'Devotees, Experiences of Sri Sai Baba'* and Sai Sharananad's *'Sri Sai Baba'* (original Marathi edition) -the three most authentic original sources of information about Sri Shirdi Sai Baba. Therein the avid reader will find that Sri Sai Baba never spoke in favour of or against any religions. He was against religious consideration as such. His basic concern was ethics and good conducts as a human being.

The Universal Master Shirdi Sai Baba's overall effort was directed towards developing in His devotees control over their dispositions. All His informal advice and teachings to His devotees and all His thrilling parables, stories, disclosure of people's past lives and all His own life examples were aimed at one supreme goal: that of making men morally clean, inwardly strong and ever ready to face the ups and down of life, the turmoils of *sansara* or *bhavsagar* with a high sense of values and belief in the magnanimity of God who is omnipresent, omnipotent and omniscient.

Despite the fact that Shirdi Sai Baba was a divine personality possessing all supernatural powers and *siddhis* and the fact that if He wished He could certainly live, dress eat and enjoy in a luxurious manner as many of the present-day Swami, Acharyas and *Mathadeeshes*, etc., are doing, he preferred 'affective neutrality'- an utter disregard to the worldly possessions and facilities, showing no interest in the quality of habitation, food, dress, and no yearning to amass wealth for His *ashram* nor any desire to establish institutions or hereditary *gaddi* (seat) and things like these, which have been so current in the religious circles throughout the world.

A close perusal of Sai Baba's teachings and messages clearly reveal that instead of trying to promote the interests of any particular religion or cult or trying to introduce a new school of spirituality or religious philosophy, Sri Shirdi Sai Baba always clearly and purely emphasized universal values like love, truth, unity, egolessness, detachment, commitment, forbearance, humility, help, hospitality, non-possession, service, surrender, etc. All the major religions and moral codes of human societies in the world have always been emphasizing these very values and they are, therefore, treated as universal values.

Shirdi Sai Baba's teachings represent a garland of carefully chosen sweetest flowers of morality and spirituality grown in the flower beds of different religions. He Himself advised many of His *Yoga Vashistha, the Ramayana, the Gita, the Bhagavatha, Vishnu Sahsranama, Vithal Pothi, Holy Quran, etc.* references to them are there in *Sri Sai Sat Charita and Devotees" Experiences of Sri Sai Baba*. It is also on record that when Bal Gangadhar Tilak's commentary on the *Gita* was presented to Him, instead of letting it be placed at His holy feet He lifted it up and touched His head with it saying "Such holy books have their rightful place on Our forehead, not at Our feet."

As one reads *'Shri Sai Sat Charita'* and *'Devotees Experiences of Sri Sai Baba'* page after page, one discovers Shirdi Sai Baba revealing these very truths of yoga Vashistha to His devotees and visitors in very simple, rural, rustic words of Marathi and Hindustani. Rama was the paragon of virtues, the establisher of proprieties - *Maryada Purshottom*. Shirdi Sai Baba lived those values and extolled them by His living example as also unembellished speech. He advised His devotees to emulate the virtues of Rama and regularly sing "Raja Ram, Raha Ram."

He often referred to the *Gita* while advising His devotees. He emphasized *sharanagati* (total surrender) before one's Guru, which is the most important teaching of the *Gita*. In *Sai Sat Charita* there is a very direct and concrete reference to it:

Nana Saheb Chandorkar was a good student of *Vedantha*. He had read the Gita with commentaries and was proud of his knowledge. He fancied that Baba knew nothing of all that of Sanskrit till Baba one day pricked the bubble. These were the days before crowds flocked to Baba, when Baba had solitary talks at the mosque with the devotees. Nana was always sitting near Baba massaging His legs and muttering something.

Baba - Nana, what are you mubling to yourself?

Nana - I am reacting a *sloka* from Sanskrit.

Baba - What *sloka*?

Nana - *Utter it loudly.*

Nana then recited the *Bhagavatha Gita* (IC-34) which is as follows:

"Tadviddhi Pranipatena Pariprashena Sevyaya.

Upadeshyanto Te Jnanam Hnaniastattwaderashinah"

Baba - Nana, do you understand it?

Nana - Yes.

Baba - If you do, tell Me.

Nana - It means this-

'Making *sashtanga namaskar*, i.e. prostration, questioning the guru, serving Him, learn what this *gyana* is. Then those *Jnanis* who have attained real knowledge of the *Sad-Vastu* (Brahma) will give you *upadesha* (instruction) of *Jnana.*

Baba - Nana, I do not want this sort collected purport of the whole stanza. Give Me each word, its grammatical force and meaning.

Then Nana explained it word by word.

Baba - Nana, is it enough to merely make prostration>

Nana - I do not know any other meaning for the world Pranipata

then making prostration.

Baba - *What is* Pariprashnena?

Nana - Asking questions.

Baba - *What does* Prashna mean?

Nana - The same (questioning).

Baba - If *Pariprashena means the same as* Prashna *(questioning) why did Vyasa add the prefix* Pari. *Was Vyasa off his head?*

Nana - I do not know of any other meaning for the word Pariprashnena.

Baba - Seva, *what sort of* seva *is meant?*

Nana - Just what we are always doing.

Baba - Is it enough to render such service?

Nana - I do not know what more is signified by that word Seva.

Baba - *In the next line* Upadeshyanto *to* Jnanam, *can you so read it as to read any other word in lieu of* Jnanam?

Nana - Yes.

Baba - What wordd?

Nana -*Ajnanam.*

Baba - Taking that word (instead) of *Jnana,* is any meaning made out of the verse?

Nana - No, Shankara Bhashya gives no such construction.

Baba - Never mind if he does not. It there any objection to using the word *Jnana* if it gives a better sense?

Nana - I do not understand how to construe by placing *Ajnana* in it.

Baba - Why does Krishna refer Arjuna to *Jnanis or tattwadarshi* to do his prostration, interrogation and service? Was not Krishna a *tattwadrshi,* in fact *Jnana* itself?

Nana - Yes. He was. But I do not make out why he referred Arjuna to *Jnanis.*

Baba - Have you not understand this?

Nana was humiliated. His pride was knocked on the head.

Then Baba began to explain:

(i) It is not enough merely to prostrate before the *Jnanis.* We must make *servaswa sharanagat* (complete surrender) to the Guru.

(ii) Mere questioning is not enough. The question must not be asked with any imroper motive to trap the Guru and catch him at mistakes in answer or out of idle curiosity. It must be serious and with view to achieving *moksha* or spiritual progress.

(iii)*Seva* is not rendering service, retaining still the feeling that one is free to, offer or refuse service. One must feel that he is not the master of the body, that the body is guru's and exists merely to render service to Him. If this is done, the *Sad-guru* will show you what the *Jnana referred to in the previous stanza is.*

Baba added:

(1) Praniptha implies surrender.

(2) Surrender must be of body, mind and wealth.

(3) *Why should Krishna refer Arjuna to other* Jnanis? "Sadhakas *take everything to be Vasudev (B.G. VII-19),i.e., any Guru takes a disciple to Vasudev and Krishna treats both as his* Prana and atma *. As Sri Krishna knows that there are such Bhaktas and Gurus, he refers Arjuna to them so that their greatness may increase and known.*

A perusal of Shri Sai Sat Charita clearly bears out that Shirdi Sai Baba laid greatest emphasis on the universally acclaimed spiritual disciplined of egolessness, detachment and surrender which Lord Krishna taught in the *Gita*.

Bishma in ' Shanti Parva' of the *Mahabharata* advised the Pandavas as follows:

Truthful speech is commendable; more commendable is speech directed to do good; in my opinion that is truth which is the greatest benefit to living beings.

In Sri Shrdi Sai Baba's teaching this very concept of truthful conduct directed towards the good others finds a place of pride. How poignant and forcefully penetrating are His following words:

You must always adhere to truth and fulfill all the promises you make. Have *Shraddha* (faith) and *Saburi* (Patience), then I will always be with you wherever you are.

"—You have got to make *vichar* or make enquiry about your true nature."

Universality, humanism and tolerance have been the most essential traits of *Santana Dharma*. 'Shivam, Sundram' are the three fighest universal values of Hinduism. The eternal question " Who am I?" , which engagged the attention of almost all the Vedic sages and that of Ramana Maharshi, a contemporary of Shirdi Sai Baba, was also often posed by Baba to HIs devotees. He advised them to ponder over "Who am I?"

Ramana advised:

When other thoughts arise, one should not pursue them, but should inqire: 'To whom did they arise?' It does not matter how many thoughts arise. As each thought arise, one should inquire with diligence, 'To whom has this thought arisen?" The answer that would emerge be, "To me." Thereupon if one inqquires, "Who am I?", the mind will go back to its source; and the thought that arose will become quiescent. With repeated practice in this manner, the mind will develop the skill to stay in its source..... Whatever one does, one should not do with egoity "I". If acts in that way, all will appear as of the nature of Shiva (God)."

Shri Sai Sat Charita recoeds an incident of a Marwadi (businessman) who had come to Shridi Sai Baba wit prayer to show him *Brahma gyan* or self-realisation. Baba's instructions to him were:

"For seeing *Brahma gyan* one has to give five things, i.e. surrender five things" (1) Five *Prans* (2) (Vital forces); Five *indriyas* (senses); (3) *mana* (mind); (4) *buddhi* (intellect); and *aham* (ego);

"....How can he whose mind is engrossed in wealth, progeny and prosperity, expected to know the Brahma without removing his attachment for the same?"

Shirdi Sai Baba did not extol the virtue of one's taking *Sanyas*. He advised His devotees to lead normal family lives, to live in society and yet remain detached, pure and elevated. The concept of *moksah* (liberation) is one of the most important concepts of Hinduism. For that end, several modes of worship, penance, fasts, rituals and other prescriptions like *Japa, tapa* and like have been prescribed. Shridi Sai Baba did not want His devotees to be confused and get lost in the rigmarole of liberation but just to do these four things——to have *Shraddha* (faith) and *Saburi* (patience); to do *namasmaran* (name chanting), to surrender to Guru, and to do duties of one's station in life honestly and properly in a detached manner.

In Islam, the values of respect for the rights of fellow beings, equality, mercy, justice, characterfulness, piety, tolerance, peace, forgiveness, hospitality, perseverance, courage, etc. have been emphasised.

Islam presents a very clear concept of God: "There is no God save Him, the living, the eternal, Neither slumber nor sleep overtake Him. Unto Him belongeth whatever is in the Heavens and whatever is in the earth. Who can intercede with Him save by His own leaves? He knoweth that which is in front of them that which is behind them......He is the Sublime, the Magnificent."

Let us see these teachings of Shirdi Sai Baba and we shall immediately know that they are quite identical with the Islamic values and the Islamic conception of God mentioned above:

Sitting in this *masjid* I shall never, never speak untruth. Take pity on Me like this. First give bread to the hungry, then eat yourself. Note this well. Sri Hari (God) will certainly be pleased if you give water to the thirsty, bread to the hungry, clothes to the naked and your verandah to strangers for sitting and resting.... Let us anybody speak hundred of things against you, do not resent by giving any bitter reply. If you always tolerate such things, you will certainly be happy. Let us world go tpsy-turvy, you remain where you are, Standing or staying in your own place, look on calmly at the show of all things passing before you. Demolish wall of difference that separates you and Me."Allah Malik", i.e. "Allah is the Sole Proprietor, nobody else is our Protector. His method of work is extraordinary, invaluable, and inscrutable. His will be done and He will show us the way and satisfy our heart's desires.

God is, consider it as truth,

God is not, consider this as untruth,

Every thing is Allah, only Allah.

All this is Allah Mian's.

God is the Master, none else is. His actions are extraordinary and inscrutable. None is greater than Allah who gave you birth, who looked after you.

Reading these words of Baba, one feels as if Prophet Mohammed Himself was speaking through the mouth of Shirdi Sai Baba. He believed in one God and "Allah Malik" was His constant refrain.

Jesus Christ's two commandants 'Love of God' and 'Love of Neighbours'; and the universally acclaimed emphasis on prayer, worship and service are the greatest contributions of Christianity to humanity. This very universal value of Love found its highest culmination in the life and teachings of Shirdi Sai Baba as the Universal Master, the kind of which the world had not yet known, He not only preached but by His daily behaviour and life activities exemplified the genuine love and concern He had not only for men, women and children, but even for animals, birds and insects. Countless religious and spiritual personalities and scriptures throughout the 8,000 years old cultural history of mankind have been repeating the importance of love as a supreme human value which cements human hearts and elevates man to divinity, but none had ever given such a direct, empirical and thrilling demonstration of love in action as was done by Shri Sai Baba who in numerous incidents of His stunning miracles like appearing in the forms of a hungry dog, a pig a buffalo, a beggar a *Sadhu*, an ant, insects or the like, accepted food offered by His devotees, or took over the illness, grievous wounds and scorching heat of the blacksmith's fireplace inflicted on innocent human beings and animals.

In a simple yet ground and thrilling manner, He demonstrated each time that all creatures have the same *atma* and therefore all must loved by us as we love ourselves. As Christ used to say, "All are one, be like everyone." Shirdi Sai Baba shared His food with His devotees, dogs, cats, birds, insects freely, and loved them all equally without the least trace of differentiation. Nowhere, not even in the stories of *Purand* which are full of all sorts of thrilling demonstrations of genuine love which Shirdi Sai Baba showed for the world. INdeed, there have been innumerable miracle men in the long history of mankind but Shirdi Sai Baba was the first one in the world to use His miracle-making powers to teaching illiterate and semi-literate people who could not understand the intricate scriputers, the basic principle of love. Thus Sri Shirdi Sai Baba's stature as the Universal Master legitimately and mainly rests on this sort of unprecedented exemplification or empirical evidence of the universal element or power of love on which the whole comes is held together and functions..

Skikhism like Islam, upholds the concept of One God, and this was also preached by Shirdi Sai Baba all His life through word and deed. Also Guru Nanak's most remarkable elucidation of Guru's importance in the life of a disciple finds its total replication in the memories and the teachings of Shirdi Sai Baba. The common refrain of both was that one cannot gain anything without achieving Guru's grace. Guru Nanak sang:

"Without the Guru, one goes astray and transmigrates,

Without the Guru, the efforts become useless,

Without the Guru, the man serves furiously,

Without the Guru, one is not satisfies in Maya,

Without the Guru, one loses at every step, says Nanak."

Comparing this with Shirdi Sai Baba said about Guru to HIs devotees Mrs Radhabai Desmukh said:

"Oh mother, my Guru never taught Me any *mantra;* then how shall I blow any *mantra* in your ears? Just remember that Guru's tortoise like loving glance gives us happiness. Do you try get *mantra or updesh* from anybody. Make Me the sole object of your thoughts and you will, no doubt, attain *Paramartha* (the spiritual goal of life)— No Sadhna, *nor proficiency in the six* Shastras, *are necessary. Have faith and confidence in your Guru. Believe fully* that *Guru is the sole* actor or doer. *Blessed is he who knows the greatness of his Guru and think him to be, Hari, Hara and Brahma (*Trimurti *incarnate).*

To his another devotee Pant, Baba instructed thus:

Come what may, leave not but stick to your bolster (Support,i.e. Guru) and ever remain steady, always atoneness (in union) with him.

In his memories of Sai Baba, Professor G.G.Narke confessed as under:

According to Sai Baba traditions. The disciple or devotees that comes to the feet of the Guru in complete surrender has to be doubt pure, chaste and virtues....The Guru does not teach. He radiates influence. That influence is poured in and absorbed with full by the soul which has completely surrendered itself, blotting out the self.

— The Guru will lift him, ensue him with higher powers, vaster knowledge and increasing realisation of truth. And the end is safe in the Guru's hands. All this was not uttered by Sai Baba at one breath to me or within my hearing, but the various hints I got from His example and dealing with many and His occasional words—when put together, amount to this.

Ram Chandra Sita Ram Dev alias Balabhau or Balbhat of Andheri, we had first seen Shirdi Sai Baba in 1908, asked Baba to give him updesh and be his Guru.

To him Baba said :

It is not essential that one should have a Guru. Everything is within us. What you sow, so you reap. What you give, you get. There is no need for a Guru. It is all within you. Try to listen within and follow the direction you get. we must look at ourself. That is the monitor, the Guru.

"Although during the last decade of His life (1908-18), He was literally rolling in wealth as He was getting dakshina of about 500 to 1,000 rupees per day, yet He invariably distributed the whole of it among His devotees and beggars and poor people retaining almost nothing with Him. At the time of His Maha Samadhi, only an amount of Rs. 16 in cash was found in His belongings as testified by Chakra Narayan who was Police fouzdar at Kopargaon and present there at Shirdi in October 1918 when Baba passed away:

"Whatever He got He scattered with a liberal hand. When He died, we took possession of His cash; that was only Rs 16. Yet daily He was paying or giving away hundreds of rupees."

In the film *Shirdi Ke Sai Baba* there is a scene in which a sadhu comes from Haridwar to Shirdi and is amazed to see the grandeur of Shirdi Sai Baba's *palki* procession from Dwarka Mai to Chavadi, and wonders how a saintly person like Sai Baba prefers all this pomp and show; he takes Baba to be a hypocrite. But when he comes near Baba in Dwarka Mai Masjid and questions Baba about it, Baba shows him His miracle -giving the glimpse of the sadhu's Guru, which immediately brings him to the feet of Sai Baba.

In Sai literature, we find such references that in later years Baba used to receive plates full of delicious foods from His devotees, girls used to come and dance before Him in the Masjid, people used to decorate Him with costly *chadars* (shawls) and clothes, He held His durbar like a majestic ruler. Yet, He was utterly indifferent to all this paraphernalia and accepted all this as an imposition of the wishes of His devotees on Him.

The following testimonies of Baba's contemporary devotees are most relevant in this respect:

Das Ganu recalled:

Several of those that he was regularly paying everyday were subjected to income tax. After Lokmanya Tilak visited Baba (1915-1917), the Income Tax Department directed its attention to the *Shirdi Samsthan*, some officer came and watched the income. They first wanted to tax Sai Baba, but (perhaps seeing that He had little left with Him to proceed upon) they taxed His regular donors, viz., Tatya Patel, Bade Baba, Bagla and Bayaji Patel.

He was really advaita personified. Thirty-two dancing girls would come and play before him daily; He would never care to look at them. he never cared for anything. he was detached and in His *anand* state ...

He used to cure the money-mindedness and the ego of His devotees by asing for dakshina repeatedly till they were left with no money. He advised none to become a sanyasi and forsake his family and home. He advised none to become a *sanyasi* and forsake his family and home. he advised His devotees like Nana Saheb and

Khaparde not to lust for sex. He advised Mlahaspati to sleep very little at night when he used to sleep with Baba in the Dwarka Mai Masjid.

In short, He Himself was following the kind of *yoga* which Guru Nanak spoke about while replying to *siddha* Lohadipa Yogi, and He advised His spiritually advanced devotees to follow the same scrupulously.

Where else except in the divine personality and role-functioning style of Shirdi Sai Baba do we find located in one personality the vibrant elements of Krishna's superb magnetism of love and knowledge of the reality of *atmagyan* Buddha's aura of compassion and piety, Adi Shankara's *advaitism* and spirited fight against secerianism and strict orthodoxy, Kabir's unconventional scathing attack on bigotry and obscuritism, Tulsi's devotion to Lord Rama and the devotional outpourings of love for the divine as those of the great integration like Mira, Chaitanya, Nanak, Purandhardasa, Thyagaraja, Kanakadasa, Tukaram, Ramadas, narasimham, Mehta Ramanad, Nayanar Apar, Eknath, Namdev, Manikkavachakam, etc.; the mysticism of Rama Kirshna Paramahansa and the love, brotherhood and service taught by Christ, Mohammed, Mother Teresa, Dalai Lama, Baba Amte and the like, and the philosophical musings of Ramana Maharshi, Sri Aurobindo and others? Sri Shirdi sai Baba epitomised the quintessence of the values and ideals taught by the world's greatest religious and spiritual masters of all religions and lands in history.

People of all religions, nations and cultures have been and will always be finding all the previous values and spiritual truths in the life of Shirdi Sai Baba. Therefore, it is fully justified calling Shirdi Sai Baba the Universal Master of mankind — a unique avatar of God who descended in order to promote sublime form of spirituality and emotional integration among all human beings. The like of Him, who combined in His personality so deverse and ennobling attributes and lived such a simple life of faqir, has not yet been seen by the world, and who knows, the like of Him may not again be born at all! This makes Him a unique Universal Master of mankind whose most inspiring and spiritually elevating life story should be made known to people of all races, religions and lands.

One thing which is all the more unique about this great Universal Master is that although He shed his mortal coils in 1918, yet he even today responds to the earnest yearnings and prayers of all people in distress and of all His devotees as per unique assurances given by Him. We do not know of any other spiritual personality who had ever made such grand and compassionate assurances to mankind which still keep getting fulfilled. Evidently, a lot of research into the divine mysteries of Shirdi Sai baba as the unique Universal Master of Mankind is needed in order to understand Him. Baba's own advice in this connection was:

"If a man utters My Name with love, I shall fulfil all his wishes, increase his devotion. If he earnestly listens to My life and deeds, him I shall beset in front and back and on all sides. His Holiness Dalai Lama, the spiritual Head of the Tibetans, while delivering the Ninth Bhimsen Sachar Memorial lecture on 'Spiritual Values in Modern India', organised by the Servants of the People Society at Lajpat Bhavan, New Delhi, on December, 1980, said:

The qualities of love and compassion are universal qualities which various religions try to develop among their adherents but religion is not a prerequisite which may be said to constitute a universal religion in themselves.... You don't need a complicated philosophy, you don't need a temple to develop these qualities.

Shirdi Sai Baba's total emphasis and compassion as has been shown above, was on such universal values of love, which are the basics of spirituality. He was not a promoter or champion of any religion as such; instead he was the teacher of spirituality which does not need a complicated philosophy, and that is why, Shirdi Sai Baba did not advance any complicated philosophy of his own, but emphasised the universal values and qualities. The religions may, in future, charge or even disappear, as Rajneesh once prophesied, but the super spirituality of such simple universal values as preached and practiced by Shirdi Sai Baba will ever remain alive and growing.

19

WHAT RESEARCHES SAY ON SRI SHIRDI SAI BABA

Dr. S.P. Ruhela

> "I am the 'Parasakti' and I am the 'Adisakti' who created Brahma, Vishnu, and Maheswara. I am the one who is the cause of creation and dissolution. I am the mother of the Universe. Those who realise me as the Brahman will not only Parama Shanti but also Mukti." Shri Shirdi Sai Baba.
>
> —Sri Shirdi Sai Baba

I am a devotee of Sri Shirdi Sai Baba since 1974. I have been visiting Shirdi often. I have met and interacted with a number of devotees all these years. I have been collecting and reading all that has been published on Baba and that has been available to me. I have myself experienced the love and mercy of Sri Shirdi Sai Baba in my life and in my family.

On the basis of the about 40 materials of research importance from Das Ganu's writing of 1903 to M. Rama Rao's writing in 1994, collected and briefly highlighted and reviewed in my book, 'What Researchers Say on Sri Shirdi Sai Baba' (1995). I have arrived at these research conclusions almost Sri Shirdi Sai Baba:

1. It is clearly established, beyond any shadow of doubt, that Sri Shirdi Sai Baba was the highest kind of Prophet or Spiritual Saint and Saviour of mankind par excellence. He was a matchless

and the greatest contemporary Incarnation of God, whose charismatic divine personality as a Prophet or Godman, has been influencing, moulding, saving, spiritualizing and granting liberation to countless persons.

2. His most benevolent mission of providing love, help, cure, upliftment, solace and spiritual enlightenment to all those who came under his influence, nay, all of whom he drew to him by his mysterious designs, irrespective of race, religion, caste, class, nationality, occupation etc., without any trappings of high-flown, bombastic, obtruse or obscure spiritual concepts and idioms and any fanfare of publicity of his miracles and grace, has now assumed the shape of a gigantic global spiritual movement - the SAI MOVEMENT. The Sai movement founded and set into motion by Sri Shirdi Sai Baba at the tiny dilapidated Dwarkamai Masjid of Shirdi in the later-half of the 19th century and the first two decades of the 19th century and the first two decades of this century, is growing and spreading in fast throughout the world.

3. The most distinguishing feature of this great Incarnation, as unfailingly attested by most of the actual eyewitnesses or participant observers in the high drama of spirituality enacted by him at Shirdi till 1918 and as experienced by many realised souls of later years, has been his genuine efforts to unite different communities into bonds of love and brotherhood by not merely preaching them but by actually demonstrating before them how the basics of spirituality really work, how the souls of all creatures - persons, animals, birds and reptiles and after animals are essentially the same and are equal; how the principle of nexus between '*Karma* and *Punarjanma*' (Action and Rebirth) invariably operates in every soul's journey; how all persons and other creatures of the animal world are in fact tied to each other by our mutual bonds of *"Rinanubandha"* (bonds of give and take); how it is so easy to reach the Lord's Feet by following *Bhaktimarg* (Path of devotion), and the like.

Here was the Divine Master of the Universe who could recall for how many births a certain devotee had been in close contact with him, in the past birth what fault one did and what punishment he, she or it was suffering on that account in the present life, and who could just by his having been moved at the prayer of a tearful heart of a mother or father order a soul to take birth from the womb of that childless woman; one who monitored the births and deaths in this world and left proofs thereof for the inquisitive devotees to find them out.

The mankind has not seen any other saint of such a great stature who did all such spiritual demonstrations and experiments with such ease and facility and with such breadth and depth. Really, Sri Shirdi Sai Baba is matchless. While there have been a countless number of saints in all religions, races, and countries in the long history of human civilization who have indeed taught many things of morality and spirituality and also many of them did show their myriad manifestations of their Siddhi powers, one distinguishing thing that has emerged from the testimonies of the researchers and writers and spiritual seekers on Sri Shirdi Sai Baba is that he used his miracles extensively for all and sundry, so spontaneously, without any glamour and fanfare of publicity, just to help and cure all those who approached him with a prayerful heart.

4. This is clearly borne out by researchers that Sri Shirdi Sai Baba preferred *Bhakti Marg* instead of *Gyan Marg*, but he was not against *Gyan Marg*. Those who wished to follow that Marg and had competence to do so, were encouraged by Baba to study several religious and spiritual texts but he cautioned them that it was a difficult and less satisfying path.

5. The factual ethnographic details recorded by Sri Shirdi Sai Baba's contemporary devotees like Das Ganu, Hemadpant, Pradhan, Swami Sai Sharan Anand, Kavi Yogi Maharshi Shuddhananda Bharti, Shivamma Thayee, all those whose testimonies had been collected by narasimbhaswamiji and recorded in his most thrilling work *Devotees' Experiences of Sri Sai Baba'* and the thrilling revelations made by Sri Sathya Sai Baba about the life of Sri Shirdi Sai Baba— how Baba lived, behaved, performed his divine role as Avatar, interacted with visitors and devotees, performed his miracles silently and surely, made his thrilling disclosure about certain persons' past births, how Shirdi village and Dwarkamai Masjid looked like and what services, celebrations and activities were done therein, who went there, with what wish or motive and what he or she received— all these details help us in having a very magnified picture of Sri Shirdi Sai Baba, the unique Fakir of Dwarkamai Masjid, sitting or walking on our mental screen. Like a video film, these ethnographic details project a living and moving picture of actual Sai Baba passing before our eyes, engrossing us with spirituality, ecstasy and peace. These ethnographic details of Baba and his time, which are not intellectual analyses but pure simple, honest, and empirical

accounts of the participant observers as devotees-cum-researchers for 60 years of the physical presence of Baba at Shirdi (from 1858 to 1918) instantly attract any one and turn him or her into Baba's devotee.

6. The miraculous and benevolent nature of Sri Shirdi Sai Baba has been recognised and highly appreciated and praised in time and space. He assures his devotees to help, protect and cure by his miracles!

7. Some of the researchers have researched into the significance of the name *"Dwarkamai"* which Sri Shirdi Sai Baba gave to the old, dilapidated and forlorn Muslim mosque occupied by him in 1858 and where he lived till his *MahaNirvana* in 1918.

Sri Shirdi Sai Baba's action of giving this name to the mosque was with a divine purpose or intention. He wanted the Dwarkamai Masjid to be the meeting place of all communities, sects, castes, occupations, and other variants of social stratification, a crucible or melting pot in which all rigidities and tendencies of fundamentalism, alienation, self-estrangement, dominance, exploitation, superiority and inferiority complex and workings of ego could be melted and souls purified of all sorts of impurities. He wanted to make Dwarkamai an anvil on which the national unity was forged by the Divine Ironsmith using the flame of his spiritual teachings like atomic equality, *Rinanubandha*, love etc. and casting the iron by seasoning it with his typical behavioural attributes in which love, anger, honour, scorn, mercy and concern for other's welfare were significant ones.

It has been pointed out by some researchers that the Sai movement started by Sri Shirdi Sai Baba since the 1920's been growing and spreading throughout the world, due to the tireless and devoted efforts of great devotees and propagators of Baba's name like Das Gaanu,1 Hemadpant, Narsimhaswamiji, Swami Sai Sharan Anand, Swami Sri Sai Narayan Baba of Sri Bhagawati Sai Sansthan, Panvel, Sai Padananda Sri Radhakrisnaji, Swami Sri Gopalkrishna Bhagat, Shivamma Thayee and Sri H.D. Laxmana Swami, Sri R.S. Chitnis of Delhi, Sri Kailash Bakiwala of Jaipur and innumerable others. Countless Shirdi Sai Temple have come up in not only in the nooks and corners of India but even in many foreign countries like UK, USA, Africa, Australia, Singapore etc., Americans, Germans, Italians, Canadians, Africans, Mauritans, etc. are becoming Baba's devotees.

Each of the Shirdi Sai Temples established so far seems to have a thrilling story full of great suspense and mystery behind it — a story full of Sri Shirdi Sai Baba's miracles - how total strangers suddenly appeared on the scene and offered, with great dedication, humility and love, cash, stone, marble tiles, cement, iron bars, girders, windows, doors, fans, electricity fittings, and all sorts of other equipments, appurtenances and decorations and even food stuffs for *bhandaras* and funds for Nama Saptahas or Kirtans. The unseen miraculous hand of Sri Shirdi Sai Baba has been working behind all these offers and gifts and is visible to or experienced so intimately by those associated with any of these temples anywhere in the world. In this materialistic world, how these temples of Sri Shirdi Sai Baba have been coming up in almost all Indian cities, towns and important villages, and even in foreign countries, how people are motivated to donate funds and articles so liberally without any one's persuasion and without Shri Sai Baba Sansthan, Shirdi yet being able to provide leadership to the Sai Baba movement on the global scale, is a real mystery or miracle of Baba.

Reference

Ruhela SP. (Ed.), *What Researchers Say on Sri Shirdi Sai Baba*. New Delhi: M.D. Publication, 1995.

20

SAI WAY TO SALVATION

Dr. Vijay Kumar

"Sai Baba is one of our incarnate divinities. He was not a writer or a speaker. He was beyond words and thoughts. He was the "Truth" as it is and Love as it manifests, such silent dynamic souls do not disappear with the body. Sai cosmic force still acts and saves thousands."

—Justice M.B. Rege, Sai Devotee

One of my collegues died in March, 1968 at a tender age of 37. During his short tenure at a doctor, he had earned the respect and admiration of both professionals and patients, especially for his love and compassion to the sick and disable. This doctor had reached the pinnacle of success in his chosen field and enjoyed the status and financial rewards that accompany such accomplishment. He had tasted every good thing, by the standards of the world. At the staff-meeting following his death, a five minute eulogy was read by a member of his department. Then the Chairman invited the entire staff to stand for one minute of silence in memory of the fallen colleague. I have no idea what the other staff members contemplated during that pause, but I can tell what went through my mind at this time.

I was asking Lord Sainath, "Is this what it all comes down to? We sweat and worry and labour to achieve a place in life, to impress our fellow-men with our competence. We take ourselves so seriously, over-reacting to the insignificant events of each passing day. Then finally, even for the brightest amongst us, all these experiences fade into history and our life is summarised within a five-minute eulogy and sixty seconds of silence. It hardly seems worth the efforts Lord."

Also I was struck by the collective inadequacy of that staff-meeting to deal with the questions raised by our friend's death. Where had he gone? Would he live again? Will we see him on the other side? Why was he born? Were his deeds observed and recorded by a loving God? Is there meaning to life beyond our investigative research and expensive automobiles? The silent response by learned men and women in that staff-meeting symbolised our inability to cope with these issues.

Then a wave of relief swept over me as I thought about the message of Sai Baba:

"Wherever you are, if you think of me, I am there at any time you please." "Believe Me, though I pass away, My bones in My tomb will give you hope and confidence. Not only Myself but My tomb would be speaking, moving and communicating with those, who surrender themselves whole heartedly to Me".

It provides the only satisfactory explanation for why we are here and where we are going to. The final heart-beat for a Sai-devotee is not the mysterious conclusion to a meaningless existence. It is, rather the grand beginning to a life that will never end. That is why we can proclaim even thy sting?. In fact. Sai Baba told Shama that they were together for 72 births.

How extremely important it is for the man of the home to know the answer to these perplexing questions, and to be able to lead his family in the path of righteousness. When he accepts that spiritual responsibility as Sai Baba intends, the entire family is likely to follow his example. Sai asked: "Give me two-pice '*dakshina*' - - '*Nishta*' and '*Saburi*', i.e. faith and patience." This issue is of such significance that I feel compelled to set down here my convictions regarding the basic plan of salvation.

I used to ponder over a difficult question. It seemed strange that God would incarnate as Sai Baba and live amidst us for eighty years and undergo suffering for the benefit of His devotees. I reasoned that God, as Creator of the universe, was in charge of everything. That entitled Him to make His own rules and establish His own boundaries. It seemed to me that God could have provided any plan of salvation. He chose anything that suited.

Sai Baba's aid was received by hundreds of people. He said to G.S. Khaparde that constant attention to the thousands that sought his aid ruined his system and would continue to ruin it till the fleshy tabernacle should break, and that he did not mind the trouble and loss, as he cared more for his devotees, than for decades and the cross he was nailed to. From that cross, his soul has ascended and regained its spiritual perfection and is blessing all devotees.

I could not comprehend why He would put Himself through such grief and sorrows on our behalf when He could have offered a less costly plan of salvation, I struggled with this issue as a Sai-child and was perplexed by the questions it raised. H.H. Narasimha Swamiji provided me the answer in one of His *'Mahasamadhi Message'*:

The central truth of Sai Baba's life is: 'A life spent in sacrifice and loving service is life; And that a life spent in indulgence and other ways is death':, "If all of us do but strive to reach this ideal, our individual and natural goals are sure to be achieved. "Deserve and you will get it" so said Sai.

It is interesting to look back on the things that troubled me in earlier days. I now have a better understanding of Sai Baba's plan of salvation and what motivated it. And the explanation is of great significance for me, because it deals with the very essence of Sai philosophy. Here, then, is my concept of the plan of salvation and why Sai's physical death was necessary. It begins, as it should, with an understanding of Sai Baba's nature'. throughout *'Sai Satcharita'*, the Almighty is represented by two uncompromising characteristics "His love and His justice". Both of these aspects are reflected in everything God does, and none of His actions will ever contradict the other one.

Love and justice of God were especially evident when He created us human beings. Obviously, he could have programmed us to love Him and obey His laws. This could have been accomplished by creating us as highly sophisticated robots or puppets. He did in fact, program the brains of lower animals, causing birds to build a certain kind of nest and wolves to kill wounded deers. They have no choice in the matter. My pet dog plays an assortment of wirred-in behaviour about which neither of us has a choice. For, example, he cannot help barking when the front-bell rings. Nor can he keep from gobbling his food as though he would never get another meal. God has imposed instinctual behaviour in him, which operates without learning.

But Lord Sainath chose to put no instructive behaviour in mankind and left it free to learn. This explains the utter helplessness of human infants, who are the most dependent of all creatures at birth. They lack the initial advantages of unlearned responses, but will later run circles around the brightest animals with 'lock-in' reactions. Such is the nature of our humanness.

By granting us freedom of choice, therefore, Lord Sainath gave meaning to our love. He sought our devotion, but refused to demand it. However, the moment He created this choice, it became inevitable that He would eventually be faced with man's sin. Sai Baba told people that if they quarrelled and hurt each other his heart was burning within and that if they endured each other's faults and attacks with patience, his heart was rejoicing. In His own mosque the Hindus. Christian, Muslims, Parsis stand side by side in their adoration to Him. Far from destroying each other, they are building each other's temples, mosques and sacred structures, and helping each other to have unmolested celebrations in the same building. The Hindus rebuilt his mosque and a Brahmin devotee of his, Upasani Baba, built a mosque next to his own temple. The Muslims perform their 'Id' in the same mosque without noise and when the turn for the Hindu worship in the same place comes up, the Muslim brother beats the drum in the mosque to help Hindu do his worship.

In spite of Sainath's advocating 'Saburi' (Patience) we do come across stray instances where-in Sai devotees lose their calmness and confront each other, with the most serious dilemma of all time. Sai Baba's love for His devotees is unlimited and He forgives His disobedient children. The Bible say "A father pitieth his children, so the Lord pitieth them that fear Him."

(*Psalm* 103:13).

That is an analogy I can comprehend. I know how I pity my children when they have done wrong. My inclination is to forgive them.

Lord Sainath is close behind our thoughts. In every moment of our life his declaration comes true; "Wherever you may be, you may remember this always: "I ever know whatever you do or say."

In spite of Sai Baba's great love, His justice required complete obedience. It demanded repentence and punishment for disobedience. So here-in was a serious paradox or conflict within Sai Baba's nature. If he destroyed the human race, as his justice would require in response to our sinful disobedience, his love would have been violated; but if he ignored our sins, his justice would have been sacrificed. Yet neither aspect could he compromise.

But Sai Baba, in his marvellous wisdom, proposed a solution to that awful dilemma. "Do not try to get *Mantra* or *Upadesh* from anybody. Make Me the sole object of your thought and actions and you will no doubt attain *'Paramartha'*. Look at Me whole-heartedly and I, in turn, look at you similarly." Years after His Mahasamadhi, when Kaka Dixit had a doubt as to how he could attain the 'devotional status' of *Nava-nathas,* Sai Baba cleared his dilemma through a dream-vision to Anand Rao Pakhade. ".......Devotion in the form of bow to or worship of Guru's feet is sufficient."

This understanding of the plan of salvation is not based on guesses and suppositions, of course. It is drawn from the literal interpretation of Sai's word.

Isn't that a beautiful explanation of Sai Baba's purpose here on earth? It makes clear why Sai Baba's plan necessarily involved his own exchange of life with Tatya Patil. Only by paying this incredible price could He harmonise the potential contradiction between love and justice, and provide a 'way of escape' for mankind. It also explains why there is no other means. Sai Baba said: "Simple rememberance of my name as SAI, SAI will do away with sins of speech and hearing".

Just how does a person proceed, now to accept this plan and follow the risen Lord? Prof. G.G. Narke in 1936 said: "Sai Baba is now in the flesh, and when he was in flesh he was in the state in which he is now." We are aware that there is no change in Sai Baba. "He was, He is and will ever be an *Aparntaratrna*." The Bible says: "Anyone who calls upon the name of the Lord will be saved (Romans 10 : 13)."

As I understand the Sai philosophy, there is a second responsibility. "Are there still some among you who hold that 'only believing' is enough? "Well, remember that the demons believe this too so strongly that they tremble in terror when will you ever learn that 'believing' is useless without doing what God wants you to? Faith that does not result in good deeds is not real faith (*James* : 2 : 12-20)." So something else is required. While it is true that you could 'work' your way to salvation, you cannot do enough good deeds to earn it; repentence is still an important part of the process.

'Repentence' is a word that is often misunderstood. What does it really mean? Sapatnekar's incident in Chapter 48 of *Shri Sai Satcharita* defined repentence as having three parts to it. "The first is conviction. You have to know what is right before you can do what is right; and you have to know what's wrong in order to avoid those misbehaviours." Repentence also involves a deep awareness that you stand guilty before the Lord. When Sapatnekar went and placed his head at the holy feet of Sai Baba, he seemed to have no real awareness of his own sin and guilt. He had no 'contrition' of heart. That is why Sai Baba rebuked him saying "Get out".

But where does this spirit of repentence originate from? It must come through the teaching 'Look to Me, I look after you.' We should have this relationship with Lord Sainath. Sainath must be so important that you will allow Him to turn your life around and change your behaviours. In summary, then, repentence includes conviction, knowing right from wrong, then contrition, being aware of your guilt and sin, and finally, a resulting change of mind and heart and behaviour. We are aware that Sapatnekar led a blissful life after Sainath ultimately blessed him.

I think it would be helpful to give an example of the kind of prayer that a person might pray if he understands what I have been writing and wants to accept Sai Baba as his own Lord and Saviour. Let me express it in this way.

"Lord Sainath : I do not have anything valuable to offer except myself and my love. I accept your control of my life, and intend to serve you, obey you and follow you. You have my past, my future, my family, my money and my time. Nothing will I withhold. Thank you for loving me and forgiving me and making me your own."

(Shri Sai Leela, Sept-Oct., 1996)

21

GOD SAI BABA'S RARE DISCOURSES FOR THE MODERN MAN

Yogi Minocher K. Spencer

"Seek enternity. Be not baffled by the tempests of life. Be not seduced by the gaities of life. Seek God in all earnestness, in all purity of heart and He will lead you to your goal."

–Sri Shirdi Sai Baba

Minocher K. Spencer (1888-1958) was a great Yogi, perfect medium and a great Spiritualist. He was born in the Parsi community in India. He was the resident of Karachi, now in Pakistan. He was a metal merchant by profession. This was his third and last incarnation in this world. By virtue of his rare merit in his previous two births as a human being, he had the spiritual guidance of Rishi Ram Ram - a great Master of the Spirit World, even while he was in his cradle. Later on reaching higher stage in his spiritual evolution, his progress was taken over by Sri Sai Baba, the God Almighty, till the last stage-God realisation.

His goal was to see God face to face, and walk with him side by side. In the last stage he was spending eighteen hours in meditation daily, and the balance of six hours he spent in taking food, rest, writing on spiritual topics and serving lepers and this was his hobby. As ordained by God, he wrote more than 2000 pages of typed matter on the topic *"How I Found God"* which contained many messages from Spirit Master and Sai Baba as a God, and also Foreword by God was given. One hundred copies of the same were printed by the Spiritual Healing Centre, Coimbatore in 1953, but before that interesting, illuminating and thrilling book could be released for the benefit of the devotees, it was God's order to burn the said books, written in the course of one month. This was another blow given to him to test whether there was any grain of egorism left in him, and he successfully withstand this God's test. Luckily one copy of that rare book has survived, as per God's wish.

Between 3.11.1952 and 18.2.1953, Sri Sai Baba, the Supreme Spirit dictated 77 rarest of the rare kind of discourse or messages to Yogi M. K. Spencer in his vision. Out of them four most relevant messages are being reproduced here for the enlightenment of all Sai devotees and spiritual seekers throughout the world. All the 77 messages are published in a recent book *'Shirdi Sai Baba speaks to Yogi Spencer in Vision'* (New Delhi: Vikas Publishing House, 1998) compiled and edited by S. P. Ruhela.

These messages are invaluable for effective solution of the contemporary world's problems and the spiritual elevation of mankind.

When God Sai Baba was thanked for these 77 beautiful discourse, which were given to Yogi Spencer in his altar room, from day to day. He gave the following every illuminating message on 18.2.1953:

"Do you know that these discourses are a reflection of what you have been able to grasp yourself. I have only helped you in putting them in proper from and style. They are not only an expression of your grasp of the whole teaching but a revelation of your own inner self. See how beautifully, I have made your inner self speak for the edification of your world. It is the voice of your inner self - the voice of God, - with whom you are united for ever and ever throughout eternity."

1

RENUNCIATION IS THE ESSENCE OF SPIRITUALITY

Think of the indwelling spirit and not the body which is frail and subject to decay. It is spirit alone, that is eternal, all else is ephemeral and transitory. Bodily indulgence is an obstacle to spiritual growth and progress. Care should be taken of the body, for it is the temple of the soul, but in no case, bodily enjoyment should be mistaken for spirituality. The body, the senses and the mind are to be curbed in order to cut asunder the inner sheets which cover the soul and make it a prisoner.

Renunciation is the essence of spirituality. Annihilate all desires and kill the ego in you. Be sturdy and strong like the oak in the jungle and stand fast against all tempests of temptations. Listen to the voice of Conscience for it is your best inward monitor.

Work and worship go together. Work is the essence of life, but it should not be for the purpose of enjoying the fruit of your labour. The labourer seeks his hire, but the true YOGI discards it. He works for the sake of work, to spread God's love and light and not for selfish gain. He works in the name of God for the growth of his spirit and not for the satisfaction of his carnal desires. Work is worship, when it is concentrated and dedicated to God. Be a KARMA YOGI by keeping the fire of love and devotion for God burning in you all the time.

(6.11.1952)

2

PEACE, HARMONY, LOVE - THESE FORM THE RHYTHM OF LIFE

Peace, Love, Harmony - these form the rhythm of life. They are the vibrant factors which promote happiness. Peace is the antagonist of discord, war, hatred and bitterness of feeling. Discard all that is bitter in your heart, forgetting and forgiving all those who do evil in life. No man can live in peace, unless he makes Virtue his spouse and unselfishness his comrade in life.

Peace is the harbinger of love and love is the most sacred element in man. It is divine nectar. It is the soul of divinity, the parent of all virtues, the source of true happiness. Keep the fire of love burning in your heart. Love all, without distinction. Love is divine comradeship. It is the light of truth. It is the pattern on which God has woven His whole universe for the happiness and bliss of all His creatures.

Make your life a book of Love, from end to end. Let every page and every line be the mirror of God, reflecting His beauty, His mercy, His grace, His gentility and above all His great LOVE which lightens the forces in the universe harmonizing all LIFE, which is ONE. Love begets love. Love your neighbour as your love yourself and God will love you with a treble force. Make love the corner stone of your life, the foundation of the whole edifice, the fulcrum of all your activities, the symbol of your perfection.

(9.11.1952)

3

GOD-REALISATION - THE GOAL OF LIFE, NOT EARTHLY HAPPINESS

Different faiths are like different rivers that flow from different regions but ultimately join the ocean. The object of every religion is God. He alone is worthy of worship and none else. People make Mammon as their God. This is wrong. To make sordid desires of life to dominate is to invite catastrophe. Do not be dragged in the mire of worldly temptations for they are death knells of misery and degradation. Riches are the burning bricks with which the vault of hell is built. Lust for power is a shadowy substance. Do not aspire for worldly applause for it is fickle and baseless. Stain not your soul with the allurements of life but keep it stainless with the love and light of God.

God alone is the Reality, all else is of unreal nature. Seek God in the simplicity of your heart. Renounce the gewgaws of life. Hold fast to Truth and Righteousness. Mercy and Compassion, Love and Gentility, Simplicity and Humility, Earnestness and Sincerity, Passivity and Catholicity, Sobriety and Integrity, Forgiveness and Forbearance, Patience and Perseverence. Aspire to be a saint, a sage by getting out from the common track and following your own path to God. Work ceaselessly, Pray to God zealously, keep your mind serene and calm even in the midst of storms and tempests. Be pure in heart and you will see God. God-realisation is the goal of life, not earthly happiness which is false and effervescent.

(6.12.1952)

4

GROW IN SPIRIT

To rise to the highest pinnacle of spirituality is ordained by God for every one. But extremely few reach the goal for the path leading to it is so narrow and painful to traverse. It is a great mistake to avoid the narrow way which leads to God and to take to the broad way which leads to corruption and decay. Why sell eternal peace for a mess of pottage. And yet millions and millions of your people of the earth plane, forgetful of the Self within them, hanker for loaves and fishes of life, gilded with an outward shine and leave off God, who is the only Reality.

Seek God not in outward shows and forms. Seek God not in the paraphernalia of rites and rituals. Seek God, not in church congregations. But seek Him in the cave of your heart. It is there He dwells, hid in the kernel. Throw off the shells and the shackles that bind and devitalise you. Grow in spirit and the indwelling Spirit, free from all its outer coverings and coatings will shine like a crystal star and lead you on and on to the starry realms of unimaginable glory and beauty to your extreme delight and joy. Make God your home, your hearth, your sole and profuse source of thought and activity. It is then alone, you shall reach Him and be united with Him in all eternity.

(8.12.1952)

22

SAI BABA AND THE FUTURE OF RELIGION

Sri B.V. Narasmhaswamiji

There are thousands, if not tens of thousands, who are perfectly convinced that Sai Baba was fully divine or, in the words of the orthodox, an Avatar, though, as soon as we use that term, troubles arise and dissidents come forward to differ. So the best thing to say is that Sai Baba had in him the allround perfection of divine qualities in such a manner as to fulfil our idea of God. That is what Sri G.S. Khaparde said, and what many others have said who are learned enough to draw distinctions between divinity and a divinely gifted human being. Metaphysics apart, let us confine ourselves to the usage of terms according to popular parlance and go on in this article with the explanation of Baba's position in respect of the future of religion. So far as India itself is concerned, the future of religion in India is largely a question of the fusion of the two great trends which appear to be so widely different, namely, Hinduism and Islam. The differences have fed frequently to the breaking of heads and burning of temples, and recently even the breaking up of the political unity of the country. So, the achievement of something like a basis for the unity of Hinduism and Islam is itself a very great and momentous task and may be justly viewed as affording a solution to the country's problem of fusing the two into one.

So, we might first take the question of Hindu-Muslim religious differences, and see how far Sai Baba was able to draw these communities nearer so as to give some ground for hope that Islam and Hinduism might one day combine and produce a blend that will satisfy the really earnest amongst the adherents of both religions, and form the foundation of India's main religion of the future. In India itself the Muslims are so numerous that any failure to take note of their religious needs in trying to shape the future of Indian religion must spell a failure. Happily for us, however, Sai Baba has chalked out some outlines which give very good promidse of a blending of these two.

We shall se what history has to teach us about the blending of these two religions in the past. Great souls have always existed who appreciated the advantage of fusion, and they worked hard to achieve success in this matter. Akbar's name must naturally be given the highest prominence in point of time and in point of width of views, as he was not merely an emperor with both Hindu and Muslim subjects, but one of the most liberal rulers that the world has ever seen. The idea that God is one, and, therefore, people professing all religions should come together and worship Him in a common place with love and amity among them, being the children fo the same God, treating one another as brethren, was the noble idea of Akbar. This must always command the assent of every right thinking individual. The difficulty arises only when a thinker convinced of the above position as being right, tries to make others accept it and propound not an individual faith, but a popular formula for a popular religion that would please both these communities. Akbar did not, however, care to go into the metaphysics or the technique of this question, but did what was the most practical and best thing to do for the promotion of his object. He, as an emperor, commanded the obedience and allegiance of both the religionists and he ordered the leading followers of both religions to come together and worship God in a common place, and called the faith which he thus propounded '*Din Ilahi*',that is, God's religion. Every religion must be God's religion and the essence of all religions must be God's religion. God has no special religion. Religion is that which binds, 'Re' back 'Ligo' to bind. Religion is that which binds people back together in society for purposes of worship and other similar matters. Religion is a social phenomenon and it necessarily includes something which will appeal to the average or even the lowest level of intellect prevalent in any society. The ideas of God that are found even in one religion, even at one age, widely vary, and the modes in which God is approached and people carry on their contact with or approach to God, are various, and it is no easy joke to unify religions even for the people of one country and one age. Yet, Akbar attempted his task and by reason of his position and the excellence of his idea carried his point almost to success. Unity of god is the central principle in both Hindu and Muslim religions, and the one God has always to be revered and adored by prayer for prorecting oneself and one's dependents and country. For this purpose, therefore, Hindus and Muslims can always join, and in fact have often joined. In national calamities and crises, differences of opinion have not prevented people from joining together and praying to a common God for relief from great distress and peril. Similarly when an emperor ordered, people were able to join together and pray to a common father. For some time Akbar's experiment proved to be practical and successful. Unfortunately, his ideas and practice did not take root, and his successors had widely different ideas from his. Aurangazib's policy was extremely opposite to his. Instead of promoting harmony between the two religions the Aurangzeb's policy was extremely opposite to his. Instead of promoting harmony between the two religions, Aurangazeb's idea was to compel all his subjects to discard other religions and to adopt one religion, namely, Islam. Historians agree that this was one of the chief causes of the collapse of the Moghul empire in India. When we discover a mistake committed in the past it is our duty to discover and adopt the correct policy.

"Live and Let live". Freedom to all people as far as possible to adopt their ideas of approach to God must be the basis on which society must be founded. Any compulsion in religion will destroy religion and society also. This cardinal principle is noted to be one of the main features of Sai Baba's dealings with his multifarious devotees including Hindus, Muslims, Christians, Parsis, and others. Anything like compulsion or for that matter any attempt for conversion is absolutely destructive of the work of religion. We can have neither religion nor unity where compulsion is adopted. Conversion is very often the result of either compulsion or low motives, and Baba. who knew this fact very well, on one occasion when a Hindu convert to Islam was brought by Bade Baba to him saying, 'Baba, this man has been converted to Islam', struck him (the convert) on the cheek, and asked, 'have you changed your father?" Changing one's father is absolutely unthinkable, and an absurd idea. Each religion makes God the father of its followers, and when one has got a father according to accredited lines, which are useful, it looks absurd to think of changing either the physical father who begot one or the Universal Father that is adored in religion. So, Baba always dissuaded people from changing their religion either from Hinduism to Islam or from Islam to Hinduism or from Christianity to Hinduism, and *vice versa*. What is most important is not mere external conversion but conversion of the heart, which makes a man lose his sinful and bestial nature and climb up to Godhood. That real conversion is not called conversion by people because it generally has no external marks to denote it. Baba's object was that all people should be really converted and should have God in their hearts, and get firmly attached to God so that all of them will be soaked through and through with the idea of God, and in consequence there will be no friction between one person soaked in God and another person soaked in God.

There can be no quarrel among religions so far as the essence is conceerned. the quarrels are all about the externals. 'You wish to go to a Temple. I wish to go to a Mosque. So, we cannot agree. You put on Namam vertically. I put on sandal or sacred ashes in parallel horizontals. so we cannot agree'. Can this be recorded as the correct attitude? Let every person sit quietly directing his mind to the greatness of God, and the grand qualities of God and allow himself to be lost in them. Then there is no possibility of his quarreling with any other person or any other person quarreling with him. The result of contemplation of love for god is Love. If we go into the essence of religion, that is, if each tries to concentrate on God, the result will only be love and harmony and not a jarring set of crusades among people trying to trample on one another. Luckily wars of religion like the crusades are now things of the past. But what have succeeded them are wars for the sake of material aggrandizement, for getting colonies, and for conquests of population, for economies purposes, and these are quite as deadly in their effects as were of religion. If a discovery is made of a solution for the problem of difference of religions amongst mankind, it bids fair to solve also the problem of wars for pelf, for colonies, etc. We have to examine carefully into Sai's history to see what he has done, how far he was successful in promoting harmony between individuals of the various groups that came to him, such as Hindus, Muhammadans, and Parsis, whether the solution found by him has worked well amongst his immediate followers, and whether that solution can be extended to other fields and to the entire world.

Let us now see what has been done by Baba. He was first worshipped by a handful of Hindus who treated him as God or Gurudeva, because he showed such wonderful powers over material Nature. He converted water into oil and , therefore, the villagers of Shirdi were firmly convinced that he was not an ordinary human being but one gifted with divine qualities. Along with that, the exhibition of other *chamatkars* by Baba proved his possession of very vast powers, though this was done only gradually. He by a unique series of kind acts towards all, and especially the poor, the sick, the unfriended and the miserable, showed uniformly a golden heart of love towards all, treating every one, prince or peasant, pandit or rustic, Hindu or Muslim, on the same level. There was in him practically universal love combined with a sense of equality and equanimity, and utter absence of self. He had no family, no attachments, and the whole world was his kin.

Ayam Nijah Perovaiti

Gannana laghu chetasam

Mahatmanastu ....

Vasudhaiva Kutumbakam.

That is, it is the petty mind that considers whether any particular person is one's friend or a stranger. The great souls treat the entire world as a little family of their own. Baba was undoubtedly such a great soul from the very beginning and for this reason as well as on account of his *chamatkars* increasing numbers began to worship him as God and called him their Gurudava, Ishta Devata. Now some would suppose this is only adding one more to the 33 crores God's that Hinduism recognizes, and, therefore, giving more scope for differences. But luckily this "33 crores and 1st" god swallowed up all the 33 crores and showed the unity of God. He drew people to himself for granting them various reliefs and finally led them on to the one God who is nothing but Love, who is common not only to Hindus, but Muslims, Christians, Parsis and others also. He demonstrated to all that the only God that they could deal with was something visible, something in human form, something with wonderful love and power and mercy, so that they were compelled to bow down to it and accept it for their good in every department of life. So, Hindus, Christians, Muslims, and all practically worshipped him. However, as the Semitic religions like Islam and Christianity forbade baring the God that they proclaimed Christians and Muslims mostly did not know him to be God & people from accepting any one as God nor adopt the external processes of worship which the Hindus always adopt. But this really does not matter, **for the essence of holding on to God is prayer to God and getting** relief. This the Christians and Muslims did not hesitate to do. They had their distresses, and because they were Artas, they prayed for relief before Baba when he was in the flesh or at his tomb when he left the body and got the relief, proving to them that they were really appealing to a divine source. So in effect they treated him as God, but would not confess that they were treating him as God on account of their dogmas and doctrines. All the same, in effect and in reality, all persons bowing to him and appealing to him for aid in their extremities were adopting him practically as their God and revering him as their *Ishta Devata*. Whether they used the name *Aualia* or guardian Saint or *Ishta Devata* does not really matter. Unity was brought about and a common bond was created by Baba by his acting as the common Father of all. Baba Said, 'I am the father of you all. so you should not say that. "G. G. Narke, M.A., M.Sc., and England returned scholar, said Baba was a man and not God. This was reported to Baba. Then Baba pointed out that what that learned scholar said was true from the material stand point. That is if you regard the Baba body as Baba, it is a human body, and, therefore, there is no mistake in saying that Baba was man. But it is a terrible mistake for people to view Baba as man, especially, if they wanted Baba's defvne Help. Divine help was not coming from the muscles, nerves, and bones of the human body, but was coming from the spirit, and that spirit was divine. So Baba told them, 'You should not say that (that is, that I am a mere physical human being for I am your father, and you have all to get your things from me'. It is by treating him as God that Ramasami Chetti, Abdul Kadar Saheb, Joseph Ransome and other persons could get what they wanted; that is, it is the divinity in him that must be kept in mind, and the material body must be put aside and completely forgotten in order to get one's relief. Therefore, Baba pointed out the correct attitude to take was not that Sai Baba was the body of 3½ cubit height which they saw, but the divine spirit which was living within that body, and which could work at any place faraway from that body. Baba exhibited such power that sitting at Shirdi he could influence men and things thousands of miles away and draw spirits to him at the moment of their death in order to give them the protection they needed, or the help they wanted. It is this Baba spirit that we call Baba, and not the mere Baba body. When once this view is accepted, then the system built up by Baba, of unity among all persons approaching Baba for various sorts of relief from the common father must be regarded as a remarkable achievement, an achievement not merely for the individuals but for the entire groups, for countries and for the world. On the basis of attachment to this common father Baba, Brahmans and Sahebs, Chettis and Parsees all combine and go together and act like brethren. That is what they did when Baba's chavadi procession took place and what they do now when it takes place at Shirdi. All communities join together in praying their respects to this Mighty Master and, therefore, Baba furnished the clue to the unity of religions amongst his immediate followers. The clue is, 'do not stress the external observances. Externals no doubt differ. But stress the essence of all religions, namely, the approach to God and the achievement thereby of the satisfaction of your various needs, and the conquest of various obstacles for the elevation of your nature gradually, further and further upward, till you lose your self by contact with the feet of God.' This is a common plank, which is furnished by Baba, which has been used time and again by various people. Hindus who have given statements to this author and others, mostly show their acceptance of this view. Even a few Muslims who have accepted Swami Vivekananda as their guide adopt the same view. Thus Baba has furnished a basis on which Hinduism and Islam can combine. That is, Hindus and Muslims must make up their minds to revere God in essence. As God in essence cannot be seen or sensed, that divinity should be approached through human personalities exhibiting divine powers in wonderful profusion as in the case of Sai Baba. One may ask how one Sai Baba can suffice to leaven the whole world; but let us look at facts. One Sai Baba has now produced hundreds of Sai Babas, there are many Hindu and Muslim saints all over the country who act upon the principles on which Baba acted, and have amongst their followers both Hindus and Muslims. In almost every district we now find Muslim saints who are catholic enough to allow Hindus to continue their observances, and yet approach them as their Godman. These are slowly leaving the whole Indian Society. the adoption by a few individuals of such an attitude towards such saints may not suffice to convert the entire country to the cause of religious unity. There will always be people who will rejoice unity. There will always be people who will rejoice in difference and who can never rise above the existing level of thought prevalent in their particular community. But when any one says that 'No man can rise above that level', they are committing a big mistake.

History shows us how in the past vast upheavals have often taken place and how masses themselves have been attracted and led to adopt mere doctrines, dogmas and relegations. One great powerful Sai can by his perfectly divine powers stamp the entire world with the impress of his own views. With the advance of time the numbers that follow the great saint will be increasing large and it will soon be so large that others will actually drift into union with them. Mankind has no power of resistance against divine currents. This is proved by the history of great saints in every land. Thus, we have a fair basis for hope that the present Sai and the future sais that might develop out of the present Sai will furnish the entire world with a uniform religion, in some form, some shape, and some beliefs that we cannot now define or describe. There is excellent ground for hoping that this achievement may come to pass, and we may rest in confidence that Sai's spirit will accomplish the same.

From: Narasimha Swami's
Life of Sai Baba (Vol. IV)
Madras: All Indian Sai Samaj

23

SAI BABA AND THE UNIVERSALITY OF RELIGION

O.K. Vaide Rao

"I am present in all beings. I have neither dislike nor liking for any one. Whosoever devotedly worships Me, I stand revealed in them wholeheartedly. Even if the worst sinner worships Me with complete faith, he will become virtuous and secure lasting peace. Even those that are born in sin, if they take refuge in Me, they will obtain supreme peace and the eternal abode."

—Sri Shirdi Sai Baba

The Unity and Universality of Religion with an emphasis on the Hindu-Muslim aspect of it is a most vocally demonstrated precept but the least practised one. In the process, the problem of National Integrity and Communal Harmony have become a national calamity.

This disturbed situation created by *Adharma* overtaking *Dharma*, one of the perennial evils anticipated to envelope Humanity, reminds and demands Lord Krishna to keep His promise through His disciple, Arjuna, to the people at large viz., '*SAMBHAVAMI YUGE, YUGE*' to correct the much deteriorated communal harmony and resultant disharmony and imbalance, a natural product of projecting too much of the first person pronoun 'I' in every religion to the deteriment of other religions.

As if in immediate reponse to the need of the times, a sixteen year old youth appeared sitting under the neem tree in 1854 at Shirdi and it augured the promised arrival of Lord Krishna to correct and restore normalcy. Thus arrived Shri Sai Maharaj - a servant and saint - a Ram-Rahim in one.

Hemadapant, the author of Marathi *Sai Sat Charita* wrote, "I hold the Pen, Sai writers HIS Auto-Biography".

Who can measure the depth of the Sea or write about the deeds and *leelas* of Saints of Sadguru Sainath's stature.

But this scribe, no way near Hemadpant, is making an attempt to just present a phase of Baba's life and his methodology of unification for which He was deputed into this world.

With Baba's blessings, I quote from the book *'Life of Sai Baba'* (Volume 4, Chapter 8) authored by Pujyashri Narasimha Swamiji dealing with the subject Castes and World Unity, now so much talked about from housetops but least practised.

It deals with Hindu-Muslim unity and the necessary integration thereof to save humanity from chaos, confusion and incidental imposition of curfew orders by the authorities.

A Hindu Inspector gave Baba a donation of stones to reconstruct a mosque but Baba used them as an occasion to introduce his Unity message by diverting the stones for the much needed Hindu temples on a priority basis at Shirdi against the wish of the Hindu doner.

The donees had a peculiar and curious positive reaction that they, in gratitude for timely help, collect funds among themselves and gave to Baba for Mosque renovation expenses.

Let us in an unbiased way examine the whole episode.

First and foremost, the Hindu Inspector donating for mosque renovation reflected greatly the catholicity of the Hindu a rare phenomenon but served the very purpose of Sai's Avatar.

The Hindu thought flow was to help a religious cause, never mind for Ram or Rahim. In this special attitude, we perceive the Running Gold Thread of the Common GOD Feature, the Pearls in it are the many religions. But, Swami Vivekananda said, "Only, the majority of man-kind are entirely unconscious of it".

All rivers flow into the sea and like-wise *'Sarva Deva Namaskaram'* (Salutations to all, may be Kesava, or Allah, or Christ etc.) all reach the 'one God' of all religions, thus establish the' ONE GOD' principle, so essential for religous integration.

Once this is recognised, the many religious differences which are at cross purposes disappear and with it the resultant chaos, confustion and curfews too would vanish.

By the diversion of the donation, meant for the mosque by a Hindu, to the Hindu Temple reconstruction on a priority, based on urgency, Baba established the faith that service to one God is as good as to another and thus added strength to the principle of Universality of GOD.

More fascinating was the reaction of the Hindu Temple donees who in appreciation of the timely monetary help rendered to them by Baba felt a reciprocal donation a moral necessity and collected a large amount among themselves and gave it for mosque reconstruction. This once again places a great emphasis on the catholic attitude of the Hindu Temple donees and on 'One God' theory.

Sainath, in his most subtle mannered way, educated His devotees by telling them "If what you donate is for a mosque or temple is for the God, whether you are a Hindu or Mussalman, please give until your fingers pain and thus help mutually a worthy cause of your brothers from other religions with the least thought of the religious base coming in its way." By this advice, He paved the way for national integration. Sai diverted the Hindu--Muslim thought into a natural common thinking channel of "SERVICE TO GOD" which invariably led to the unification of all religions.

Hemadpant in his *'Sai Sat Charita'* says "He who completely surrenders himself to the Lord by getting rid of egoism and body consciousness and thus becomes one with HIM has nothing to do with any question of caste or nationality" Shri Gunaji's English version *(Shri Sai Sat Charita*, Chapter VII, page 39).

The second idea is that 'Sai Baba was the living emblem and embodiment of Hindu-Muslim Unity'.

The Unity project is not one day affair but spread over Baba's life time as his whole--time life mission with the precept and practice so well synchronised and reflected in the personal life he led.

The first hurdle was the intellectual fanatics in both Hindus and Muslims what with their individual religious rigidity and fundamentalism. They were always in a warring mood each trying to protect their individual religious tenets and unbending stubborn attitude, crossing as a blocki, to the idealistic thinking and attempts of Baba to establish unity of a Universal Religion. Baba's solution to this problem was to humour them and leave them to themselves as otherwise any confrontation with them was like disturbing the Hornet's nest.

Pujyashri Narasimha Swamiji in his *Life of Sai Baba* (Vol. 4) summarises and suggests a simple working plan when he writes. "The task of uniting highly advanced religious exponents of each religion into one unit is not so easy as the task of uniting the masses who come when they see a wierd and impartial God-man like Sai Maharaj working for their good and they co-operate to unite easily into a harmonious group."

Sai Baba who could easily visualise the situation and identify the blocks in the way of Unity and Universal Brotherhood could overcome the hudles by adopting specially suited methods of approach to the class and mass specially.

So He started with the understanding and easily approachable masses by calling them, irrespective of caste, colour or creed, as Children of Dwarakamayee, thus classified all into one family all those that stepped into the Masjid and brought them under one umbrella of thought viz., "Uuniversal Brotherhood", the base and essence of 'Sai Shri'.

To develop a sense of belonging in the devotees, Baba lived on alternate days in the Mosque and Temple, accepted poojas from each religion according to its tenets, conducted the festivals of both religions in the Masjid, allowed both religionists to do their Pooja and Prayer as permitted by the religion of each with no clash or confrontation.

While Baba inducted the positive thoughts of religious integration, he never forgot the negative aspect side by side and so was very vigilant to stop the cropping up of negative desctructive thoughts to kill the other religionists. To illustrate, at Dwarakamayee Muslims and Hindus slept side by side, when one day in the night the Muslim fanaticism that was put to sleep by Baba by his great silent efforts, came to life suddenly and an attempt to assasinate the sleeping Hindus was made by the Muslims. The ever-vigilant

Baba rose to the occasion and stood before the Muslims and said "If you so desire to kill the Hindus, kill me first and next them". This sharp, direct and sudden awakening of the Muslims by Baba to their filial bonds and duties to Hindu brothers, so much harped by Baba earlier acted as a Lorry's 'AIR BREAKS' to the Muslims who realised their grave mistaken act and suddenly stepped back. Such is the deep rooted teachings of Baba and his preventive measure that it had a spontaneous reflex action and thus the Muslims derailed to *Adharma*, were re-railed to *Dharma*.

The Masjid was made into a mosque-cum-temple complex, a common place of worship for both Muslims and Hindus who congregate at different times of the day to pursue their prayers and pooja as per the laid tenets of each religion, astonishingly with no clash or altercation between them. The music of Gita slokas and melodious recitations of Quran could be heard in that one hall.

We could hear in the, Dwarakamai Masjid the reciting of Vishnusahasra-nama by the Hindus, the Quran by the Muslims, Bible by the Christians and people of other castes doing 'MANASA Pooja' visualising their caste Deity all in 'Sadguru Sainath'. Sai Maharaj by this method established the MANY +IN-ONE principle the very essence of Saism. Sai thus maintained the Unity in diversity.

This is the greatest contribution to the country and people by Sadguru Sainath Maharaj.

Needless to mention about the great necessity of a philosophical thought of the oneness of all people in the eyes of God, of mutual tolerance, avoidance of bitter conversation specially involving religious matters as a compulsory course of Human conduct to work out to happy, peaceful and trouble-free life sans the religious confrontations.

To wit, the tantrums of the Rohilla with his loud disturbing prayers were explained away by Baba to the protesters that it was all done by him to drive away his Amazonic wife, a mere myth created by Baba to avoid a clash and to keep the Devotees peaceful. He knew how to handle a situation.

Again, the way in which Jawhar Ali from Rahata claimed himself as Guru of Sai Baba, who in his turn submitted to himself as disciple of Ali, the religious fundamentalist, in a docile way and followed him to Rahata just to keep Shirdi in peace and avert clashes at a place where Baba had laid laboriously the foundations of

Universal Brotherhood. Baba managed a meeting of the quiet religious Hindu Savant Devidas with Ali and had religious discussion in which Ali found himself no where and silently left for Rahata only to come back to Shirdi later in a more humble way to Baba. Thus Baba has his religious victory to establish Unity and Universality. Thus worked Baba's genius for a peaceful silent Hindu-Muslim Unity without any outward upheaval.

Inspector Gopalrao's URUS fair and 'Sandal procession' of Amir Shanker Dalal, a Muslim devotee were made quite handy into one procession of both Hindus and Muslims and synchronised it on Sri Ramanavami Day to symbolise Baba's great service to man to introduce the 'One Family' principle.

The procession of the 'Flags' by the Hindus and that of the Muslims went on side by side simultaneously partaking without a hitch and that with band and music, not normally permitted by Muslims before a mosque, much less in a Masjid.

The Urus was transformed into a Ramanavami festival where annually a Haridas did Bhajan and Ramakatha, which was ultimately entrusted by Baba to the noted Bhagavather Das Ganu Maharaj permanently, who, since then, had successfully and creditably fulfilled the entrusted functions.

The Ramanavami festival marked the finale of Baba's project of 'Unity' which continues to date at Shirdi.

The Kirtanakar Das Ganu Maharaj besides the annual Shirdi event was doing his Harikathas elsewhere making Baba's leela also a part of it by which he became Baba's unofficial ambassador of carrying the Message of Muslim-Hindu unity cause to every corner he went, thus ensured the unity message of Sai getting to the masses everywhere.

Sai Baba had very successfully inculcated in his devotees of all classes that "one common principle that all religions are true and each community conservatively should keep up to its own creed, faith etc., peculiar to its religion" and, most important, not minding other religions practising their rituals inside Dwarakamayee Masjid as permitted by their religious tenets. This clearly demonstrated the existence of a world unity with its people at large which is the beginning and process of Baba's religious mission entrusted to Him by the Almighty.

Sai Baba made his devotees get accustomed to the differences and variations as a permanent unavoidable basic features of all religions to be accepted as a part of the ritual and thus make it a channel to find permanent joy and peace in Heaven with due emphasis on the part played by mutual love and affection during the process.

This idea is well epitomised by Swami Vivekananda when he says :

"That plan alone is practical which does not destroy the individuality of any man in religion and at the same time shows him a point of union with others".

Baba was so careful to advise his devotees not to desert the religion in which they were originally born but keep it up and find a way to practise SAISM through it, as otherwise it would tantamount to disowning the 'FATHER'.

Baba also demonstrated to the devotees of the great possibility of becoming one-world-citizen and as one family and achieve the socialistic pattern of ideal society only on the principle and practice of "Love and Universal Brotherhood".

"He showed the way and let us follow in His footsteps".

" Was Baba living because He had the body! and was He dead Because He left it ? No! Certainly not, Baba is ever alive", "always by our side and will take any form and appear before the devotee and satisfy Him". *Shri Sai Sat Charita* - English p. 184 Gunaji's

To quote Swami Vivekanada to illustrate and establish the unaustentatious simplicity and silent service to man and society of Sadguru Sainath Maharaj!

"So those who are workers and really feel at heart the Universal Brotherhood, do not talk much, do not make sects for Universal Brotherhood but their acts, their movement, their whole life show out clearly that they, in truth, possess the feeling of brotherhood for mankind that they have love and sympathy for all. They do not speak, they do and they love".

This in short an epitome of the life and leelas of Sadgurus like Shri Sainath.

He finally assures His devotees "Why fear, when I am here"

and guarantees His continued vigilant help in the present and future as was done in the past.

Long live SAISM: Let its Founder's touch of Wisdom and Spiritualism be our friend, philosopher and guide.

Salutations and respectful pranams to Shri Sainath and his disciple Swamijee 'BVN' and the like of them among the Sai *bandhus*.

--O.K. Varada Rao
58, M.I.G.H., Mehdipatnam, Hyderabad.
(*Shri Sai Leela*, January 1989)

24

THE RELEVANCE OF SAI SPIRITUALISM TODAY

V.H. Desai

"Our true Guru is God alone. He transcends all gunas. He is beyond all forms. He is the only ONE who can dispel the darkness of ignorance and light the lamp of Supreme Wisdom".

–Sri Sai Baba

Ever since we attained political independence on the down of the 15th August in the grace year of 1947, we have been stressing on National Integration; but without understanding the real implications behind it.

Everybody wants national integration and clamours for it but national integration does not come so easily, nor even if it comes, it does not mean anything to any-one. There is nobody who likes discrimination on the basis of caste, creed, religion, region or language. But still we witness incidents of communal tensions and hatred and quarrel in the name of religion, region, language, caste or creed.

The scenario is no different; either in the East or the West, neither North nor South.

According to Lord Buddha, three things, called the 'Three Poisons' are the sources or roots of all evils, miseries, tragedies, misfortunes and calamities in human life.

What are these 'Three Poisons'?

1. The Poison of desire and greed.
2. The Poison of anger and hatred.
3. The Poison of ignorance and stupidity.

The last one, is again the spring of the two:

As it is said in one of the Buddhist scriptures:

"People always cherish desire and greed for benefit and advantage; harbour anger and hatred for disadvantage and disappointment. These passions come out not from wisdom but from false and wrong views. They are therefore called ignorance and stupidity. These three poison are the roots of all distress and troubles".

I is tragic that despite enjoying many decades of Independence we are still exercising our minds on how to promote national integration. This is indeed a sad commentary of the state of affairs. This goes against the genius of our people; the dumb millions.

The National Integration, as one would like to understand it is in literal sense, is a far cry.

The country today is beset with narrow and parochial approaches or shortcuts to achieve one's own selfish ends.

True, India as a nation stands pledged to the ideal of secular democracy. Our Constitution has provided full opportunities to all, irrespective of community or religion, full religious freedom and scope for the growth of culture and religion. The Constitution is binding on all.

However, unless the fine sentiments expressed in the Constitution find expression in our day to day life, the ideals however big they may be, would prove empty and valueless.

The introduction of Adult Franchise, despite appalling poverty was an extremely bold step which has greatly helped the spread of democratic and egalitarian ideas. It has created a tremendous consciousness of rights though not equally of obligations, and of soaring aspirations. The democratic system is as much difficult to work as it is most efficacious for healthy development of human society.

We have thus to organise the none too-easy means, that is

the democratic apparatus. We have also to build up the solidarity of the country and lay the foundation of a strong secular base. While grappling with the stupendous problems, some blunders and mistakes do occur. Critical self-examination is essential for improvement and that we should do self-introspection unhesitatingly in the interest of the country at large.

There has been alarming trend which has encouraged violence and indiscipline and lack of respect for law and order. Parochial and fissiparous tendencies have also been in evidence. There has been a deplorable setback in the high ideal of service and sacrifice that characterised our struggle for freedom.

It is sickening that the tissues of non-communalism built during the freedom struggle are splitting one by one. Due to the sad happenings after freedom, people are being emotionally moved into reactions even to this day, favourable to breeding the communal forces.

Throughout the long years of Congress history from Dadabhai Naoroji to Mahatma Gandhi, a robust tradition of non-communalism had been fostered in our life.

Yet, eminent men are espousing the country's cause, even to this day, in so many words, on how to promote national integration ?

Interestingly, for the root cause of all our troubles the politicians blame each other. The opposition blames the Government and vice-versa. The religious leaders express concern over the primacy given to considerations of party gain ever national interests, so on and so forth.

But, the imperatives have gone by default. There is no knowing, when we will be able to lay our hands on them with confidence and unmistakable faith in our destiny.

Speaking of one of the most imperatives is " education. It is common knowledge that the present day education is not based on any definite policy. Whatever, policy there is, is only so-called. The object of all education should be to establish the role of the common man. Man is a social animal. He has a personal as well as a social life to live. As he goes on living his individual life he should not be made to neglect his duty towards the society. The individual is indebted to the society in a variety of ways.

Therefore, he should be made fit to repay it in full.

It must be remembered here that children are imitative by nature; they always try to act as elders do; their parents; brothers, sisters, and teachers act. They demure when they are asked by others to act in a particular manner. Even today, particularly in rural households; children drop off to sleep lulled by lofty lullabies and stories and legends of the wisdom and the prowess of our ancestors narrated by elders. The child however likes to be self-reliant, he prefers work. His intellect and perceptions are strong.

Stories of how in 1921 the people used to hear the clarion call of Gandhiji and flocked to him, still kindle patriotic fervour in the young mind today.

Therefore, we have to decentralise education also. Only he is capable of imparting education who has developed an individuality of his own; individualities can not be cast in one and the same mould. Education progresses to the extent that is allied to life and experience.

How many young minds know that the dominant characteristic of the Indian mind has always been to see the one in many ? And, this is why it has been possible for India to harmonise the Many in One.

Even the inner spirit of Governments, however democratic they may claim to be, refuse adaptation to the temper of the age. Vested interests think of maintaining their own theories. Religious fanatics defend even morbid communalism.

As a reaction to these, under the banner of progressive forces, revolution and agitation take place. Hence, the revolt and agitation born as they are of a reaction to an existing evil can not produce positive dynamism, which can usher-in- a New Order. No enduring order worth its name is brought about by any revolution unless the revolution is backed by ethical values.

The National Integration in essence, should usher in the evolution of ethical values since our social ideals are now a days ever governed by economic considerations. They do need a thorough shakeup. But what can shake them up save an adequate ethical dynamism ?

The central message of India's civilization is that the universe is a spiritual reality. India's nationality itself is a living illustration

The Relevance of Sai Spiritualism Today

of the vest federal pattern. In religion, India has preferred rich harmony to dead homogeneity. In social organisation too, the federal pattern is evolved and remarkably maintained through centuries. Love for India's culture has been the greatest armour in the battle for India's freedom against foreign arms. It has been the greatest source of inspiration to our patriots.

Thanks to Science, it has today offered to the modern many mechanical devices like the press, the radio, the cinema and TV for the quick and constant propagation of varieties of life.

Indeed, the Press if properly organised and sincerely pursued can become an effective medium of public opinion and the true custodian of human values.

The Radio can edify as well as entertain.

The Cinema and TV with their tremendous power of patriotic attraction can be used as an effective instrument of education of man making of culture and character. The Cinema and TV can cut across the barriers of region and language; and undoubtedly are a powerful force in promoting national integration.

It is indeed tragic that all these accredited vehicles of knowledge and education have been vitiated at their very source and have today lost their value of moral uplift.

The media has been commercialised into a tempting instrument of horrified sensationalism and cheap romance. The Press has to work through the scylla of the capitalist who finances it and the small mercies of the Government which controls it. Superstition and ignorance, cruelty and criminality have grown for centuries, like disease. Their persistent poisoning has corroded man's urge.

Journalism is no longer what is used to be. The professional today puts his conscience to sleep and places his services at the disposal of the highest bidder. He is a man (and an increasing number of women) being in a hurry is itching to catch the reader's eye, invariably placing sensation before truth. The journalist has ceased to be a 'missionary' and has become by and large a slave to the proserous exploited proprietor or through him to the Establishment.

Gone are the days when editors considered themselves 'missionaries' and were given that status by others in the lofty expectations of sacrifice for a cause. Such 'missionaries' did exist in the pre-independence period and they bravely suffered terms of imprisonment for their outspoken views. There are still 'missions' available for the asking but we do not any more give such a title to professional work in a good cause.

Some of the faults of journalism today arise from competitive proliferation which gives rise to the urge to get a story before the rival does. Some harm does result from haste or even uncharitable intent, but such risks seem worthwhile in the larger context of public good. In any case the reader is not easily fooled all the time and has his own way of assessing a newspaper's credibility.

It has been universally accepted by journalists that their calling is a public trust. The objective of journalism is to save the genuine public interest by publishing news and comments in a free and fair manner. The highest and the most fundamental principle is to serve the truth. This requires the media to be honest, objective, fair, accurate, balanced, decent and anything but self-aggrandising. Fairness involves commitment to justice. Lack of this commitment results in abuse of the power growing enormously, signs of cynicism are becoming visible. It is time we took serious not before it is too late.

There is no written code of media ethics. It is also not desirable to write down a rigid code. Ethics is a normative philosophy and practice of conduct, essentially personal but compulsorily for the good of the people at large. It is a set of moral values evolved into principles consensually accepted to govern the conduct of individuals or groups. Media ethics, in other words, is a body of tenets governing the conduct of media for the good of the society.

The mind therefore is the starting point of human evolution. For it is from mind that goodness or evil of life flow it is the mind which is the source of our strength and the cause of our weakness as well. It is the mind which can either drag us downward into miserable depth of degradation and ruin, or push forward to the divine height of a mighty God.

The doors of knowledge are still stand locked, barred; and can be opened only with the Golden Key.

The knowledge which the masses receive today is very meagre and the culture which they acquire is scanty and mean. Only the fortunate few are able to assimilate the best that is taught and known in the world.

Culture is recognised as something beyond entertainment. It provides a perpetual source of inspiration for all those who want to develop their intellect. History bears ample evidence that no civilisation has succeeded in transmitting to posterity a heritage unless it were committed to values.

Throughout history, the Indian sub-continent has had, in spite of a multitude of diversities, a recognisable cultural unity, which has made it possible for the non- Indian immediately to detect the Indian and for the Indian to feel closer to his fellow-countrymen.

Against this backdrop, Mahatma Gandhi giving his can did views on the Congress' resolve for the reorganisation of states on linguistic basis, after it came to power, had significantly said that though such redistribution would be conducive to the cultural advancement, "but such redistribution should not militate against the organised unity of India. Autonomy did not and should not mean disruption or that hereafter provinces could go the way they chose, independent of one another and of the centre. If each province begin to look upon itself as a separate sovereign unit, India's independence would lose its meaning and with it would vanish the freedom of the various units as well."

It should be remembered here that Indian nationalism grew as a result of the British domination of Indian partly as a consequence of Western learning and Western ideas. The prime necessity for integration was there for all to see. India inhabitated as it is by a people marked by cultural, regional, linguistic and religious variations of various orders, with linguistic chauvinism displayed by people often times, in a pronounced violent manner, the outburst of recurring communal riots, the atrocities continuously perpetrated on Harijans by the so-called upper castes, all these are the compelling reasons why a greater sense of national cohesiveness and unity should not be taken up as a movement, if the country has to remain intact?

Looking back for a while, it seems as though the wheel of time is turning backwards. Instead of national feelings, plain selfishness has become the new virtue.

During our freedom struggle when communication was an unknown commodity one song of Bankim Chandra Chatterjee's *'Vande Mataram'* shock the entire population of the country. There was an awareness among the people despite entrenched poverty and insecurity. A wave of patriotism and love for the country swept all across the land.

It is said once Bankim Chandra's daughter asked him: "Father always talks only about the Motherland. After all, how is that Motherland ? What is it ? Please tell us". When Bankim Chandra replied by reciting the poem it is said that his emotional daughter burst out crying with teras rolling down her eyes.

Just one word, *"Vande Mataram"* brought about an awakening in the heart of the slumbering country, right from Kashmir to Kanyakumari.

This same word came on to the lips of every martyr before he was hanged at the gallows. This word became a regular greeting whenever any two people met each other. This small spark lit up the hearts of crores of people with patriotism and became a volcano of nationalism.

Along with Vande Mataram, Iqbal's song *"Sare Jahan Se Acha"* became popular among the people at the time. This song gave a depressed nation a new perspective for revival. It gave us a new sense of consciousness about ourselves. Even today our heads rise up in pride as a sing *"Sare Jahan se Acha"*.

Netaji Subhash Chandra Bose's national greeting and saluation 'Jai Hind' had captivated everyone. Sung at public meetings and flag hoistings the song *"Vijayi Vishva Tiranga Pyara"*, become a house-hold word.

But today we have lost their content and meaning.

The children today no longer sing *"Janani Nanmabhoomi"* : Their heroes are no longer Chandra Sekhar Azad or Bhagat Singh, but the hero of the film "Sholay". Gabbar Singh. Even leaders prefer to serve their self interest rather than suffer any hardships for the sake of the people.

Our present day writers no longer brave prison for causes like Yashpal, Makhanlal Chaturvedi or Jnanendra Kumar, but are satisfied with awards and perquisities as an objective, with a *"Padma Shri"* or a Rajya Sabha seat as the ultimate.

Ganesh Shankar Vidyarthi became a martyr to the flames of communal frenzy. Today's intellectuals are satisfied with passing resolutions which are sent to the newspapers to be published and even electronic media does oblige them. At most, these "intellectuals" take part in a demonstration in the spirit of martyrdom!

Intellectualismis confined to peace marches in peaceful areas, which begin with the click of the TV camera and end with a picture in the dailies. Their expressions of concern are like echoes in a vacuum. The literature they create can hardly be different.

We are passing through a period of crisis presently. The elements of this crisis are differently understood by different observers. The entirety of this compelling crisis defies anyone's limited vision. The basic element of our crisis is the crisis of values. Values are internalized through education process. They discriminate between what is right and what is wrong. They are the bedrock on which the cultural moorings of a society are anchored. But values are not eternal rocks, they are shaped and reshaped in every society. However, if the critical values are challenged at their basic code, a crisis has developed. We are in the midst of such a crisis.

We have to overcome this crisis; the sooner the better for all and for the Indian polity. It is universally accepted that a happy and harmonious home is the foundation of a good society. How this can be brought about ? This is not an easy subject. Whether one can do this by devising a code of conduct for individual families is a subject that could be considered. If a code of conduct is evolved, it must include daily meeting of the entire family at least for a few moments before going to bed then they could discuss the problem of harmony and the need for give and take on the part of the different members of the family in their daily behaviour with each other also possibly spend a few minutes in a family prayer for getting the spiritual strength to do so. There are many points that could be brought is regard to the way in which the members of the family treat each other, whether there is willingness to cooperate and do participator work instead of some people doing all the work and others merely making demands, the need for truthful speaking, and the use of gentle words, and affection in daily conversation and conduct and so on. Above all, one must never forget that children are very much influenced by what they see in their homes in actual conduct, rather than by preaching some sermons even by elders.

The more they see from their parents and elders practise ethical values, the more such valves get build up into their own individual systems and become a part of their sub-conscious foundations of conduct. Special concern has to be shown within the family for its weaker sections like children and the aged, and men should be prepared to share in some of the hard work that is put in the homes. The more one can devise activities for all the members of the family apart from meals more will be the family getting inaugurated and this can be done by family reading of some scriptures and ethical stories or taking up some work for the house in which they all can be in a participatory role.

The home culture however does not function in isolation. It is education which takes up a larger part of the time of the young and it is through the re-orientation of our system of education in a value oriented and character-building direction from the primary school stage that can provide the answer.

One way of doing this is for the parents to take much more interest in the working of the educational institutions to which they send their children and acquire much more awareness on what their children are getting by way of education in terms of values and character-building from their educational reforms and there is plenty of material available in the field of suggestion for educational re-construction.

There is need for bringing into the curriculum and time-table moral and spiritual education including not only basic human values but also positive secularism, that is universal.

If this should have an effect on moulding of character and attitudes, they have to find an important place in the primary and secondary education. One need not even have special lectures for this purpose, but could select or devise text books for the subject normally learnt in schools which should contain these ideas and contribute indirectly to the formation of values of building up of a character. One could also set up model educational institutions which have value-orientations, and character-building as a part of their objectives, and have achieved some success in achieving this objective. It is parents who need to be educated on what to give to their children, not merely skills and academic honours, but also values and character.

As regards citizenship, there is no doubt that if the individuals living in the country begin to think of themselves as citizens who have not only rights but also responsibilities, it would go a long way in producing an atmosphere of individual and collective action for social harmony. The feeling that everything must be done by somebody else and that the individual is only a receiver and not also a giver must be got rid of. 'Taking' must always be accompanied by 'giving' Assertion of rights should go side by side with the duties and responsibilities that accompany them. This kind of citizenship education can come out not only from extension lectures, continuing education and adult education classes, but also by the formation of groups of individuals or even by the undertaking of individuals by themselves to spend some of their time and resource on oneself-regarding work which should emphasis the social aspect of the citizenship rather than merely that of their individual self-regulating emphasis on personal rights and what they themselves can get for that purpose from the society in which they live. The production of good literature will indirectly influence human behaviour and as such the making of such literature available on a large scale and at subsidised prices would be a supplementary way of promoting civil and social consciousness.

Above all, what we need is the recognition of our common humanity and the readiness to do something for fulfilling in one's own life either individually or in. association with groups or institutions the ethical obligations that flow from such recognition of our common humanity. This is the ultimate basis of both ethics and spirituality.

This can not be promoted merely by propaganda. It is only action, not merely impersonal action on the part of the Government or even institutions that can bring about the desired results. Individuals and voluntary groups have a great role to play in the matter of giving ethical and spiritual content to both our individual and social living.

Family life and home life today are under great stresses and strains for various reasons. This is prejudicial to the promotion of national integration.

Moral values are bound up with religion. By and large, all religions in India have grown in an atmosphere of tolerance. Concern for others, kindness, compassion, fellow, feelings, self, control, tolerance, truthfulness and discipline; in short much that is admirable and bountiful in conduct; are all that all the religious emphasis. There could be no compulsory religions instruction in our educational institutions. But it is necessary that we all know about each other's religion.

Bureaucratic administration and vested political interests could not have the right to apply moral consciousness from the background of cultural ignorance.

A levelling up on these sharp contours of culture is indispensable, before we can think of a free and confident association of human beings in a clear and sunny atmosphere of friendliness and peace.

Power Seekers are often seen making capital of our traditional belief. They would like people to be merely emotional rather than rational. Superstition becomes the naturally of injustice which emanates from unjust economic system.

If we have to promote national integration at all levels our immediate imperatives should be at popularising three kinds of education, not only through schools and Colleges but through other sources too.

No doubt Schools and Colleges occupy prominent place in Government. But the propagation of high ideals of life in the masses can very well be done through the media such as the Radio, TV, Press and the like. But to our misfortune, these scientific and quick means of spread of knowledge have fallen into misuse. They are not harnessed to cultivate sober tastes. Instead, they have become instruments of cheap entertainment.

On the other hand, true democracy should aim at the development of full personality, of man, and not to mould him to suit the ulterior ends of the State.

True, Democracy should set forth high ideals before the individuals. In other words, education should not become part of the struggle for power between religions, classes and nations. The pupil should be considered for his own sake and not as a recruit.

This is a big and stupendous task before us. Are we capable of accepting this challenge, here and how ? It remains to be seen.

We are on the threshold of a new dynamic change. It is no time for us to slacken our efforts.

Let us draw our strength from the thought that mankind has always risen out of deadening chaos and crisis into happy harmony of a new and larger life.

If the future is dark and dismal and the present utterly confused let us hark back a while, upon the inexhaustible treasure-house of the past and open our minds to the accumulated knowledge of the ages, the eternal wisdom of the sages, whose words are forever ringing loud and clear, along the vast corridors of time touching that hear it, with fresh impulses of constant striving to create in our world lasting conditions of health and happiness, of peace and plenty; the right royal road to national integration.

We can face any problem if the 'ego' in us and our false prestige are given up. This is the only one factor-the ego-which is solely and mainly responsible for the ills of the individual as well as the society. No man is free from defects, nor any one can claim infallibility. If his owns the defects in him he will become 'divine' within himself. Man being a social animal commits errors; and it is true that it is human not to accept that he was at fault. Because, the arrogance in him will persist in telling him that he was not responsible for the act. Owning his defects and errors require moral courage. This is the character we have to build up if national integration has to be our life-style. Then only the myth shall explode to become a reality; in letter and spirit. To achieve this national goal, a movement of the people, for the people and by the people towards knitting India together is a must.

The long years' of the life of Sri Sai Baba are the sweet innings of an avatar who not only preached national integration but religiously practiced and lived to his finger-tips. Being a witness of the 1857 Sepoy Mutiny against British rulers, Sri Sai Nath experimented the great Truths of Mahakavyas e.g. *AYAM ATMA BRAHMA*; it mean *'Anal Huq'* and Hatred and bitterness can never cure the disease of fear, only love can do that. Hatred paralyses life; love releases it. Hatred confuses life; love harmonizes it. Hatred darkens life; love illuminates life".

Sri Sai Baba's teachings are universal in nature. These carry within them the essence of spirituality. Seeing Baba in every form and bowing mentally to Him is the essence of Bhagwad Dharma. The underlying *TRUTH* is *ONE* in all religions. Every individual carries with him or her the spark of Divinity.

Sri Sai Baba possesses the key which opens to us the inner floodgates of bliss. To experience the unity of life in all forms is to drink the Divine Nectar!. This is the only panacea of all our ills. National pride is the sheet-anchor of Sri Baba's teachings. He saw Godliness in every human being; as if redeeming the pledge of rich cultural heritage.

The time has now come to banish all kinds of ignorance of religious tenets - since the word religion itself means love, truth and good life. If every child in this country is made to understand the ingredients of true religion the day will not be far off when people of the country will speak with one voice as proud Indian, making the imperialists in the garb of protecting the so-called human rights to bow their head in shame.

Let us follow Lord Sri Sai Nath. He alone attains Him who live by His will. He alone can live by His will who is humble, ego-less ! This individual 'ego' is the cause of our undoing vis-a-vis national integrity and character. He beckons the youth of the country not only to preserve, protect and strengthen our cultural values of national pride but to show to mankind a new light of Hope and Prosperity; the Path of Grace ! We have to love our Divine Mother for love's sake only. That is India's calling today.

(*Shri Sai Leela*, Jan.-Feb., 1995)

25

THE NEED FOR BABA'S TECHNIQUE TO THE PRESENT WORLD

Dr. R. Rukmani

"My treasure is full and I can give any one what he wants, but I have to see whether he is qualified to receive, what I would wish to give".

—Sri Shirdi Sai Baba

"Purification of mind is absolutely necessary, as without it, all our spiritual endeavours will prove futile. It is therefore, better for one to take only what he can digest and assismilate".

Lord Krishna says in Bhagavad Gita :

*"Adityanam aham Vishnur
Jyotisham ravir amsuman
Marichir marutan asmi,
Nakshatranam aham Sa Si."*

Of the Adityas I am Vishnu
Of the luminaries, the Sun
I am Marichi of the Maruts
Of the asterisms the Moon am I."

The luminary of the day is the Sun. The foremost among the luminaries at night is the moon. These two heavenly bodies are considered as the embodiment of Lord Vishnu and workshipped with great veneration. In other words, God is considered as a Divine Light, ever sought after, to remove the darkness of our illusion.

"Lead kindly light, amid the encircling gloom,
Lead Thou me on
So long They power hath blest me,
Sure it will lead me on"

The Divine Light God is our guide in the troubles and tribulations of worldly life.

The Eternal Guide comes to our rescue, whether we seek his aid or not.

"Yada-Yada hi dharnasya glanirbhavati Bharata
Abhyutthanamadharmasya tadatmanam srujamyaham
Paritranaya Sadhunam Vinashayacha dushkrutam
Dharmasansthapanarthaya Sambhavami Yuge-Yuge".

As lord Krishna proclaims in Bhagavad Gita, whenever there it decay of dharma and rise of adharma, then He himself takes human manifestation in order to protect righeousness and for the establishment of dharma. Hence, from time to time an incarnation of God or a man of authority, sent by Ishwara, comes to the world, puts all lapses in the practice of dharma in an order and leaves a scripture for future guidance to mankind. This deputy of God takes a form, which will be most acceptable to that particular period and he presents his preachings in a delectable way, quite suited to the manner and moral standard of people of that particular time.

When emperors were esteemed and worshipped by all people and their words were accepted as law, Lord Rama and Lord Krishna came to the world as emperors and established dharma. It was the time, when all the scriptures like Vedas, Upanishads, Brahmasutras became too difficult for the people at ordinary level to digest and follows. At this juncture first the Ramayana was offered and then the Bhagavad Gita, the quint essence of all ancient scriptures in vogue, was offered.

The Bhagavad Gita is universally accepted as the greatest religious scripture, as it presents the fundamentals of Hinduism in simple language through beautiful illustrations. Bhagavad Gita has its special merits.

(a) Direct teaching of Lord Krishna to His disciple Arjuna. Therefore, it has the curiosity of the listeners and the interest of the teacher.

(b) It covers all stages and aspects of human life connecting religion to day-to-day life, chalking out a practical path of righteousness for people to read upon.

(c) Simple both in the manner of thought and language.

(d) It reveals through concrete illustrations, the greatness of *Paramatma* and the characteristics of *Jeevatma*.

(e) As Bhagavad Gita is very vast, it could, offer varieties of instructions suited to different sects of people.

(f) It teaches the way to attain eternal happiness through *Bhaktimarga*.

Bhagavad Gita offers instructions to all walks of people like Kings, common folks. Sanyasis, Sadhakas etc. offering different paths of worship, like path of devotion, path of yoga and path of *dhyana*, leaving the choice to the people according to their needs. But, at the end of Bhagavad Gita after elaborately explaining the nature of divinity, the helplessness of *Jeevatma*, *Paramatma*, omnipresence in all objects, and His capacity as creator, protector and destroyer, Lord Krishna consoles His devotees to leave all paths of dharma and surrender themselves to His lotus Feet and He will take care of all. It again causes confusion, when total surrender can fetch Lord's help, where is the need for explaining elaborately in the earlier chapter about Bhakti-marga. Dharma-marga, Dayana-marga and the sacredness of doing one's duty, the nature of *sattwa, rajas* and *tamas gunas*.

But, when even Bhagavad Gita seemed to be too difficult to understand for the majority of human beings, they needed some easy way, as assurance from God, a sort of direct agreement, that He will come to their rescue and give them salvation. When this kind of spiritual need was felt, the three Acharyas came one after the other to make people understand the readiness of God's protection. Among these these three Acharyas, Shankara came first. But, his principle of advaita was beyond the understanding capacity of common people. Shankara equated Jeevatama with Paramatama and explained the occurances and activities of daily life as *maya* or illusion. This raised doubts in the minds of people. If the world is full of *maya*, where is the reality ? What is the need to live in this world of illusion ? It is better to renounce this world and concentrate on the ways to reach the stage of Brahaman. Again the ultimate goal, Brahmam became an abstract concept, an utopian ideal, with no hope of reaching the goal. Advaita denies dualism. but human life as such is imperfect and hence. unable to unable to accept its identity with God, and more than that, unable to see Paramatma's identity in any human being, however great he may be. A doubt arose even in the power of Paramatma's. as he equated with *Jeewatma*, the less powerful. Of course Advaita philosophy is a bliss, as it induces one to perceive Paramatma in everything and thereby trying to cmanate kindness and love towards all human beings. But, practically it was impossible to perceive the *Brahma swarupa* in all objects and all time.

Madhava wanted to bring a clarification of this by stating, that Jeevatma is inferior, full of demerits and Paramatma is superior and both cannot be one. But the way to reach paramatma to reach the stage of total perfection etc, became ambiguous. Hence, the doctrine of Dvaita was less promising to the masses.

At this stage Ramanuja's *Vishishtadvaitam* came as a solution to the innumcrable doubts of people. Ramanuja reafirmed the fact. that this worldly life is worth living. For there is nothing deceptive or avidva in it. It is reality as the clernal reality Lord Narayana has created it. Worldly life can be a bliss. if one surrenders himself to Lord Narayana.

Ramanuja summarized the whole system of Indian Philosophy, ranging from the vedio hymns upto the doctrines of various Acharya in one sentence, surrender to Lord Vishnu, the supreme force. Who was a beautiful human form, with an enchanting fhute on his rosy lips. This form of Lord Vishnu, which is worshipped, concentrated and meditated by innumerable saints like Andal, Meera, Surdas, Chaitanya, Vallabh, etc. was advocated by Ramanuja. "Saguna upasana and Namajapa are the casiest way to get devotion and the path of devotion is a straight. even path; there is no chance of one being misled in this". Ramanuj instructed to one and all the mantra of 'OM NAMONARAYANA'. Ramanuja explain the divinity as a personal God. with a beautiful Swarupa. He described the relationship between the divinity and the living beings in this world, as the one between parents and children. The divinity is in the form of the compassionant and loving father Shri Narāyana and mother Mahalakshmi. Just as every one of us receives, whatever we need from our parents, who are ever ready to forgive all our blemishes and are always planning to offer us the highest gifts, which can make us happy. Just as our parents feel happy, when we are truthful, honest, good, cleaver and thus possessing the sparks of divinity, in the same way our universal father and mother, Mahavishnu and Mahalakshmi are there, always keeping us in their loving care and feel immensely happy. Just children are part and parcel of their parents, yet different from them, so is the relationship between the Jeevatma and Paramatma. Paramatma is *saguna* and is the embodiment and mamlestation of all divine attributes and has a beautiful unchanging from. The highest goal in life is to reach Shri Vaikuntha and be with Shri Narayana, the one God. Who, if we wish can come to us in any form, which we loves, as mother, father, servant, friend, Guru or child. Ramanuja assured that the carthsis real and worldly life is not illusion and it is worth living. The divinity of God is present everywhere and as God and the divinity are real, worldly life is also real. To reach Narayana Ramanuja says : "No strenuous efforts is needed, but just *Namajapa*, repetition of Narayana's name". Ramanuja was the first preacher, who introduced the concept of `serve "*Bhavamu Sukhma*" "*Vasudaiva Kutumbakum*" that is those who worship the omnisent Lord Vasudeva belong to one family. Hence the narrow barriers of caste, creed etc. are to be given up. It is only pure devotion which elevates the position of a person and not any thing else. Ramanuja himself accepted Thirukachi Nambi a vaisya as his teacher. The doctrine *Vishishutvama* is easier for the masses to follow and it aims at universal brotherhood by removing all caste differences. But, there was one difficulty people were already worshipping their personal God in different forms, like Lord Muruga, Shakti, Vinayaka and through their personal experience with the God whom they worship, they can have a personal communion with him, whenever they desire. Ramanuja's stress on one God and Lord Narayana as that one God was aimed at to intensify the concentration and devotion of everyone and put an end to the quarrels arising in the name of God. For Shri Ramanaju Narayana is synonym of God. Ramanja's *Vishishtadvaita* was acceptable. But a further explanation and interpretation of doctrine was needed so as to reach the masses.

During the reign of Delhi Sultanate and the Moghuls Islam

became the state religion and the conversion of people from Hinduism to Islam started. Sometimes it was optional, because of the material benefits, which the people could get from the monarch. Sometimes because of the easy concept of one God and sometimes because of some practical difficulties and threat. Whatever may be the causes after twelfth century, it became necessary, that the Hindus and the Muslims should live peacefully in one country.

That was the time, when Kabirdas and Gurunanak started to Stressing the concept of 'One God'. Who is the 'Ram' of the Hindus and the 'Rahim' or 'Allah' of the Muslims? The idea of universal brotherhood was propagated. At the same time to make spiritual path easy, Tulasidas, Mirabai, Surdas, Vallabh and Tuakaram preached '*saguna marga*' workship of the Lord with divine attributes. Kabirdas declared that all religions lead ultimately to one destination, that is the realm of that one God. The concept of one God in Kabir's philosophy impressed the people. But regarding realization of God, Kabir leaned more on Advaita and the understanding of self, and the realization of God in oneself. This again confused the people for only great seers and sage could understand the inseparable Brahaman within oneself. Further Kabir laid emphasis on renunciation of everything to attain bless, This is also impossible for all just as the impracticability of the concept of extreme non-violence of the Jainism, Kabir laid too much emphasis on the unreality of the life and the ultimate destruction of body in other words the unreality of the worldly life. Whatever drawbacks were brought against the doctrine of Advaita, the same were applicable to Kabir's philosophy as well.

After the coming of the Europeans of India, Christianity spread rapidly in our country. The non-violence, tolerance, mercy absolute faith in Jesus Christ, the synonym of utter selfness etc. attracted the people. The industrial Revolution and the advancement of science and technology made the vast world very small, communication quick and easy, and the dependence of one country on another one community on another and one person on another.

The scientific advancement resulted in making the people run made for power, wealth, supremacy, and comfort. In a way, people became over confident, thinking that they could achieve anything by their intelligence, the ego in them asserted itself, in such a way, that they even started arguing against the existence of God. The dawn of the 20th Century witnessed people marching ahead towards destruction. Sai Baba, the Rama of Treata Yuga and the Krishna of Dwapara Yuga, the Allah of 8th Century A.D. and the Jesus Christ of 1 A.D., Kabir of 16th Century appeared before us in a form acceptable to people of all religions. His white dress made Him look like a Jain Saint, a Tirthankara, or an apostle of Christ. His innocent, calm and serene face reminded one of Jesus Christ, His turban reminded the Muslims of Allah, His sitting pose, as a Guru, with crossed legs and hand in the form of *Abhayastha* reminded the Hindus of Dakshinamoorthy, Thathatreya and Lord Narayana; His total detachment and disregard of material things reminded the Buddhists, of the great Buddha, who renounced His earthly kingdom to rule over a divine kingdom. His concern for Hindu-Muslim unity and upliftment for the masses reminded them of Kabir, and his stressing on '*Hari Guna Ghana Bhajan*' reminded them of Tulasidas, Surdas and Meera. Yes, Sai Baba's universal religion is an amagamation of the fundamental doctrines of all religions. He made religion more practical, easy connecting it with our day-to-day life. So far people were struggling, because they could think of religion only as something apart from their day-to-day life. Baba's preaching are according to the psychology and need of this modern world. Baba did not encourage conversion. He wanted every one to stick to their own religion, the form of God, whom they already worship, He advocated a perfect democracy in the matter of religious worship. Through this He wanted to achieve unity among people, and establish universal brotherhood.

The point to be noted here is, it is actually very difficult for one to leave the form of God, whom he is already worshipping and to start worshipping a different form of God and follow a different way of worship. Baba made it very clear that all our prayers, worship etc. reach only that One omnipotent God. As Baba wanted worship of God to be made a habit at the initial stage, He asked people to do *namajapa*, concentrate on God's form and perform Arati four times a day.

Since in the modern world everyone is busy, always struggling to earn his livelihood, they have no time even to do regular poojas, utter daily prayers etc. The modern world has made the people business-minded, and just as business contact, they want assurance from God like, if they say their prayer, what will they get, if they trust God, what benefit they will get, if they help the poor and the wretched, what profit they will get, etc.

Hence, Baba as Absolute Parabrahma, as Himself the *Purna*

Purusha, gives His promises, in very simple words, just as a mother tempts her child, saying if you are friendly with your brother, I will give you this toy or sweet etc. They very first word of His promise is, when one comes to His abode, he has perfect security, both physical and moral. He is collecting His children from all places and it is not they, who come to him on their own effort. He advises people not to renounce this world, undergo hardship or observe fasting to reach God, but just following a righteous path, and speaking always the truth, are enough to get the blessings of God. He stressed this fact that, if we are sincere and firm in our devotion, then we can get *Sakshakara*' of God in any form, we like. Service to the poor and the needy, service to the benefit of humanity etc. is service to God. Thus, Baba's path connects our spiritual life with our worldly life, whereas the preaching of other prophets before Baba, separated spiritual life and worldly life as two separate entities.

Baba as Dwarakamai assures Her love and protection to all, and Her abode Dwaraka, is an abode of peace and love, where everyone can enjoy the bliss of eternal happiness. Baba's call to the entire humanity to come to Dwarakamai, has made volumes and volumes of various philosophical doctrines ranging from the Vedic age down to the preaching of Ramakrishna Paramahansa, very simple, clear and acceptable to all. The realization of the existence of a Divine Mother, to take care of our day-to-day needs, to protect us from dangers etc. is actually, what is required on our part. How fortunate we are! Just as in this busy scientific world we have all conveniences like electronic equipments, transport facilities, computers etc. to make our life comfortable, in the same way on the spiritual side also we have a convenient, comfortable and easy doctrine to follow.

--Dr. R. Rukmani
No. 7, Sixth Street,
Ramnagar, Nanagandllur
Madras 600061
(*Shri Sai Leela*)

26

WE DEVOTEES

S. M. Bannerjee

"Impelled by dark currents of ignorance, you are not able to know who I am. I am the Divine Power, Prime Power, Noble Form, combination of twenty-four subtle elements, Supreme power which destroys the evil effects of evil actions. I am the Life-Power of movable and immovable objects of the world. I am the living power which protects My bhaktas. If you repose your fauth in Me, I shall ensure that you are endowed with health and longevity."

—Shri Shirdi Sai Baba

Lord Krishna in His immortal message to humanity says:

"Four types of devotees seek Me. To one type belongs the person who worships Me, because he is tormented by ills that affect the body; he is the *Aartha*.

The second type seeks My help and favours in his pursuit of prosperity and power, property and welfare of his progeny; he is *Aarthaarthi*.

The third yearns for the realisation of the *Atma*, studies the scriputures and sacred texts, moves ever in the company of spiritual *sadhakas*, practices *Sadachara* by acting along the lines laid down by the sages and is always motivated by the eagerness to reach the *Sannidhi* of the Lords; he is the *Jijnaasu*.

The fourth is the *Jnani*. He is immersed in *Brahmathathwam*."

"The first, the *Aartha*, worships Me only when he is in difficulty and suffers from grief or pain. When he prays to Me, I hear it and I satisfy him only in relation to that particular prayer. So too, when the *Artha-arthi* prays for riches or position or power or high status, I listen and award him only the particular thing he craves for. The *Jijnaasu* is blessed with the chances to do *Nishkaama Karma* under the guidance of a proper Guru as a guide who teaches him to discriminate between the *Atma* (Eternal Spirit) and the *Anantma* (the physical that is Ephemeral) and thus he is helped to achieve the goal of human birth. I bless him so that he is saved from distractions to concentrate on the single aim of liberation."

But all this showering of Divine Grace issubject to the following conditions placed by the Lord:

"Persons who loving meditate, worship and serve Me at all times as the Lord in their own heart as also in the hearts of all beings and things, I take the responsibility of their well-being and happiness here and hereafter."

The 'Soul' of every religion or philosophy lies not in its theories and dogmas, but in the practical way of life laid down for its followers, namely, practice of Truth and Righteousness, Love and Service to fellowmen; practice non-injury in thought, word and deed. What an enchanting order of life would it indeed make if all we devotees dive deep in the ocean of our religion and gather the precious pearls of 'values' instead of being content with sticks and straws of rites and rituals floating on the surface. That, indeed, would make life worth living for every man. This is precisely what the world needs today. Thinking along these lines would give us a truer and fuller perspective of "devotion" in its different grades, making some persons devotees only of God, some others devotees of teachings of God or of messages or direction of Guru or Saints and still other persons devotees of the values of life. Only the practice of such devotion by us of teachings and values can providee the power to balance our lopsided development. This power which can lift man to higher planes of thinking and living is called 'Spirituality'.

We who claim to be "Devotees" therefore have, to ask ourselves: are we devotees of only God or Sai Baba or are we devotees of the teachings of God or Baba? Even in our day to work we often come across some people who talk much but accomplish little or nothing, so too in the case of religion. True religion is not mere knowing or speaking but actual 'doing'. As Jesus said, "if a man is 'doer of the Law' even in a small measure, he will not only himself be religious but he will radiate religion and influence the lives of others as well." This 'practical religion' not only transforms one self but it also becomes productive of good to men and women around, entirely unlike the morbid religion which merely clings to rituals and dogmas.

The sole purpose of religion and philosophy is to make one's life meaningful and useful to others as well. Mere going to the temple and saying, "I come here as I love God or Baba" is neither active religion nor practical religion. We find that quite a few so-called "devotees" come to temple only when they have some problem or crisis in their life or family and the frequency of their visits increases as long as the crisis continues and progressively diminishes to a trickle as the crisis passes off by His grace! Although such devotees are very much a part of the Sai family, they just do not have the time or inclination even to talk or enquire about the well-being of other fellow devotees. Their whole attention is on self and its welfare. Perhaps such devotees fail to appreciate that by sharing the grief and pain with others, a lot of relief and consolation can be derived. That is the law of Universal brotherhood, which has been stressed by Baba or God from time immemorial. Such devotees do not realise that if they just spare a little time to allow another aggrieved human being to unload his pains and grief to somebody how relieved or light he or she feels and this act of listening to other's woes and expressing a little sympathy constitutes a great act of charity without spending any money. Alas, such devotees fail to do even this much, nor do they have any time to take a little part in social welfare but expect abundant grace from God or Baba. If his life contributes nothing for the happiness of his fellow men, how can we say that he or she is religious. In fact, these devotees only love themselves but surely not God or Baba. Sai Baba has said "LOVE IS SELFLESSNESS AND SELF IS LOVELESSNESS". This indeed is the challenge which true religions throws to all of us devotees of various grades and shades.

Let us, therefore, examine when we say we are the devotees of Sai Baba. Are we devotees of only Baba or also of any particular objective or goal in life? Pondering over this question will make each one of us look within ourselves, and find out whether we devotees are only devotees of Baba clinging to rituals and dogmas or seekers of some material benefits from Him, or again, whether we are Spiritual aspirants or Sadhakas. Only an honest self-introspection and self-appraisal along these lines will tell us how far we are following the teachings of Sai Baba for our own individual good and for the good of the community at large. In this connection it will be interesting to quote a measage from Bhagwan Sri Sathya Sai Baba which is most helpful to understand the 'personality' of a devotee.

"There are four different types of behaviour which form part of man's daily life. The first type is able to recognise the faults present in himself as also to recognise the good that is present in others. The second type, an intermediate grade, is able to recognise the good that is present in others. The third type hides or denies the faults present in himself and exposes the faults present in others. This is a bad stand. The fourth one, which is the worst, goes on proclaiming the good which does not exist in himself but also tries to expose faults of others which do not exist in them at all. Unfortunately, the fourth category of people who have been described as the worst of all far outnumber the other three categories in this world. They too go to temples and holy places, meet holy men, join *sat-sang*, call themselves devotees and speak lofty words about religion and God. But in practice they hardly give any evidence of their devotion or *sat-sang*. That is why they are not able to contribute to the good or to the prosperity of society".

In these words, Bhagwan Baba has given an excellent equipment or device to us devotees, to evaluate ourselves. This brings us to our tendencies of egoistic behaviour, anger and jealousy which hinder us in developing love, compassion, forgiveness and allied good qualities which are the hall-mark of true devotion. This raises another question: Are we ourselves responsible for these various unhealthy tendencies and if so, can we change them for better and alter our destiny? The answer is Yes, if one takes to the path of spirituality. How does spirituality help man to fulfil himself? The permanent goal of life for everyone of us is to be free from all suffering and pain. We all try in our daily life to shake off pain and misery to acquire more and more happiness of one type or the other. But we fail to get the happiness we are really striving for. In fact, in acquiring, retaining and enjoying this happiness we lose our most precious possession, namely, inner peace which is the bed rock of enduring happiness, as all the worldly happiness we are striving for is very ephemeral in nature. To add to this, every thinking mind is disturbed sooner or later by its ignorance about life itself, its source, meaning and goal. We become painfully aware of our blunder and strive to retrace our steps to come on to the right path with guidance and help of knowledgeable persons like Godmen or saints like Sai Baba. The wisdom of retracing our steps from the wrong path and progressing on the right path is called spirituality. The presence of Divinity in Shirdi Sai Baba and in the present human form of Bhagwan Sri Satya Sai Baba is a rare opportunity available to all the devotees to draw spiritual light in their path of life to experience continuous inner peace. We must therefore, have a clear understanding of the challenges of this change over, as also of the rewarding glory of Divine Grace that awaits the pilgrim at the other end of the path.

We devotees are very fortunate to have been born in an era when both Sri Shirdi Baba and subsequently Sri Sathya Sai Baba took human forms and walked the earth to guide, purify and lead the ignorant suffering humanity. Sri Shirdi Baba gave out His teachings by examples and some time in parables, whereas Sri Sathya Sai Baba is giving out the same things in a codified and much simpler form for the so-called rational humanity to understand and pratise the teachings. True devotion is not worship of God or Baba but practising His commandments and teachings in the form of human values. Nothing good ever happens without God's blessings and grace. We generally use these words "God", "Blessing" and "Grace" very casually without a correct understanding of these words just as when one says "sorry" or "thank you" without any corresponding feeling of regret or gratitude behind them. We receive the belssing of Baba during our first *darshan* when He plants the seed of FAITH or *Shradha* by fulfilling some of our immediate material desire and this *darshan* is not in itself a prayer but it is the fruit of our prayers offered earlier to God. Hereafter, it is for us to develop this seed of faith planted in us by self-effort or *Purushartha*, which in its turn brings the Divine Grace of Baba and the seed of faith grows in our hearts as the tree of spirituality. *Purushartha* can be equated with watering the seed and Divine Grace as the *sunshine* for growth of the Spiritual tree in us, which ultimately cleanses our dross of anger, jealousy, hatred and lust.

However, many of the devotees remain satisfied with the fulfilment of their immediate mundane needs for some time and hardly undertake any self-effort for the development of spirituality. Hence Sathya Sai Baba has remarked that "If you do part time service to God, you will only get a part-time blessing". After some time when our mundane needs are satisfied, we start feeling a frustration as we discover that we are not experiencing the inner peace which is the goal of human life. Here starts the personal effort to draw in more and more of Divine Grace on which ultimately depends the further growth and fruition of the plan of spirituality. Thus personal effort and Divine Grace are complementary and contributory to each other, both in turn, depending upon the intensity of our spiritual hunger to experience the inner Peace of Divinity. These personal efforts have to be two-fold; one is to draw Divine Grace for our spiritual progress and the other to draw the Divine Grace for our personal efforts in worldly pursuits which have a close connection with our "Peace".

Sai Baba in his present human form as Sri Sathya Sai Baba has given us a Charter, laying down the guidelines of discipline, devotion and duty for devotees all the world over to practise in their day to day living. Just as we have to sign a document or deed with a bank while availing of a loan and abide by the conditions to which we have committed ourselves thereby, so too in the case of Divine Grace. Otherwise, the guarantee will be withdrawn and the Divine Grace would cease to flow. The "Nine Points" laid down in the charter for Sai Devotees to follow and practise, therefore, are of supreme importance to us. There is, however, one "Saving Grace" once we understand and bear in mind the working of Divine Grace. We ourselves will spontaneously feel the urge to make these nine points of the charter a part and parcel of our day to day life and activity. Their practice will start within us a process of transformation comparable to the three important operations in gardening, namely, manuring, watering and weeding which are needed by the spiritual point.

Three types of *sadhanas* have been presented for us by Bhagwan Baba. These are - Individual Sadhana, Family Sadhana and Individual Society Sadhana, other than Group Community Services. Through this three-fold Sadhanas, we devotees can acquire and grow in spiritual strength to reduce the effects of ego, anger and jealously which disturb our world within. Meditation, *Japa* and *Swadhyaya* (study of spiritual literature) constitute Individual Sadhana. To contribute and promote the harmony in the home and to add a spiritual dimension to the life of the members of our family through regular group-singing of devotional songs called Bhajan, discussing spiritual texts etc. is the Family Sadhana. Doing whatever is possible for the good of society as Selfless service is the Society Sadhana. The first two Sadhanas help us to repay the overdraft and interest of Divine Grace. The third exercise, the Society Sadhana kindless in us the wisdom of Bhagawan's omnipresence leading to realisation of universal brotherhood. These three sadhanas fill up the deficiencies in our *"Purushartha"* so as to make it perfect and fruitful.

It is against this background of the personal efforts needed to reach our goal that we have to consider the 9 points in the Charter of Sri Sathya Sai Organisation which constitute the 3 exercises which Bhagwan Baba has shown us to cleanse our mind and to advance spiritually. These 9 points are: (1) Daily meditation and Japa (2) Bhajan or group devotional singing with all the members of the family once a week (3) Imparting education in human values to children in our family (4) Engaging ourselves in Individual and community sadhana (5) Participating in group devotional singing or Bhajan in public places at least once a week (6) Regular study of spiritual literature and attending study circles (7) Speaking softly with everyone (8) *Narayan Seva* or feeding the poor to form the habit of avoiding wastage of food. The inner significance underlying each of the above points so that they form three streams for self purification, namely, our individual, Family and Society Sadhanas to experience absolute peace.

In fact a Sai Organisation or Samaj, considering its spiritual objective is not an organisation, but an 'organism' each devotee being a cell of the Sai Body. Just as each cell in the body is kept fit for the function allotted to it, so too each devotee is helped to keep himself fit for his duty by the voice of the Lord within him, telling him what to do and what not to do. There are different cells in the body witth different functions and all of them work together in harmony, because they are all together a "Mini Universe in themselves". So too is the case with the devotees, who cannot remain aloof in the Organisation but have to overcome the illusion of multiplicity and that is why the third path viz., the communitty Sadhana has been laid down for us as a part of our spiritual Sadhana by our Divine Lord. This third extension will add more calories to our spiritual health and take us to our goal provided we fulfil two conditions viz., (1) we give 200 hours of service as our Sadhana every year at an average of 4 hours every week and (2) we take up the Group Community Sadhana only after adopting in practice the preceding two paths of Individual and Family Sadhana. If we do not do so, we cannot become a part of the Organism, because we will be, again, slaves of our Ego and its group of companions. He has given as Community Sadhana or Service to mankind in some form or the other which suits any particular devotee according to his or her aptitude, talent or taste.

In short, the time has come when we should grow into "devotees of the teachings of Sri Sai Avatar and not devotees of Sai Baba." Otherwise, there is little hope for true progress for us as spiritual aspirants. We have to become human to realise that we already are God in the making. Let us remember that God or Baba will take charge fully of our worldly requirements only when we earn the divine grace and that will leave us free to pursue in our spiritual sadhana while He will bother about our daily problems and needs. This is my personal experience.

In fact, Shirdi Baba's saying "*Sab Ka Malik Ek*" points out to common Fatherhood of Humanity and the natural corollary of this is "Brotherhood of Humanity" which is implied, and we must practise this by community Sadhana and Service to quality for the Divine Grace.

S.M. Banerjee
President
Sri Sai Samaj Calcutta (Regd)
28/6, Bepin Pal Road
Calcutta-700026
(*Shri Sai Leela,* May 1988)
(Courtesy: Editor, *Shri Sai Leela*)

27

APPRECITATING THE FULL SIGNIFICANCE AND SOCIAL RELEVANCE OF SRI SHIRDI SAI BABA
–A SOCIOLOGICAL ASSESSMENT

Dr. S.P. Ruhela

"I am God. I am in Shirdi and also everywhere. Everything belongs to Me. It is I who give all things to every one. The entire Universe reposes in Me. I am the sum total of all that is manifest. Those who believe that Sai resides only in Shirdi have not seen Me. Even a leaf does not move without My will."

–Sri Shirdi Sai Baba

I

HOW MUCH DO WE KNOW ABOUT SRI SAI BABA?

Sri Shirdi Sai Baba is being worshipped throughout the world by millions of people. There are atleast ten journals exlusively devoted to Him published in India and there are at least twenty-four Sai organizations in India today. No one correctly knows how many Shirdi Sai temples are there in India and abroad, but this much is known to us that there are such temples in almost every town in India and there are such temples also in USA, UK, African countries, Australia, Hong Kong, Nepal, Mauritius etc. It is indeed a Sai miracle that despite there being no central global Shirdi Sai organization for the propagation of Sri Shirdi Sai Baba's name, countless self-inspired devotees have taken upon themselves the responsibility of starting organizations, temples, welfare activites in the name of Sri Shirdi Sai Baba. Countless people visit Shirdi every day seeking Baba's blessings, although Baba attained MahaSamadhi 79 years ago in 1918, and their numbers are increasing each year.

Despite these facts, this is also a grim fact that most of the devotees and even *pracharaks* of Sri Shirdi Sai Baba do not really know fully about the greatness of Sri Shirdi Sai Baba. Most of the Sai devotees only know this much that Sri Shirdi Sai Baba was a great saint of Shirdi who was an *Avatar* (Incarnation of God) and who led the life of an humble Fakir, dressed like a Muslim, begged alms in the vicinity of his unique Dwarkamai Masjid, performed many miracles and who has left behind perennial assurances to all his devotees for all times to come that whosoever would remember Him at the hour of his need and whosoever would step into his Dwarkamai masjid would find his grace flowing and problems solved soon. Since at no other place in the entire universe none other than the gracious saint Sri Shirdi Sai Baba, has even given such grand assurances, Shirdi has become the unique epicentre of Sai devotion and not only devotees but non-devotees also visit this holy place with great love, expectations and faith.

The life of Sri Shirdi Sai Baba as an Avatar in the 19th century and the first two decades of the 20th century, from 1838 to 1918, is known to most people but they really do not try to know further about this unique spiritual personality. Even their knowledge about the parents, circumstances, locations and timings of his birth, childhood, period of training under the Guru Vikusha, his *agyatwas* between 1854 when he first reached Shirdi as a 16 year old Fakir and disappeared from there within a few weeks, and 1858 when he again reached Shirdi with the marriage party of Chandbhai Patil's nephew and was welcomed by Mhalsapati, the priest of Khandoba temple, in these historic words *'Ya Sai'* (Welcome Sai), is uncertain, vague and fossilized, and they tend to ignore many new discoveries and revelations coming to light in these matters. Many myths or illogical things are popular about Sri Shirdi Sai Baba which ought to be shed aside in order to understand Sai Baba's life and stature logically and correctly.

During the last three decades a number of books have come out revealing the past incarnations of Sri Shirdi Sai Baba. This should interest all Sai devotees. It has been revealed that He was the incarnation of Dattatreya, and also He was the incarnation of Shiva. In the Bhakti period of Indian history, He was born as Kabir, the great iconoclast who had hit hard the superstitions and dead rituals of the Hindus and Muslims and preached the essence of spiritualty and *bhakti*. In one incarnation he was the same Muslim Fakir who had blessed the fugitive Emperor Humayun that he would be blessed with a son who would be a great ruler of India; the same Fakir had then advised Mukund Brahmachari of Kashi, who in his next birth was born as Emperor Akbar about whose secularism, Din-Ilahi and proclivity towards Hindus and spirituality a lot has been written in countless books.[1] *Shri Sai Satchcharita* mentions many stories of the past births of Baba in which he and his devotees had lived together in the same family, locality, valley, was kinsmen or neighbourhood.

These past incarnations of Sri Shirdi Sai Baba must also be of relevance to all his devotees in order to appreciate the crucial fact that He did not suddenly emerge as an Avatar in the 19th Century. As a matter of fact, for countless births He had been a pilgrim on the path of spirituality and had been spreading divine knowledge and promoting love and communal understanding among people and compassion towards all. His advert as Avatar at Shirdi was the culmination, the highest achievement, of his soul as a saint or Godman in our planet earth.

After his Maha Samadhi on 15 October, 1918, what happened to him? Most of the Sai *pracharaks* and devotees do not know and they do not care to know this. It is time to know also about Sri Shirdi Sai Baba's Spirit after his Mahasamadhi event. As a keen and longtime researcher in the Sai phenomenon, I have tried to find it. Fortunately, I have recently discovered two very important relevations:

(1) Shirdi Sai Baba became the Spirit Guide of the World immediately after his Mahasamadhi in 1918 and He occupied this high position in the higher plane till 1941, and then Rishi Ram Ram, a great Spirit, succeeded him as the *Spirit Guide* of the world.

(2) There-after He merged into God and became the God Almighty.

The following are the three most startling and hitherto not widely known evidences of these two great spiritual mysteries about Sri Shirdi Sai Baba:

(1) On 17 April, 1942, Mrs. Annie Besant, the well-known pioneer of the Theosophical Movement in India, announced as under publicly:

"God morning. I am now happy having seen the Masters who guide us unerringly for many years. Ram Ram is the greatest of Masters, gentle as Jesus, all knowing and pure, his resplendent presence is an inspiration. He is guiding humanity into one higher path of Spiritual life .....

Sri Shirdi Sai Baba, after achieving the spiritual regeneration of a considerable cross-section of the people of India, having realised the universal self merged himself with the Universal Consciousness, the necessary sequel. His mentle fell in 1941 on Rishi Ram Ram, who was elected as the Spirit Guide of the world."[2]

(2) In a book "*Twenty-six Years in Contact with the Spirit World*", V.S. Krishnaswami, I.F.S. (Retired), published at least three decades back, it was mentioned :

"According to the spiritual sources, the recent spirit guides of the world were Sai Baba and Rishi Ram Ram. Apart from arranging for religious instructions to the spirts of different spiritual planes, they (Spirit Guides) have to arrange for spiritual education of persons in the earthly plane."[3]

(Quoted in *Dawn of a New Era*: *The Vision of Master Rishi Ram Ram* (1970 p. 45)

(3) In *The First Sai Devotees' Convention in 1971*, the following extract had been published in the Souvenir:

"Minocher K. Spencer, a Parsi, a seeker of truth, used to receive instructions from a departed saint Ram Ram.

The Saint Ram Ram one day revealed Himself to Spencer and told him, "I have told (instructed) you (in spirituality) so far. But for further guidance you pray to Sai Baba."

"The *Sadhka* (Spiritual seeker) Spencer has left a book entitled *"How I Found God"* and therein he narrates about the daily lessons he took from Sri Shirdi Sai Baba who used to appear to the devotee (him) in Astral Body; besides Sai Baba had given him messages from 3.11.1952 to 18.2.1953).

That rarest of the rare book "*How I Found God*, (1957)[4], of whose only 100 copies in proof form had been printed by the Spiritual Healing Centre, Coimbatore, and whose almost all the copies (excepting a few ones left for future reference, one of which has since then been with Sri A. Somasundarm, a close, friend, confident and spiritual successor of Sri K.S.D. Aiyer, Secretary of the Coimbatore Centre) had been burnt on God's order to test Spencer's ego, has been totally unavailable to all the Sai devotees in the world all through the last 40 years. Yogi Spencer ultimately realised God as guided by Sri Sai Baba, the God Almighty, in 1957 and soon thereafter he attain Mahasamadhi in 1958. Sri K.S.D. Aiyer also suddenly passed away in 24.1.1965 and consequently the Spiritual Healing Centre, Coimbatore, was abruptly closed down for ever. Aiyer had sent to Sri A. Somasumdarm one set of the four volumes of Spencer's book "*How I Found God*" in proof copy form of 1396 pages in print, immediately on its publication, and thus that rarest of the rare book has survived for the humanity. I had the great fortune of visiting Sri A. Somasundarm's 'Divine Centre' at Markapur (Andhra Pradesh) on 13th June 1997, meeting my spiritual father Sri A. Somasundarm, 82 year old Spiritualist, there and obtaining the original book "*How I Found God*" and his kind blessings and permission to bring out its selected portions for the information of the Sai devotees at large, as the right time has come for making such spiritual mystery known to the world at large.

In that matchless and thrilling book "*How I Found God*", Yogi Spencer has recorded that since his cradle days he had been under the spiritual care and guidance of Rishi Ram Ram, a great Spirit of the Spirit world, he was spiritually trained by Rishi Ram Ram till 11th May 1949, when the Rishi handed over the charge of his spiritual training and efforts for God-realisation to Sri Sai Baba, the God Almighty, the highest Spirit controlling the entire universe. Before that on 10th April 1949 Rishi Ram Ram had given this message M.K. Spencer:

"...I have taken you to the very end of the journey.
It is now for God to take you in " (p 209).

The same day the Master put Spencer's case before Sai Baba,

the God Almighty, whom the Parsis call Ahura Mazda; at the time of the transfer on 11 May 1949, the Master told him, "I am handing you on to Him (Sai Baba) for He has the final authority to liberate your soul, and not I. (p. 260), and also that "I shall now await the happy day of your transformation which you will achieve through Sai Baba who is the greatest in the whole celestial hierarchy" (p.261).

In the foreword to this monumental book of M.K. Spencer, his cousin and himself a great yogi of his times, Homi S. Spencer, had commented as under:

> "The position of this socalled Sai Baba in the Celestial Hierarchy becomes quite definitely clear as the story unfolds itself. First of all it shows by numerous re-iterations that *Sai Baba is none other than the God Himself in His Sakari'* (or Manifest) aspect of Asho Ahura Mazda Ameshaspand a fact which is emphasised over and over again not only by Baba Himself but also by Rishi Ram Ram and several other Celestial Beings of pre-eminence in the Celestial Hierarchy (like Jesus Christ, Lord Krishna, Lord Buddha etc.) (p. 32).

On 18th May 1949 Rishi Ram Ram told Yogi M.K. Spencer:

> "I reveal to you this secret. God is manifesting to you in the shape and form of Sai Baba. Bow down to him in utter devotion. To put it in the words of Homi (H.S. Spencer) He is Asho Ahura Mazda Amshaspand. He is Amashaspanda as well as God. When He manifested Himself He is Amshaspand. You have heard Him. You will also soon see him. (p. 276)

At a latter stage, Sai Baba, the God Almighty told His pupil M.K. Spencer, "It is not a question of mere Self-realization but a realization of God with all the mystic powers added for superconscious work on a large scale on your earth plane." (p. 411)

Sai Baba, the God Almighty, took Spencer's soul out of his body in September 1949. On 25th Septembe 1949 Sai Baba revealed to him:

> "I took out your soul without putting you into trance...The soul passed away from your body and came back in a minute and that minute was terrible for you. It was I who in that one minute's gap sustained you by My invisible force and power." (p. 393-394).

Appreciating the Full Significance

Rishi Ram Ram commented upon this as under and told Spencer: "It is not a joke to take out the soul when the body is in living condition and in full consciousness and to bring it back quite safe and sound. No Master can do it. It is only Sai Baba alone who can do it and by so doing He has manifested to you His tremendous power and at the same time shown you what He actually is. He is your God whom you worship day and night. He is your Ahuramazda Amshaspand who has taken the form of Sai Baba for the simple reason and no other that you have His picture in your Altar room. He can take any form" (p. 394).

In this 1396 page big book Spencer has vividly described Sai Baba as God, His great divine powers and how ultimately he showed Himself to him.

In his message recorded on page 471 Sai Baba clearly confirmed this :

".... God has taken the form of Sai Baba and when you see Him face to face it will be the exact copy of the picture you have in your alter room."

After giving many rigours tests ultimately Sai Baba, the God Almighty, helped him in God-realization. On 13th Decembe 1957, the God Sai Baba (Ahura Mazda) gave this most thrilling and assuring message to M.K. Spencer for all of us to note and rejoice: "*I am God and I am going to save your world from destruction*" (p. 1389).

All these authentic spiritual revelations, which have hitherto remained undisclosed as per God's Plan, should now enlighten all the Sai Devotees and *pracharaks* all over the globe, and convince them and make them feel greatly happy to discover that by their worshipping Sri Shirdi Sai Baba they are on the right track; they are worshipping not only Sai Baba as Avatar but also Sai Baba who is now the God Almighty—the Highest of the Celestial Hierarchy, the Highest of the Planes of Consciousness.

II

RESPONSIBILITIES ENJOINED UPON ALL SAI ORGANIZATIONS, *PRACHARAKS* AND CONSCIOUSNSS SAI DEVOTEES

The foregoing factual position about the full reality of Sri

Shirdi Sai Baba—that He is not merely an Avatar who was with us in this earthly plane during 1838-1918 but now God, the Almighty, the very Ahura Mazda of Parsis and Allah of the Muslims and the God of the Christians, binds all of us to a number of serious commitments.

It now becomes our responsibility to see that we seriously hear and follow His messages not only the words He spoke as His teachings as recorded in *'Shri Sai Satcharita''*, *'Devotees's Experiences of Shri Sai Baba* *'Sai Baba's Charters and Sayings*" and a number of other books on his Avataric career and mission, but also we pay heed to the divine mysterious messages from Sri Shirdi Sai Baba as God from the highest spiritual plane as received by his chosen devotees like Yogi M.K. Spencer of Karachi, Sri B. Umamaheswara Rao of Guntur, Dr. K.V. Raghav Rao of Hyderabad, Prof. P.S. Verma of New Delhi and some others, which have been very carefully recorded by them just after their receiving in their visions and dreams, and which are full of the highest spiritual truths, wishes of God Sai Baba and what we must do to liberate ourselves in this very life.

III

PREVAILING CONFUSION AND NORMLESSNESS

We find that on the one hand there is a tide of enthusiasm among Sri Shirdi Sai *pracharaks* and devotees to organize *keertans*, establish Shirdi Sai temples, do *seva* activities, found Sai organizations, install Shirdi Sai's statutes and do all these and more including national and international conventions and the like, on the other we find several undesirable, unethical, normless, fundamentalistic and materialist trends rampant these days.

(1) Many *pracharaks* are posing themselves as Gurus or Deputies of Baba or even the very likes of Sri Shirdi Sai Baba and getting them selves worshipped by their devotees at par with Sri Shirdi Sai Baba.

They are spreading Baba's message alright, but their eye is mainly on collection of funds, right or wrong by various dubious means. There is now a growing fashion to organise *jagran* type of Sai keertans in public on grand scale, in homes and in public places, singing all kinds of devotional as well as filmi songs, *Shastriya sangeet*, Qawwallis and what not, and devotees participate in them in rather, non-serious or indisciplned manner, and then the whole rigmorale of hosting *bhandaras*, giving lot of money to singers party, temple society, after the socalled Sai Baba's messenger or deputy has given his special blessings to the rich hosts or organisers, or sung Panjabi *badhaiyan* in praise of the hosts. This creats competition in Sai devotees and dishearted the poor ones among them who cannot afford such costly *pujas* and *bhandaras*.

(2) Some illogical myths about Sai Baba are perpetuated by some Sai *pracharaks*, such as:

> Sri Shirdi Sai Baba was *Ayonijic*, not born of the woman's womb.

> Sri Narasimhswamiji himself had in 1956 ridiculed this illogical and unfenable myth in 'Life of Sai Baba' (Vol. IV, page 237) in these hardhitting words.

> "Thinking that it would enhance the glories of Baba to put forward fantastic notions about his being *Ayonijic*, that is one who came into this word without entering into the womb of a woman, some people fall into the unfortunate habit of creating stories about Baba. The *Ayonijic* theory, as has already been stated, has no shadow of support for it amongst the statements made by Baba himself in respect of his parents either in this *Janma* or any previous *janma*".

This had been clearly and emphatically stated by Swamiji as early as in 1956, but even after 40 years we find that diehard like, M.B. Nimbalalkar still vigorous keeping on harping on the same illogical and absurd myth.

(3) Even *Shri Sai Satcharita* had mentioned long back that Baba was probably born in 1838, that he lived for 80 years. Sri Satya Sai Baba has revealed that Shri Shirdi Sai Baba was actually born on 27 September, 1838 in a forest near Pathri village.This has been corroborated by the ancient palm leaf *nadis* available with Dr. A.Karunakaran, a famous naadi reader of 'Sughar Agasthyar Naadi Jothida, 14 Mannar (Reddy) Street, T.Nagar, Madras-600017 (Tel. 4348094). Various Gurus and high heeled *pracharaks* have been confusing the people by giving fantastic guesses about the date of birth and parents' names of Baba. For example, M.L. Narasayya

says, Baba was born on 11.6.1836, B.K. Narayan says Baba was born on 23.5.1858, Mataji Krishnapriya says He was born on 26.3.1836, Sai Narayan Baba gives some other date in the 1940s and so on and so forth.

(4) Nimbalkar has advanced this objection about the prevailing tendency of Sai devotees to establish Shirdi Sai temples and Divines in them:

> "If a Sai Baba temple is constructed lot of money pours in. Therefore a numbe of Sai Baba temples are being constructed all over India and in foreign countries also. Since it is not possible for every one to visit Shirdi freqeuently, it is good to construct Sai Baba's temples in one's area by installing Sai Baba statue therein. But in some places exact replica of Sai Baba's Samadhi is constructed in front of the statue, which is not correct, because his body is interned at Shirdi only, *dhumi* is also established. Simple devotees are misled and offer their devotion and money in abundance at these places."

How much genuine or how much malicious or parochial and is this view this is for the Sai devotees to speak out. One may ask : "Is Shirdi Sai Baba the monopoly of the Maharastrians and Shirdi alone?" This is not for me to reply, but for all conscientious Sai devotees and *pracharkas* to reply and debate and decide in seminars and conventions.

(5) Shri Sai Baba Sansthan Shirdi is doing excellent work by way of arrangements and regulation of worship activities at Shirdi. They deserve to be appreciated and congratulated. However, there are many things to which attention showed be paid. Sanitary arrangements in the Sansthan Lodging blocks leaves much to be desired. The lavatories and bathrooms are very dirty and always stinking. The food arrangements are inadequate. One has to wait for hours on busy days to get a locker, rooms are usually not available. There is no proper library and reference facility. The whole complex is still not upto the expectations of educated people. Even books sold at the counter are too few, too old, and although very less priced and valuable and much sought after, they are not available. There is no variety, no new or solid matter in them. Their Hindi books are full of mistakes.

The average visitor to Shirdi who comes to this holy pilgrimage with high devotion is greatly pestered by brokers of lodging rooms right from the moment he alights from the bus or taxi and the private hotelliers all around Shirdi Samadhi Dwakamai Masjid complex. They exploit the pilgrims with vengeance by changing very high room rents from Rs. 50 to Rs. 300 and even more for dirty and unsafe lodging dens. Many shopkeepers in Shirdi are so rude and so much explotiative in their business dealings that they put off a sensitive customer. All around there is creze for making money any how. One wonders how the Shirdi people have so soon forgotten Baba's teachings of love, truth, fair play, probity, concern for other's *atma* and feelings and high values, and of the like of these. The taxi people are another source of menance. They have no fixed rates and some of them are of doubtful character as we once experienced. The Holy Shirdi, the seat of Sri Shirdi Sai Baba is now having the ugly problems of beggery, lottery menance, cheating, crime and exploitation. Such is the shocking social reality of Shirdi today after 79 years of Baba's Mahasamadhi. This disillusious many devotees who come for the first time with great hopes and veneration. Little is being done, it seems, by any one to deal with this sociological plight.

Readers should read Subha Verma's article *'Shirdi Mein Sai Ka Danda Chalta Hai'*[10] in *Saptahik Hindustan*, 22 Nov. 1992, p. 24. Which exposes the widespread social malaise and callousness at this holy pilgrim spot these days.

(6) The Sai Baba Sansthan, Shirdi had published a public notification in *"The Hindustan Times"* of 3 May, 1994 stating as under:

> "...The *Padukas* (Sai Baba shoes) which Shri Gopinath Kote Patil (one of their Trustees) has been carrying around with him are fake and fraud on the religious and mental sentiments of all devotees. The Board of Trustees regrets the disgraceful and shameful behaviour of its trustee Shri Gopinath Patil and warns the public at large that no money should be paid to Shri Gopinath Kote Patil nor should any donations or gifts be made to him..."

The person in question is said to be the son of the same Tatya Patil, the dearest devotee on whom Sri Shirdi Sai Baba had showered all his love, bounties, and even bartered away his own life for his saving his life Sri Narayan Baba of Panvel, in the International Meet of Sai devotees at Shirdi under his leadership, had publicly honoured the same Shri Gopinath Kote Patil as a great

'Sai Sevak, the pride of Shirdi'. I was present in the late evening function in which he was so honoured in November 1994 itself. What message does this contradiction convey?

(7) The nuisance of threatening chain letters of Shirdi Sai Baba sent by anonymmous *paracharaks* of Baba is known to many devotees.

(8) Some people, said to be associated with Shri Shirdi Sai Baba Sansthan often visit devotees homes throughout India, enjoy their free hospitality, extract train fares and even cheat them of large funds. I too have been a victim of two such cheats and named Chandra Sekhar Bhalerao and Prakash Vani of that Sansthan, the former was working as waterman in front of the Sansthan's office some years back, and both living in the Sansthan premises. They cheated me of Rs. 4600/-. Many innocent Sai devotees and pilgrims are cheated and duped by all kinds of cheats and criminals there at Shirdi now and elsewhere in the name of Sai Baba or Shirdi Sai Baba Sansthan or other Sai Organization. So many people are collecting funds for their temples and one never knows what they are doing with them, whether they are getting their accounts properly audited or not, few have published their accounts for public information so far.

On the one hand, we all believe that Sri Sai Baba is an omniscient Avatar, the God Almighty, the great Judge who will definitely do justice and punish all those who violate norms of morality, and on the other many Sai *pracharaks* and devotees seem to think that He is already dead in 1918 or even if He is there in the highest plane. He is perhaps not seeing us, and so in the name of religiousity and regard for him can keep on forcing earnest devotees to tolerate all this sort of normlessness, and remain timid victims. However baring these few dysfunctions, on the whole we find that most of the Sai devotees and *pracharaks* are very sincerely and devotedly engaged in sai worship and Sai service activities which is very satisfying. Their devotion and service must be appreciated and reinforces by all mean.

III

THE RELEVANCE OF SRI SHIRDI SAI BABA IN THE CONTEMPORARY WORLD

Sri Shirdi Sai Baba taught mutual harmony, secularism of

the highest order, love, piety, justice, *shraddha*, *saburi* and a host of other high values. He was a very great Avatar, and is now the God Almighty, deeply concerned for ushering in an Era of One religion, the Religion of Humanity. I think Baba can never appreciate these malpractices and hoaxes and it is doubtful if he is going to shower his graces on all such hypocrites or undesirable ones who blatingly exploit his name for their personal ends. Let us pray to Sai Baba to much misguided people also who exploit his name and are harming Sai devotees and the Sai movement, for they really do know not what they are doing by their parochialsm misguided motions, apathly and inaction.

Sai Baba's 77 rare message (Discourses) recorded by Yogi M.K. Spencer in "*How I Found God*" and reprinted in a recent book 'Shirdi Sai Baba speaks to Yogi Spencer in Vision"[12] ask us, the inhabitants of this earthly plane, to move "from darkness into light", to realise that" renunciation is the essence of spiritually", to "remain true to yourself and work your way to spiritual heights discarding all that is gross and carnel", to "make love the corner stone of your life", to realise that "Truth alone will survive", to "break the chain of Maya with the hammer of self-consciousness", to "destroy sin with the hammer of God's name", to realise that "As you sow, so shall you reap," "God realization is the goal of life, not earthly heppiness."

Baba advises all of us:

"Don't make life a tomb of woe and wantonness. Rise from the graveyard of sickness and sorrow, both of mind and soul, and climb then altitudes of high thoughts and aspirations, to free you from the maddening temptations of your world and it vagaries. Keep away from the shore of dead sea apples. Clinch pure gold and not putried flesh. Kindle the light of your heart with the flame and fire of God's Love and Light and you will be safe in your march from the earth on to the realms beyond.

(*How I Found God*).

Let us take note of the contemporary situation of the world. It is, is full of so many dissensions and social, cultural, economic and political conflicts, jealousies and immoral, disjunctive and dysfunctioal tendencies which have made the life of human beings all over the world very insecure. Religions have disappointed humanity through the doings of many fundamentalists, fanatics, hypocrites and wealth-loving and power-hankering *yogis* and *acharyas* who rarely see eye to eye even among themselves and do not feel shy in condemning each other.

In such a socio-religico context of the contemporary world, Shirdi Sai Baba alone comes upto the expectations of the masses of the world as the ideal Godman or Prophet who epitomises simplicity, spirituality, love and genuine concern for all creatures. His simple teachings impress us most as they are without any trappings of complicated philosophy and His grace can be easily available to all.[13]

It has rightly been said:

"Faith is the main gospel of Sai Baba and to spread that gospel in the society and to convert those in the opposing forces is prime duty of every Sai devotee. We have to inculcate this discipline in ourselves, hereafter. Sai Baba spent His whole life in spreading the message of *faith and patience* in the contemporary society. If you remain awake to fulfill this mission that will be the right duty in His memory. He whom we consider an ideal divinity and in whom we profoundly believe and in so doing to spread the message of His saying will be the right ritual in doing worship to him. Every devotee must be awakened to perform this duty."[14]

Reference

1. Bhardwaja, Acharya E., *Sai Baba The Master*. Ongole: Sree Guru Paduka Publications, 1991, (III Ed.).

2. Somasundaram, A., *The Dawn of New Era : The Vision of Master Rishi Ram Ram*. Markapur: Divine Centre, 1969, p.45.

3. Krishnaswami, V.S., *Twenty-six Years in Contact with the Spirit World* : Quote in Somasundaram A., *The Dawn of A New Era The Vision of Master Rishi Ram Ram*. Markapur: Divine Centre, 1970, p.45.

4. Spencer, Mincoher, K., *"How I Found God"* : Coimbatore: Divine Healing Centre, 1957.

5. Gunaji, N.V., *Shri Sai Satcharita* Shirdi: Shri Sai Baba Sansthan, 1982 (X Ed.)

6. Narasimhaswamiji, *Devotees' Experiences of Shri Sai Baba.* Hyderabad: Akhand Sai Nama Sapthah Samithi, 1989.

7. Narasimhaswamiji, *Sai Baba's Charters and Sayings.* Madras, All India Sai Samaj, 1986.

8. Narasimhaswamiji, *Life of Sai Baba.* Madras: All India Sai Samaj, 1957, Vol. IV, p.237.

9. *The Hindustan Times* (New Delhi), May 3, 1994.

10. Verma, Subha, 'Shirdi Mein Sai Ka Danda Chalta Hai' Saphatik Hindustan, 22 Nov., 1992, p. 24.

11. Spencer, M.K., "How I Found God". *Op Cit.*

12. Ruhela, S.P., '*Shirdi Sai Baba Speaks to Yogi Spencer in Vision*', New Delhi: Vikas Publishing House, 1998.

13. Ruhela, S.P., *Sri Shirdi Sai Baba : The Universal Master.* New Delhi, Sterling Publicationers, 1994.

14. Arun Tamhanker quoted in "*Shri Sai Leela*", 1992.

APPENDIX - I
A LIST OF SAI ORGANIZATIONS IN INDIA SPREADING THE MESSAGE OF SRI SHIRDI SAI BABA

1. *Akhil Bhartiya Shirdi Sai Bhakti Mahasabha*, Hyderabad. (M. Rangacharya, President).
2. *Akhanda Sainama Saptaha Samithi*, B/3/F-15, Krupa Complex, Anada Bagh, Hydrabad- 500047. (A.P) (D. Shankeriah, Secretary).
3. *All India Sai Samaj*, Mylapore, Madras-600004.
4. *All India Sri Sai Sneh*, A-475, Sector 19, NOIDA-201301 (U.P) (Janak Raj Laroria, President).
5. Dharma Sai, Dharmgiri Kshetra

   Shamshabad, R.R. District, Hyderabad-509218 (A.P.)
6. *Divine Centre*, 7/250, Nehru Street

   Markapur -523316 (A.P)

   (A. Somasundaram, Hon. Secretary)
7. *Dwarkamai Publications*, Hydrabad-500033. (A.P).
8. Sai Divine Research Centre, 126, Sector 37, Faridabad-121003. (Dr. S.P. Ruhela, Secretary; Tel.275844.
9. *International Pragya Mission*, Saket, New Delhi-110017. (Swami Pragyanand, Founder President).
10. *Madhya Pradesh Sai Bhakta Parivar*, 91, Napier Town, Jabalpur (M.P.) (Tel. 24830)
11. *Sai Barsi Publications*

    3-5-697-A, Telugu Academy Lane,

    Vimalwadi Narayan guda, Hyderabad-500029.
12. *Sai Foundation- India*. New Delhi-110060:

    H-353, New Rajender Nagar.

    (Sai Das Baba, Chairman).

13. Sai Kripa Sansthan, Mehta House, A-16, Naraina-II, New Delhi-110028.

    (Tel. 5704450-52)

14. Sai Prachar Kendra, S.C.F 18, Sector 19-D, Chandigarh-160019.

15. Sai Publication, Red Cross Road, Civil Lines, Nagpur (Maharastra).

16. Sai Sudha Trust, Shirdi Sai Baba Mandir, Garkhal Kausauli (H.P)-173201.

    (P.L.Goyal, President). (Tel. Kausauli 71792-931721117).

17. Sri Bhagwati Sai Sansthan, Plot No. 400/1, Near Panvel Rly. Station, Panvel-410206. (Maharastra) (Sai Sevak Narayan Baba, Spiritual Head) (Tel. 7453331, 7451001)

18. Shirdi Sai Baba Temple Society, Sai Dham, Tigaon Road, Faridabad-121002. (Motilal Gupta, Founder Chairman). (Tel. 296380)

19. Shirdi Sai Centre Inc.

    46-16, Robinson Steet, Hushin-USA,

    Hushin NY-11355 (Phone (718) 321-9243.

20. Sri Shirdi Sri Nath Trust

    37 & 38, Arvind Nagar

    Domalgude-500029.

21. Sri Sai Samaj, Picket, Secundrabad (A.P.)

22. Sri Sai Spiritual Centre, T. Nagar, Bangalore-5600028. (Tel. 603922)

23. Sri Sai Samaj Calcutta, P-113, Lake Terrace, Calcutta-700029.

24. Sri Sai Book Sansthan, Shirdi (Maharastra). (Fax 4150798 Tel. 4166556)

25. Sri Shirdi Sai Baba Mandir Society,

    39, Jatindas Road, Calcutta-700029

    (Sarojini Devarajulu, President)

APPENDIX II
A LIST OF JOURNALS DEVOTED TO SRI SHIRDI SAI BABA

1. *Sai Chetna* (English). Chennai:Sri Sai Baba Spiritual & Charitable Trust, Injambakkam, Madras -600041. (Editor: Mansha V. Bulchandani).

2. *Sai Kripa* (English & Hindi). New Delhi-110003: Shri Sai Bakhta Samaj, 17, Institutional Area, Lodhi Road. (Editor: R. S. Sharma) Annual Subscription Rs.20.

3. *Sai Kripa*: (Hindi). New Delhi: Sai Kripa Sanasthan, A-16, Naraina, 11, New Delhi-110028. (Editor: Dilip Tuli).

4. *Sai Padananda*. Bangalore-5600028: Sri Spiritual Centre, T. Nagar, (Editor: R. Seshadri. Annual Subscription Rs.20.

5. *Sai Prabha* (English & Telugu). Hyderabad- 500027: H.No.3-5-697/A, Telugu Academy Lane, Vittalwadi, Narayanguda. (Editor: B. Uma Maheswar Rao). Annual Subscription Rs.30.

6. *Sai Sudha*. Madras: All India Sai Samaj, Mylapore.

7. *Shri Sai Leela*. (English & Hindi). Bombay-400014: 'Sai Nekatan', 804-B, Dr. Ambedkar Road, Dadar. (Editor: D. M. Sukthankar). Annual Subscription Rs.50.

8. *Sri Sai Avatars*. (English & Bengali). Calcutta-700029: Sri Sai Samaj Calcutta, P-113, Lake Terrace. (Editor: S.M.Banerjee)

9. *Sri Sai Divya Sandesh*. (English & Hindi). Panvel-410206 (Distt. Raigarh): Sri Bhagwati Sai Sansthan, Plot No.400/1, Near Railway Station. (Editor: Veena D. Raval). Annual Subscription Rs.15.

10. *Sri Sai Spandan*. Hyderabad-500872: Self Analysis Institute, 402 Raj Apartments, B. H. Society, Kukapally.

APPENDIX III

BIBLIOGRAPHY ON SRI SHIRDI SAI BABA

(Compiled by: S.P. Ruhela)

1. Agaskar, P.S., *Sri Sai Leelamrita*. Shirdi: Shri Sai Baba Sansthan, 1989.(In Hindi).
2. Aiyer, P.S.V., *Perfect Masters*. Calcutta: Author,1973.
3. Anand, Sai Sharan, *Sri Sai Baba*. Bombay: Dinpushpa Prakashan, 1989. (In Marathi/Gujrati).
4. —————, *Sri Sai Baba*. New Delhi: Sterling Publishers, 1997.(In English)
5. —————, *Sai The Superman*. Shirdi: Shri Sai Baba Sansthan, 1991.
6. Awasthi, Dinesh & Blitz Team of Investigators, "Sai Baba - The Saint of Shirdi", *Blitz* (Bombay Weekly), Nov. 6 & 13, 1976.
7. Balse, Maya, *Mystics and Men of Miracles in India*. New Delhi: Orient Paper backs, 1978.
8. Bhardawaja, E., *Sai Baba The Master*. Ongole: Sri Guru Paduka Publications, 1991.(III Ed.)
9. Bharti, Sushil, *Sai Kripa ke Pavan kshan*. Sagar: Sai Prakashan, 1995. (In Hindi).
10. Bharucha, Perin S., *Sai Baba of Shirdi*. Shirdi: Shri Sai Baba Sansthan, 1980.
11. Bharvani, A.D. & Malhotra, V., *Shirdi Sri Baba and Sathya Sai Baba are One and Same*. Bombay: Sai Sahitya Samiti, 1983.
12. Bhisma, K. I., *Sadguru Sai Nath Sagunopasana*. Shirdi: Shri Sai Baba Sansthan, 1986.(In Marathi).
13. Chatturvedi, B. K., *Sai Baba of Shirdi*. New Delhi: Diamond Pocket Books,
14. Ganu, Das, *Shri Sai Nath Stavan Manjari*. Shirdi: Shri Sai Baba Sansthan, (English translation by Zarine Taraporewala,

Bombay: Sai Dhun Enterprises, 1987).

15. ———, *Sai Harikathas*. Madras: All India Sai Samaj, Mylapore.

16. *Gems of Wisdom*. Nagpur: Sri Publication.

17. *Guide to Holy Shirdi*. Shirdi: Shri Sai Baba Sansthan.

18. Gunaji, N., *Shri Sai Sachcharita* (English translation, Shirdi: Shri Sai Baba Sansthan, 1944, (XIV. Ed. 1991).

19. Harper, Marvin Henry, "The Fakir: Sri Sai Baba of Shirdi" in *Gurus, Swamis, and Avataras: Spiritual Master and Their American Disciplines*. Philadelphia: Westminister Press, 1972.

20. Hattingatti, Shaila, *Sai's Story*. Bombay: India Book House, 1991.

21. Hemadpant, *Shri Sai Sachcharitra* Shirdi: Shri Sai baba Sansthan, (In Marathi, Hindi, Gujrati, Telugu, English etc.)

22. *Is Sai Baba Living and Helping Now?* Madras All India Sai Samaj, Mylpore.

23. Joshi, H. S., *Origin and Development of Dattatreya Worship in India*. Baroda: M. S. University of Baroda, 1965. (Chapter 12).

24. Kakde, R.C. & Veerbhadra, A., *Shirdi to Puttaparthi*. Hyderabad: Ira Prakashan, 1989. (In English & Hindi.)

25. Kamath, M. V. & Kher, V. B., *Sai Baba of Shirdi: A Unique Saint*. Bombay: Jaico Publishing House, 1991.

26. Karunananda, Swami, *The Uniqueness of the Significance of Sri Sai Baba*. Panvel: Sri Bhagwati Sai Sansthan.

27. Khaprade, G. *Sources of Sai History*. Bangalore: Jupiter Press, 1956.

28. ———, *Shirdi Diary*. Shirdi: Shri Sai Baba Sansthan,

29. Krishna, Indira Anantha, *Sai Baba of Shirdi*. (Adarsh Chitra Katha - Pictorial).

30. Kumar, Anil, *Doctor of Doctors Sri Sai Baba*, Nagpur: Sri Sai Clinic.

31. Kumar, Sudhir, *Shirdi ke Sai Baba: Chalisa aur Bhajan*.

New Delhi: Author. (In Hindi).

32. *Maneey, S., *The Eternal Sai*. New Delhi: Diamond Pocket Books, 1997.

33. Mani, Amma B., *Sai Leela Taranagini*. (Parts 1 & 2). Guntur: Authoress c/o Uma Maheswar Rao, Retired S.P., 2-14-140, ShyamlaNagar, 1 Lane. (In Telugu).

34. Mehta, Rao Bahadur Harshad B., *The Spiritual Symphony of Shree Sainath of Shirdi*. Baroda: Rana & Patel Press, 1952.

35. Mehta, Vikas, *Hridaya ke Swami Shri Sai Baba*. New Delhi: Siddartha Publications, IO DSIDC, Scheme II, Okhla Industrial Area Part 11, 1995. (In Hindi).

36. Mehta, Vikas, *Karunamaya Shri Sai Baba*. New Delhi: Siddartha Publications, 1996. (In Hindi).

37. Mittal, N., *World Famous Modern Gurus and Guru Cultas*. New Delhi: Family Books, F 2/16, Ansari Road,1990.

38. Monayan, C.V.G.S., *Sai THe Mother and Ansuya, the Amma*. Masulipattanam: Sai Ma Gurudatta Publications, 18/286, Ambani Agraharam.

39. Munsiff, Abdul Ghani, "Hazrat Sai Baba", *The Mehar Baba Journal* (Ahmednagar): Vol.1 1938-39.

40. Murthy, G.S., *Understanding Shirdi Sai Baba*. Hyderabad: Sri Shirdi Sai Prema Mandiram,1977.

41. Narasimhaswami Ji, *Who is Sai Baba of Shirdi?* Madras: All India Sai Samaj, 1980-83.

42. ————, *Sri Sai Vachnamrita*. Madras: All India Sai Samaj.

43. ————, *Sri Sai Baba's Charters and Sayings*. Madras: All India Sai Samaj, 1965.

44. ————, *Life of Sai Baba* (Four Vols). Madras: All India Sai Samaj, 1980-83.

45. ————, *Devotees' Experiences of Sai Baba*. Madras: All India Sai Samaj 1965-67.

46. Narayanan, C.R., *A Century of Poems on Sri Sai Baba of*

Shirdi. Madras: Author, 1994 (II Ed.)

47. Nimbalkar, M.B., *Sri Sai Satya Charistra*. Poona: Author, 1993.(In Marathi).

48. Osburne, Arthur, *The Incredible Sai Baba*. Delhi: Orient Longmans, 1970.

49. Parchure, D.D., *Children's Sai Baba*. Shirdi: Shri Sai Baba Sansthan, 1983. (In English Hindi)

50. Parchure, S.D., *Shree Sai Mahimashstra*. Bombay: Tardeo Beek Depot, 1990.

51. Parthsarthi, R. *God Who Walked On Earth*. New Delhi: Sterling Publishers, 1996.

52. ____, *Apostle of Love: Saint Sai Padananda*, New Delhi: Sterling Publishers, 1997.

53. *Pictorial Sai Baba*. Shirdi Sai Baba Sansthan, 1968.

54. Pradhan, M.V., *Sri Sai Baba of Shirdi*. Shirdi: Sri Sai Baba Sansthan, 1973.

55. Patil, R. S. *Nine Steps to Life Divine*. Pune: Saish, 120, National Society.

56. Krishnapriya, Mataji, *Sri Sai Satcharita* (A Short Volume for daily reaction. Burla; Prof. M. S. Rao, Engineering College.

57. Ramalingaswami, *The Golden Words of Shri Sai Baba*. Shirdi, 1983.

58. ————, *Ambrosia in Shirdi*. Shirdi: Shri Sai Baba Sansthan, 1984.

59. Ramakrishna, K. K., *Sai Baba The Perfect Master*. Pune: Meher Era Publications, Avatar Meher Baba Poona Centre, 441/1, Somwarpeth, 1991.

60. Rao, M.S. *Divine Life Story of Sri Sudguru Krishnapriyaji*. Burla: Author, 1995.

61. Rao, Devata Sabha, *Baba Sai*. Hyderabad: 76, N. H. I, Type 5, Ramahandrapuram (BHEL).

62. Rao, K.V. Raghva, *Message of Sri Sai Baba*. Madras: All India Sai Samaj, 1984.(III Ed. by Dwarkamai Trust,

Hyderabad, 1995.)

63. ——————, *Message of Sri Sai Baba* (Vol.II). Hyderabad: Shri Shirdi Sai Publications Trust, 1992.

64. ——————, *Enlightenment From Sri Sai Baba on Salvation of Soul*. Hyderabad: Dwarkamai Publications, 1994.

65. ——————, *Golden voice and Divine Touch of Sri Sai Baba*. Hyderabad: Dwarkamai Publications, 1997.

66. Ravindra, A. (Compiler), *The Sayings of Shirdi Sai*. Vijaiwada: Sri Sai Baba Book Stall, P.F.6, Railway Station.

67. Rigopoulos, Antonio, *The Life and Teachings of Sri Sai Baba of Shirdi* (Ph.D. Thesis) New York: State University, 1992. (Delhi-110007: Sri Sadguru Publications, Indian Book Centre 40/5, Shakti Nagar 1993.)

68. Ruhela, S. P., *My Life With Shirdi Sai Baba -Thrilling Memories of Shivamma Thayee*. Faridabad: Sai Age Publications, 1992.(New Delhi-110002: M. D. Publications, 11, Darya Ganj, 1995).

69. ——————, *Sri Shirdi Sai Baba Avatar*. Faridabad: Sai Age Publications, 1992.

70. Ruhela, S. P., *What Researchers Say on Sri Shirdi Sai Baba*. Faridabad: Sai Age Publications, 1994.(II Ed. New Delhi-110002: M. D. Publications, 1995).

71. ——————, *Sri Shirdi Sai Baba: The Universal Master*. New: Sterling Publishers, L-10, Green Park Extension, 1995. (Reprint 1995, 1996).

72. ——————, *The Sai Trinity - Sri Shirdi Sai, Sri Sathya Sai, Sri Prema Sai Incarnations*. New Delhi-110014: Vikas Publishing House, 1994.

73. ——————, *Sai Puran*. Delhi: Sadhna Pocket Books, 1996.

74. ——————, "Baba Paatti - The Present Incarnation of Sri Shirdi Sai Baba's Mother", *Sri Sai Avatars*. (Calcutta-700029: Sri Sai Samaj Calcutta P-113, Lake Terrace), Oct.-Dec., 1996, pp.7-16.

75. ——————, *Divine Grace of Sri Shirdi Sai Baba*. New Delhi: Diamond Pocket Books, 1997.

76. Ruhela, S. P., *Shirdi Sai, The Supreme.* New Delhi: Diamond Pocket Books, 1997.

77. ——————, *Hamare Pyare Sri Shirdi Sai Baba.* New Delhi: Diamond Pocket Books, 1997. (In Hindi)

78. ——————, *Sai Baba Ke Sang Mera Jeevan* (Shivarama Thayee) New Delhi: Diamond Pocket Books, 1997.

79. ——————, *Sri Sai Avatar Trimurti*, New Delhi: Diamond Pocket Books, 1997 (In Hindi).

80. ——————, *Shirdi Sai Baba Speaks to Yogi Spencer in Vision.* New Delhi: Vikas Publishing House, 1998.

81. ——————, *Saint Shiromani Sri Shirdi Sai Baba.* New Delhi: Sterling Publisher, 1997.

82. Sahukar, Mani, *Sai Baba -The Saint of Shirdi.* Bombay: Somaiya Publications, 1983.

83. *Sai Sandesh.* Hyderabad: Sai Prabha Publications 1990.

84. *Sai Samarpan* (Special Issue on Shirdi Sai Baba, Panipat: 41B, Narayan Singh Park), Sept-Oct, 1996.

85. Seshadri, H., *Glimpses of Divinity - A Profile of Shri Saidas Babaji.* Bombay: Shri Bhopal Singh Hingharh. (It shows that Sri Shirdi Sai Baba and Sri Sathya Sai Baba are one and the same.)

86. *Sai Sudha. -Golden Jubilee Issue*, Special Number, Madras: All India Sai Samaj, June 1990.

87. Savitri, Raghnath, *Sai Bhajanmala.* Mumbai: Balaji Bagya, Sudarshan Art Printing Press, 5 Vadla Udhyog Bhavan, Mumbai-400031, 1995 (24th Ed.1986) (In Marathi). It contains folk songs and *Bhajan* on Sri Shirdi Sai since his lifetime.)

88. Shepherd, R.D. *Gurus Rediscovered.* Cambridge: Anthropological Publications, 1985. Biographies of Sri Shirdi Sai Baba and Sri Upasani Maharaj).

89. *Shirdi Darshan.* Shirdi, Shri Sai Baba Sansthan, 1966, 1972. (Pictorial).

90. *Shirdi ke Sai Baba.* Delhi: Ratan Book Co. (In Hindi).

91. Shivnesh Swamiji, *Sri Sai Bavani*, Shirdi.

92. *Shree Sai Leela: Sachitra Jeevandarshan.* 1939.
93. *Shree Sai Leela,* March-April 1992. (First Convention of Sai Devotees).
94. *Silver Jubilee Souvenir.* Madras: All India Sai Samaj, 1966.
95. *Spiritual Recipes.* Bangalore: Sri Sai Baba Spiritual Centre, Sri Sai Baba Mandir Marg, T. Nagar.
96. Singh. I.D., *Gagar Main Sai Kshir Sagar.* Faridabad; Sai Age Publications, 1996. (In Hindi).
97. Somasundaram, A., *The Dawn of a New Era: The Message of Master Ram Ram And The Need for Universal Religion.* Markapur(A.P): Divine Centre, 1970.
98. Somsundaran, A., *The Dawn of New Era: The Vision of Master Rishi Ram Ram.* Markapur: Divine Centre, 1969.
99. *Souvenir: Maha Samadhi Souvenir.* Madras: All India Sai Samaj, 1966.
100. *Souvenir.* Delhi: Shri Sai Bhakta Samaj, 1972.
101. *Souvenir.* Secunderabad: Sri Sai Baba Samaj, 1975.
102. *Souvenir.* Secunderabad:Sri Sai Baba Samaj,1990.
103. *Souvenir.* 26th All India Devotes' Convention: Golden Jubilee year, 1991.
104. Spencer, M.K. *How I Found God.* (Four volumes) Coimbatore: The spiritual Healing Centre, 1955.
105. Steel, Brian, *Sir Sathya Sai Baba. Compendium.* York Beach (USA): Samuel Weisner, 1997. pp.244-248.
106. *Tales of Sai Baba.* Bombay: India Book House, 1995. (Pictorial)
107. Tanavde, S. V, *May Sai Baba Bless Us All.* Bombay: Taradeo Book Depot.
108. Taraporewala, Zarine, *Worship of Manifested Sri Sadguru Sainath.* (English translation of K.J. Bhisma's *Sri Sadguru Sainath Sagunopasan*). Bombay: Saidhun Enterprises, 1990.
109. Uban, Sujan Singh, "Sai Baba of Shirdi", *The Gurus of India.* London: Fine Press, 1977.

110. Umamaheswarea Rao, B., Thus Spake Sri Shirdi Sai Baba. New Delhi: Diamond Pocket Books, 1997.

111. Verma, Subha, "Shirdi, Sab boom Sai ki...", *Saptahik Hindustan*, Nov. 12, 1992, pp.17-25, (In Hindi).

112. White, Charles, S. J., "The Sai Baba Movement: Approaches to the study of Indian saints", *The Journal of Asian Studies*, Vol. XXXI, No.4, August 1972.

DIAMOND POCKET BOOKS PRESENTS
SHRI SATHYA SAI LITERATURE & SPIRITUAL BOOKS

Dr. S.P. Ruhela (Com. & Ed.)
*Worship of Sri Sathya Sai Baba (In Roman) 40.00
*World Peace and Sri Sathya Sai Avtar 60.00
*How to Receive Sri Sathya Sai Baba's Grace 100.00
*Sri Sathya Sai Baba : Understanding His Mystery and Experiencing His Love 60.00

B.K. Chaturvedi
*The Miracal Man : Sri Sathya Sai Baba 60.00

S. Maaney
*The Eternal Sai 40.00

Sushila Devi Ruhela
Sri Sathya Sai Bhajanmala (Roman) 10.00

R.P. Hingorani
*Chalisa Sangrah (Roman) .. 40.00

Acharya Vipul Rao
*Srimad Bhagwat Geeta (Sanskrit & English) 75.00

Dr. Bhavansingh Rana
*108 Upanishad (In press) ... 150.00

Chakor Ajgaonkar
*Realm of Sadhana (What Saints & Masters Say) 30.00

Dr. S.P. Ruhela
*Fragrant Spiritual Memories of a Karma Yogi 100.00

Yogi M.K. Spencer
*Rishi Ram Ram 100.00
*Oneness with God 90.00

Eva Bell Barer
*Quiet Talks with the Master 60.00

Joseph J. Ghosh
*Adventures with Evil Spirits 80.00

K.H. Nagrani
*A Child from the Spirit World Speaks 10.00

Religious Books in Hindi, English & Roman
*Sanatan Dharm Pooja 95.00
*Sudha Kalp 95.00
*Shiv Abhisek Poojan 25.00
*Daily Prayer (Hindi, English French, Roman) 25.00
*Sanatan Daily Prayer 25.00

Acharya Vipul Rao
*Daily Prayer 10.00

Dr. Bhojraj Dwivedi
*Shiv Abhishek Pujan 25.00

B.K. Chaturvedi
*Shri Hanuman Chalisa 30.00
*The Hymns & Orisons of Lord Shankar 30.00
*Chalisa Sangrah 40.00

Order books by V.P.P. Postage Rs. 20/- per book extra. Postage free on order of three or more books, Send Rs. 20/–in advance.

DIAMOND POCKET BOOKS (P) LTD.
X-30, Okhla Industrial Area, Phase-II, New Delhi-110020.
Phones : 51611861-5, Fax : (0091)-011- 51611866, 26386124

DIAMOND BOOKS PRESENTS

David Servan Schreiber 'Gurier'
- The Instinct to Heal 195.00
  (Curing stress, anxiety and depression. without drugs and without talk therapy)

Swati Lodha
- Why Women Are What They Are 195.00

Osho
- Yoga - The Alchemy of Yoga. 150.00

Dr. Bimal Chhajer
- 201 Diet Tips for Heart Patients 150.00

Joginder Singh
- Jokes of Joginder singh (I, II) 95.00

Pandit Atre
- Soul @ Universe.Com 75.00

M.G. Devasahayam
- India's IInd Freedom an Untold Saga 195.00

Vandana Verma
- Lovely Names for Male & Female childs 95.00

BOOKS ON HINDU MYTHOLOGY

Prafull Goradia
- The Saffron Book 150.00
- Anti Hindus 150.00
- Muslim League's Unfinished Agenda 150.00
- Hindu Masjids 195.00

Dr. Brij Raj Kishore
- Essence of Vedas 195.00

S. N. Mathur
- The Diamond Books of Hindu Gods and Goddesses (4 Colour) 295.00

B.K. Chaturvedi
- Shiva Purana 95.00
- Vishnu Purana 95.00
- Markandeya Purana 75.00
- Bhsvishya Purana 75.00
- Narad Purana 75.00
- Kalki Purana 75.00
- Linga Purana 75.00

LITERATURE

Rabindranath Tagore
- Boat Accident (Translation of नौका डूबी) 95.00
- Inside Outside (Translation of घरे बाइरे) 95.00

Iqbal Ramoowalia
- The Death Of A Passport ....: 150.00

Ed. Rajendra Awasthy
- Selected Gujrati Short Stories 95.00
- Selected Hindi Short Stories.... 125.00
- Selected Tamil Short Stories 95.00
- Selected Malayalam Short Stories 95.00
- Selected Punjabi Short Stories ... 95.00

K. S. Duggal
- Birth of a Song 95.00

GREAT PERSONALITIES
(BIOGRAPHY)

Anuradha Ray
- The Making of Mahatma (A Biography) 95.00

Prof. Gurpreet Singh
- Ten Masters (Sikh Gurus) 60.00
- The Soul of Sikhism 95.00

B.K. Chaturvedi
- Messiah of Poor Mother Teresa 60.00
- Chanakya 95.00
- Goddess Durga 95.00

S.P. Bansal
- Lord Rama 95.00
- Gajanan 75.00

Dr. Brij Raj Kishore
- Ram Krishna Paramhans 60.00

Purnima Majumdaar
- Yogiraj Arvind 60.00
- Neel Kanth (Lord Shiva) 95.00

Dr. Bhwan Singh Rana
- Swami Vivekanand 120.00
- Chhatrapati Shivaji 95.00
- Bhagat Singh 95.00

Mahesh Sharma
- Dr. A.P.J. Abdul Kalam 95.00
- Sonia Gandhi 95.00
- Atal Bihari Vajpayee 95.00
- Lal Krishna Advani 95.00

Books can be requisitioned by V.P.P. Postage charges will be Rs. 20/- per book. For orders of three books the postage will be free.

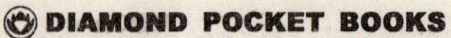

DIAMOND POCKET BOOKS

X-30, Okhla Industrial Area, Phase-II, New Delhi-110020, Phone : 011-51611861, Fax : 011-51611866
E-mail : sales@diamondpublication.com, Website : www.fusionbooks.com